advance praise for *From Script to Screen*

"*From Script to Screen* is stimulating, informative, and entertaining. In my opinion, it is a must-read for anyone interested in filmmaking, from novice to studio executive."
— RICHARD ZANUCK; producer, *Driving Miss Daisy, Jaws*

"Excellent practitioners of the craft interviewed with care by two people who obviously love film."
— GILBERT CATES; dean, School of Theater, Film, and Television, UCLA

"A phenomenal book and a must-read for everyone interested in the creative evolution of the written form. It's learning by example from some of the industry's foremost talents. Seger and Whetmore allowed me new insights with their unique format of 'sharing in the trenches'!"
— JERRY MOLEN; producer, *Jurassic Park, Hook*

"*From Script to Screen* is an affectionate book, filled with truth about the collaborative process. Reading it gave me a chance to have some wonderful 'conversations' with other filmmakers. Filmmaking can be a very isolating experience. This book unites us all in the context of our common goal: to put the best possible story up on the screen."
— CAROL LITTLETON; editor, *E.T., Wyatt Earp*

"*From Script to Screen* does an excellent job of clarifying and defining the often misunderstood role of the producer in the filmmaking process. Lively and well written, it's a unique resource for film professionals and movie buffs alike. We need more books like it."
— KATHLEEN KENNEDY; producer, *E.T., Jurassic Park*

"There is no shortage of books about how to write a screenplay, but in today's Hollywood, that's just the beginning. Any successful screenwriter will tell you the real drama comes as the script begins its perilous journey to the screen. Seger and Whetmore have captured the process perfectly. *From Script to Screen* is a treasure trove full of insight and inspiration that every writer will cherish. I couldn't put it down."

—DALE LAUNER; screenwriter, *Ruthless People, My Cousin Vinnie*

"In an era of media hype, it is a rare occasion when anything written about filmmaking can truly be said to enlighten the reader. *From Script to Screen* has woven together the unique perspective of so many talented collaborators that the result is even more substantial than the sum of its parts. A classic of its kind. Readers are unlikely to ever see the movies in quite the same way again."

—DAVID PUTTNAM; producer, *The Killing Fields, Chariots of Fire*

BOOKS BY LINDA SEGER

Making a Good Script Great

Creating Unforgettable Characters

The Art of Adaptation

BOOKS BY EDWARD JAY WHETMORE

Mediamerica, Mediaworld

The Magic Medium

American Electric

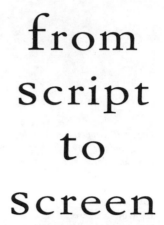

from
script
to
screen

the
collaborative
art of
filmmaking

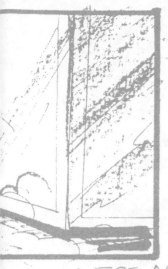

linda seger

and

edward jay whetmore

an owl book
henry holt and company
new york

*The art that appears on the title page, the chapter opening
pages, and page 119 is from the storyboards from* Backdraft *by
Peter and Eric Ramsey, courtesy of Ron Howard.*

Henry Holt and Company, Inc.
Publishers since 1866
115 West 18th Street
New York, New York 10011

Henry Holt® is a registered
trademark of Henry Holt and Company, Inc.

Library of Congress Cataloging-in-Publication Data
Seger, Linda.
From script to screen : the collaborative art of
filmmaking /
Linda Seger and Edward Jay Whetmore.—1st Owl ed.
p.   cm.
Includes index.
1. Motion pictures—Production and direction.
I. Whetmore,
Edward Jay. II. Title.
PN1995.9.P7S38   1994   93-25860
791.43′023—dc20   CIP

ISBN 0-8050-2303-8

First Owl Book Edition—1994

Book Design by Claire Naylon Vaccaro

Printed in the United States of America
All first editions are printed on acid-free paper.∞
10   9   8   7   6   5   4   3   2   1

For my friend Cathleen, and my godson,
Michael, with love

—L. S.

For my brother Vincent J. Fratello, a physicist
with a great sense of story

—E. J. W.

contents

acknowledgments

My special thanks to the people who helped make *From Script to Screen* possible: Lee and Jan Batchler; Hindi Brooks; Mimi Cozzens; Linda B. Elstad; Leonard Felder; Colin Greene; Linda Griffiths; Greg Henry; Chris Jorie; Kevin Klinger; Barbara Lawrence; Jan Lewis; Lisa Lieberman; Cindy Margolis; Carolyn Miller; Jim Pasternak; Ralph Phillips; Don Ray; Steve Rekas; Ron Richards; Tom Shoebridge; Dov Simmons; Treva Silverman; Sandi Steinberg; David Summerville; Howard Wexler; Judity Weston; and Marsha Williams.

To my readers: Cathleen Loeser; Dara Marks; Anne Cooper Ready; Madeleine Rose; Lynn Brown Rosenberg; and Helene Wong.

And to all our interviewees and their assistants and secretaries who took my phone calls and helped make the interviews happen.

—L. S.

Special thanks to all my readers: Shari Beauchamp; Kar Davis; Vincent Fratello; Crista Taylor; Chris Kawamura; Jennifer Miles; and Rachelle Whetmore.

And to two special filmmakers for their inspiration, Lawrence Kasdan and Oliver Stone.

—E. J. W.

SPECIAL ACKNOWLEDGMENT

To our editor, Cynthia Vartan, and our agent, Martha Casselman. Thank you both for your patience and support.

And particularly to Tom Schulman, who helped us all the way "from script to screen!"

list
of
collaborators
interviewed

*(listed by chapter
in the order in
which they appear)*

WRITERS — CHAPTER 1

Hesper Anderson: *Children of a Lesser God*
Pen Densham: *Robin Hood: Prince of Thieves*
Larry Gelbart: *Tootsie; M*A*S*H*
Lawrence Kasdan: *Grand Canyon; The Big Chill; Body Heat*
William Kelley: *Witness*
Babaloo Mandel and Lowell Ganz: *A League of Their Own;
City Slickers; Parenthood*
Frank Pierson: *Presumed Innocent; Dog Day Afternoon; Cool
Hand Luke*
Tom Schulman: *Honey, I Shrunk the Kids; Dead Poets
Society*
Ron Shelton: *White Men Can't Jump; Blaze; Bull Durham*
John Singleton: *Boyz N the Hood; Poetic Justice*
Oliver Stone: *Heaven and Earth; JFK; Wall Street; Platoon*
David Zucker: *Naked Gun 2½; Top Secret; Airplane!*

PRODUCERS — CHAPTER 2

Ed Feldman: *Green Card; Witness; Save the Tiger*
Brian Grazer: *Kindergarten Cop; Parenthood; Splash*
Steven Haft: *Dead Poets Society*
Gale Anne Hurd: *Raising Cain; The Abyss; Terminator*
Kathleen Kennedy: *Jurassic Park; Who Framed Roger
Rabbit?; E.T. The Extra-Terrestrial*
David Puttnam: *The Killing Fields; Chariots of Fire;
Midnight Express*
Debbie Robins: *Calendar Girl*
Richard Zanuck: *Driving Miss Daisy; Cocoon; Jaws; The
Sting*

DIRECTORS — CHAPTER 3

Martha Coolidge: *Lost in Yonkers; Rambling Rose*
Nina Foch: Actor, Director, Consultant
Amy Heckerling: *Look Who's Talking Too; Look Who's
Talking*
Ron Howard: *Backdraft; Parenthood; Splash*
Norman Jewison: *Moonstruck; Agnes of God; The Russians
Are Coming, The Russians Are Coming*
Roland Joffe: *City of Joy; The Mission; The Killing Fields*
Lawrence Kasdan: *The Bodyguard; Grand Canyon; Body
Heat*
Barry Levinson: *Toys; Bugsy; Rain Man; Diner*
Ridley Scott: *Thelma and Louise; Alien; 1492: Conquest of
Paradise*
Ron Shelton: *White Men Can't Jump; Bull Durham*
John Singleton: *Boyz N the Hood; Poetic Justice*
Oliver Stone: *Heaven and Earth; JFK; Platoon*
Peter Weir: *Green Card; Dead Poets Society; Witness*

Robert Wise: *The Sound of Music; West Side Story; Star Trek—The Motion Picture*
David Zucker: *Naked Gun; Ruthless People; Airplane!*

ACTORS — CHAPTER 4

Nina Foch: Actor, Director
Graham Greene: *Dances with Wolves; Thunderheart; Ishi*
Robert Sean Leonard: *Dead Poets Society; Much Ado About Nothing*
John Lithgow: *Raising Cain; Terms of Endearment; The World According to Garp*
Mary McDonnell: *Passion Fish; Grand Canyon; Dances with Wolves*
Leonard Nimoy: *Star Trek*
Edward James Olmos: *American Me; Stand and Deliver; Wolfen*
Peter Strauss: *Masada; Rich Man, Poor Man*
Robin Williams: *Dead Poets Society; Good Morning, Vietnam; The World According to Garp*

PRODUCTION DESIGNERS — CHAPTER 5

Bob Grieves—Sound Design: *Robin Hood: Prince of Thieves; Children of a Lesser God; Body Heat*
Ken Ralston—Special Effects: *Death Becomes Her; Who Framed Roger Rabbit?; Cocoon*
Peter Robb-King—Makeup Design: *Sommersby; The Last of the Mohicans; Patriot Games*
Ferdinando Scarfiotti—Production Design: *Toys; The Last Emperor*
John Seales—Cinematographer: *Dead Poets Society*
Marilyn Vance—Costume Design: *Pretty Woman; Die Hard; The Untouchables; Romancing the Stone*

Sandy Veneziano—Art Director: *Home Alone 2; Dead Poets
Society*
Haskell Wexler—Cinematographer: *One Flew Over the
Cuckoo's Nest; The Thomas Crown Affair; Who's Afraid of
Virginia Woolf?*

EDITORS — CHAPTER 6

William Anderson: *The Fugitive; Green Card; Dead Poets
Society*
Joe Hutshing: *JFK; Born on the Fourth of July*
Carol Littleton: *Grand Canyon; E.T. The Extra-Terrestrial;
Body Heat*
Thom Noble: *Thelma and Louise; The Mosquito Coast;
Witness*
William Reynolds: *The Sting; The Sound of Music; West Side
Story*

COMPOSERS — CHAPTER 7

Buddy Baker: Head of USC's Film Scoring Program
Bill Conti: *Bound by Honor; Rocky*
Maurice Jarre: *Dead Poets Society; Doctor Zhivago; Lawrence
of Arabia*
Henry Mancini: *The Pink Panther; Days of Wine and Roses;
Breakfast at Tiffany's*
David Newman: *Hoffa; Throw Momma from the Train; The
War of the Roses*
David Raksin: *Laura*
Don Ray: Head of UCLA's Film Scoring Program
Shirley Walker: *Memoirs of an Invisible Man*
Hans Zimmer: *Thelma and Louise; Driving Miss Daisy;
Rain Man*

recommended
viewing

The following films are those most often referred to in *From Script to Screen*. While it is not necessary to have seen them in order to understand the issues raised here, familiarity with these classic films will definitely enhance your reading experience. What's more, they are wonderful films. Each is available on video, and we recommend them to you as examples of filmmaking at its finest. Enjoy!

DANCES WITH WOLVES (1990)

Kevin Costner's sweeping western epic about an idealistic Civil War soldier who befriends a Sioux Indian tribe and eventually joins them.

DEAD POETS SOCIETY (1989)

Robin Williams stars as an extraordinary teacher who brings his inspirational message to the students of a sedate New England prep school in 1959. *Carpe diem!*

DRIVING MISS DAISY (1989)

Jessica Tandy is a cranky old Southern woman whose relationship with her chauffeur (Morgan Freeman) mirrors the civil rights movement and the social upheaval of the South from the 1930s through the 1950s.

GRAND CANYON (1991)

Kevin Kline is the yuppie businessman whose car breaks down in south-central Los Angeles, forcing him to confront the life-and-death issues that dominate contemporary American urban life. Largely overlooked when it was released, Lawrence Kasdan's intricately constructed story only gets better with time.

JFK (1991)

Oliver Stone's searing and controversial version of the assassination of John F. Kennedy. Kevin Costner stars as the investigator who unravels the threads of the most frightening conspiracy in modern American political history.

THELMA AND LOUISE (1991)

Geena Davis and Susan Sarandon are two women whose weekend getaway turns into an eccentric crime spree. Ridley Scott's deft direction transforms a familiar genre film into a poignant examination of '90s feminist values.

WITNESS (1985)

Harrison Ford is a Philadelphia cop embroiled in an internal corruption case who seeks refuge in Pennsylvania's Amish country and encounters a way of life completely different from anything he has ever known.

from
Script
to
Screen

sneak preview: the magnificent risk-takers

"That's the fun part about movie collaboration," director Oliver Stone explains with a sly smile. "You work intensely with a lot of people who are different from you and you learn a lot from them. People you don't always like. But you learn to live with them. It teaches you tolerance."

This was one of the first lessons Hollywood's most gifted and successful filmmakers provided as they tolerated our questions, responding with remarkable and precise insight into the collaborative art of filmmaking. While conducting some sixty interviews in busy offices, editing rooms, wardrobe trailers, and sound stages all over southern California, we were continuously astonished by their willingness to share what they have learned with anyone who asks.

Those of us "in the dark" are generally satisfied with paying admission, munching our popcorn, and losing ourselves for a while in the mysterious worlds filmmakers create. But if you have ever wondered what they do, how they do it, and *why* they do it, then this book is for you.

Countless books have been devoted to the creation of the story and the writing of the script. Many others define precisely what an assistant director or key grip does during production. *From Script to Screen* does neither of these. Instead, we follow the path of the script as it passes through the hands of all the collaborators. In their own words, they share with us the secrets of the alchemy they use to bring a story to life. It begins as they sit alone, reading the script. But the real magic is glimpsed most often in the ways they work with one another.

In today's Hollywood the production of a major motion picture is not the work of one "auteur" director. Nor is it the result of the latest whim of a box-office superstar who helps draw the audience to the theater. These perceptions are quite popular in the press and in certain film schools. They are wrong.

The truth is that by the time the script appears on the screen, it is a product of the collective effort of writers, producers, directors, actors, cinematographers, editors, composers, and others who have labored for years to bring it to life.

Feature filmmaking has become a *collaborative art*, a unique synthesis of artistic vision married to an unwieldy commercial marketplace populated by a volatile and fickle audience. To make a studio film you need a willingness to write checks every day for more money than most folks spend on a house. Lace it with cost overruns and sprinkle with unpredictable weather, and you've got the recipe for a major motion picture. Amazingly enough, about two-hundred of them find their way into our theaters each year.

Of these, only a handful will be considered for the major awards, and only a few of those will be remembered as "classics," films that somehow profoundly move or affect the audience. Wherever possible, we focused our investigation on these extraordinary films and on the artists responsible for transforming them from script to screen.

These are the people who have created Academy Award–winning best pictures such as *Dances with Wolves, Driving Miss Daisy, Rain Man, Platoon,* and *Chariots of Fire.* As we began to seek out those who always seem to be associated with the best the medium has to offer, the same names surfaced again and again. In these pages you'll meet them and share their personal insights into the collaborative art of filmmaking. (A complete list of participants and their credits appears on pages xv–xviii), along with a recommended viewing list.)

In her book *Uncommon Genius,* Denise Shekerjian interviewed forty recipients of the MacArthur Prize, the so-called genius award. As she combed through the transcripts, she discovered something quite interesting:

In the end the common themes linking these creative people separated and floated to the surface like cream. . . . They were all driven, remarkably resilient, adept at creating an environment that suited their needs, skilled at honoring their own peculiar talents . . . capable of knowing when to follow their instincts and above all, magnificent risk-takers, unafraid to run ahead of the great popular tide.

We found all of these characteristics among our interviewees, but the one that surfaced most often was magnificent risk-taking. These are the writers, producers, directors, and others who are willing to gamble their careers on projects of several years duration, even though the material often seems completely contrary to the prevailing wisdom about what the audience wants to see.

Yet it is *precisely* this magnificent risk-taking that produces films such as *Dead Poets Society, Thelma and Louise, Grand Canyon, Witness,* and *JFK.* Oliver Stone told us that when he first proposed *JFK,* "they" told him as politely as possible:

> "Who wants to watch a three-hour JFK murder?" They said who the hell even remembers JFK? It was unbelievable. Certainly Vietnam was a turn-off when I started. Everyone told me *Wall Street* would never play . . . there's no history of business movies that are successful.
>
> It only goes to show you—stick to your guns if you think you're right. What was it Archimedes said? "Give me a place to stand and I'll give you the world." Now, that's leverage.

Producer Steven Haft remembers optioning *Dead Poets Society* after every major studio had passed on it—many of them more than once. He was hoping to find an independent company that would do it on a shoestring but wasn't having much luck. Then a call came from Disney head Jeff Katzenberg. . . .

Tom Schulman, who won an Academy Award for the script, fondly remembers that when the Disney people started trying to market the film, industry buzz had it that the only title with less audience appeal would have been *Dead Poets Society in Winter.*

Again and again our interviewees treated us to variations on this story. It is precisely the film that goes "against the grain" and runs counter to the prevailing wisdom that provides collaborators with their greatest challenges and affords the audience its most memorable celluloid moments.

Our quest was to start with those magic moments and uncover the methods that were used to create them. Having completed the interviews, we began by identifying the steps in the process that tended to surface as the artists discussed their work.

Once an idea has been turned into a screenplay, the pages serve as a blueprint for all that is to come. Common wisdom has it that movies would be much better if producers and directors shot them as they were originally written. While the urge to order endless rewrites can and does get out of control, it is a rare screenplay that cannot be improved upon as it makes its way to the screen.

The very essence of collaborative filmmaking requires that each person who works with the script needs to be able to contribute something to the process. It's not so much about leaving a mark but rather contributing to the realization of the script's most powerful potential.

It should also be noted that there are as many different "systems" of shooting a script as there are directors. Lawrence Kasdan (*Grand Canyon, The Big Chill*) tends to stick very closely to what is on the page, while Oliver Stone tries to remain as flexible as possible and considers the editing process itself "the last rewrite." Often he will edit individual scenes so that the dialogue is delivered in an order very different from how it was scripted and shot.

Perhaps the single most important thing any director does is impart a sense of collective vision to all of the other collaborators. Everyone needs to be able to "see" the same movie if what is in the script is to find its way to the theater. Again and again we were told of projects that failed because the script's original vision got lost in its long, laborious journey to the screen.

Producer Richard Zanuck (*Driving Miss Daisy*) told us that the first decision any producer makes is the most important—the commitment to make the movie. This is not an undertaking reached lightly, for each project takes on a life of its own and most often it's a very long life. By no means does the commitment guarantee that the script will eventually find its way to the screen. More often than not it won't.

Again and again we were told that movies that got made, especially great movies, were the product of a tenacious persistence of vision. Sometimes it comes from the writer, sometimes from the director or producer—all are early collaborators involved in the development process.

Once production actually begins, there are a thousand ways for the original vision to go awry. So many people become involved at this point that problems are inevitable. Hollywood lore is replete with such stories. Suffice it to say that the pure adrenal rush of the production process takes an incredible toll on all involved. Often it takes a toll on the script as well.

In spite of everything, every so often the talent and skills of the collaborators win out and their persistence of vision prevails. In these rarified moments a new "classic" is born. Another film can be added to the small list of movies that truly make a difference.

In a speech at the Women in Film Crystal Awards, Barbra Streisand echoed the words of many of the filmmakers we spoke with: "I am committed to making films about positive transformations and unlimited growth. I want uplifting, life-affirming films, films not only about life as it is, but life as it can be."

Director Ron Howard (*Cocoon*) puts it this way:

I'm most concerned about characters and their evolution, their growth as human beings as they try to cope. Sometimes these moments of triumph are very small, sometimes they're bittersweet. I guess I'm an optimist. The mere fact that most people are struggling to do the right thing, to be happy, makes me feel optimistic.

This is not to say that all classic movies should have a "feel-good" quality or share the same philosophies or politics. Far from it. Yet in every extraordinary film, there is always a concerted effort by the collaborators to express a vision that will provide audiences with something that will help them find their own "moments of triumph." Actor Edward James Olmos (*Stand and Deliver*) puts it most succinctly. "Intent is content," he explains. Such an approach "may not always make dollars, but it does make sense."

So many films seem bent only on pummeling our emotions or providing a series of guffaws. That's not nearly good enough. Our interviewees were more than willing to take responsibility for the content of their films and discuss what they hope will be their long-term impact on the audience.

Yes, there are many things that can go *wrong* in the making of a film. Scripts get trampled, visions are shattered, egos careen out of control. We hear about it all the time. We'd be the last to deny that the vast majority of well-intended films do not succeed commercially *or* artistically. Our mission was simply to seek out those few that did and see if we could discover how and why they were successful.

What follows are the secrets of the best screenwriters and the methods of Hollywood's most effective and respected producers and directors. You'll hear about their struggles, their decisions, and the visions that keep them going through the many years it takes to move a story from script to screen.

You'll learn about the performance techniques of accomplished actors and meet the cinematographers, editors, composers, and others who are "behind the scenes" of the movies you love. Whether you currently work in the industry or simply love great films, we promise that you will never see them in quite the same way again.

It is our hope that you will come to share the vision of these talented filmmakers, a common belief that those who make movies have a responsibility to help lead the rest of us toward discovery and growth, toward a more illuminating vision of the world we return to as we walk through the exit doors and out into the light.

1
doing
the
write
thing

Audiences don't know somebody sits down and writes a picture.
They think the actors make it up as they go along.

—Billy Wilder

The battle cry of the summer of '89 was *"Carpe diem,"* the Latin phrase for "Seize the day." It came from *Dead Poets Society*, an unlikely summer hit movie about a group of prep school boys. Some audience members reported making new life decisions as a result of seeing the film. Teachers were inspired. Everyone fondly remembered the teachers of their past. Virtually no one walked out of the theater unmoved or unaffected. A new classic film was born.

The film's collaborators were among the first to feel its effects. *Dead Poets* provided new direction for the career of Robin Williams while launching those of actors Robert Sean

Leonard (*Much Ado About Nothing*) and Ethan Hawke
(*Alive*). Director Peter Weir added another gem to a consider-
able résumé that already included *Witness* and *The Year of
Living Dangerously*.

Disney's Touchstone Studios, which had taken several
years to decide to make the film, was the beneficiary of over
$100 million in domestic grosses. *Poets* was also a solid hit
overseas. *"Carpe diem"* was, literally, a message heard around
the world.

And it all happened because of one person. Screenwriter
Tom Schulman began with a threadbare premise, a few personal experiences, and a desire to write something "about
pursuing your dream no matter what."

> I was frustrated with trying to write scripts I had no real
> emotional connection with. I was writing action pictures,
> horror films, *Kentucky Fried Movie*–type comedies.
> Things I had very little aptitude for—they simply weren't
> special enough. They were like other movies I had seen
> versus something I really believed in. I never thought of
> *Dead Poets* as a commercial script. I figured it wouldn't
> sell, but as I got into it, I thought it felt awfully good.

When Schulman finished the first draft of the script, he was
one of 25,000 writers who annually register their projects at
the Writer's Guild. By the time it was all over, Schulman was
living the dream of every screenwriter: He was standing on the
stage of the the Shrine Auditorium accepting his best screenplay Oscar.

Footprints in the Dark

Unless writers are fortunate enough to win one of two Academy writing awards handed out each year (Best Original Screenplay, Best Adapted Screenplay), no one outside the industry will ever have the faintest idea who they are. Paid far less than the star or director, their names will appear "up there" for all of a second or so. And then they will be gone.

Now as ever, screenwriters labor in anonymity. "It's a monastic existence," says William Kelley, who, nevertheless, collaborated with Earl Wallace to create *Witness* and received an Academy Award for his efforts.

You have heard of Harrison Ford? He starred in *Witness*. You may even be familiar with director Peter Weir. But unless you are a writer, chances are you are unfamiliar with names like Kelley or Wallace, Frank Pierson or Pen Densham, Babaloo Mandel and Lowell Ganz, or any of the other top screenwriters whose words and ideas, characters and conflicts have produced so many of Hollywood's recent classic films.

The best screenwriters may labor in anonymity, but what they leave behind is a future all their own, the unmistakable "footprints in the dark" that will illuminate the way for all who follow.

The writer begins with a blank page and must create the story, imagine the characters, and start the long visualization process that will eventually yield a motion picture. Everyone who follows will be interpreting—for better or for worse—this original blueprint.

The journey from script to screen will be long and

arduous—and, it is hoped, will be a good collaboration. When it is, everyone along the way—producers, directors, actors, production designers, composers, and many others— will embellish and hone the ideas, adding layers to the characters and the story. Yet all will be interpreting and enhancing the original screenplay.

In order for a writer to function creatively under these conditions, a certain mindset is required, a firm belief that what you are doing can make a difference.

If you were casting the part of a veteran fiftysomething screenwriter, you'd probably want Frank Pierson. The man who gave us *Presumed Innocent, Cool Hand Luke,* and *Dog Day Afternoon* explains that the idiosyncratic nature of the screenplay all but guarantees writer anonymity as it makes its way from script to screen.

A screenplay is a very strange form of creative writing. Structured like a play, flowing like music, consisting of 120 pages or so of dialogue and a few sparse stage directions that will act as the creative impetus *for everything that is to come.*

And stay tuned, there's a lot more to come. Since the making of a studio film is a collaborative art, whatever immortality screenwriters achieve comes not from name recognition but from the work they leave behind. Pierson explains:

The fact is that a successful film, one that works on the level it was conceived and finds an audience, carries one's feelings and ideas about the life we share to literally hundreds of millions of people all over this fragile planet. I hope for some kind of future for the human race, and I'd like to illuminate that in some way.

William Kelley knows that the need to express oneself has to be guarded and nurtured. "The writer is given a little bit of madness and we must take very good care of it, preserve it, and let the world think that we're nuts. And we are, to the degree that we're willing to isolate ourselves for weeks at a time and not go anywhere."

Out of the writer's isolation comes ideas, and for Kelley, an accountability to the audience, the "final collaborators" who will eventually watch the film.

> We see darkness and we try to light a candle. We try to be proper citizens of what we occupy. We are allied in a specific time with an audience of contemporaries, and we owe them the best of our talent that we can give them.

Like many creative endeavors, a script begins in darkness. But if the writer is to leave those footprints in the dark, a candle must be lit. It begins with an idea, a creative spark. But where does that spark come from?

What If . . .

Despite his Oscar-nominated credit as the co-writer of *Tootsie*, Larry Gelbart is perhaps best known for his four years as a writer-producer on TV's *M*A*S*H*. Where do his ideas come from?

> Ideas come from within and without. They spring from your own observations or your need to say something, not necessarily a message, but the need to tell a story. It's partly a need to communicate something about the human condition, to communicate to people who might have the

same experiences, feel the same emotions, be influenced and impacted by the same stories.

So part of the writer's job is to find the idea that will speak to millions. Generally this begins with a what-if, whether the story is an original screenplay or is to be adapted from another source. What if a prosecutor assigned to investigate a murder is charged with the murder himself? (*Presumed Innocent*) What if an out-of-work actor disguises himself as a woman to get a part? (*Tootsie*)

Screenwriter Gelbart is also an accomplished playwright. His multimedia credits afford a unique perspective. "It's not the size of the idea, but the temperature of it," he explains. "Ideally it's something you shouldn't merely want to do, but something you absolutely have to do."

Computers, Cards, and Boxes

The process may begin with many ideas that must be winnowed down to one story, or a small spark that lights a fire that spreads rapidly and eventually takes over.

For writer-director Lawrence Kasdan the ideas that "bubble up to the surface" tend to be very personal. "I work out of my own interests, enthusiasm, obsessions, and neuroses." The man responsible for *Grand Canyon* and *The Big Chill* admits that for him, even one movie idea is hard to come by.

I don't have a lot of ideas floating around. I wish I did. I tend to have a few things that interest me, and one tends to bubble up to the surface more strongly than the others and demand my attention. Then I start to let my mind play with that. Of course, once you start writing, almost anything else seems more appealing, but I don't desert what I'm working on for the most part.

Pen Densham originated the story line for the rousing *Robin Hood: Prince of Thieves* and co-wrote the screenplay with John Watson.

> I probably have two or three hundred story ideas in my computer from one-liners. And they may sit there for years. And I'll suddenly go "Oh, I know how to add a theme to this one."
>
> I read somewhere that someone came up with a shoe box system, leaving little pencils and file cards around the room, and you just filled them up with ideas. It seemed like a good method. On one project I ended up with two thousand cards in the shoe box and sorted them all out and wrote a script based on them.

Though he employs a different system now, most of Lawrence Kasdan's early scripts (*The Big Chill, Body Heat*) were done utilizing a card system. He describes it as a three-step process:

> I would begin to make cards—they were just total free association—any thought that crossed my mind. It could be an image of someone on a stairwell or a bit of conversation that I overheard. It could be a joke. And I would just create a stack—no editing.
>
> Then I would go to the second stage—which was an outline for the movie. That would be a different kind of card. Those would be scene cards. And to each of those scene cards, certain of the idea cards would apply. I would literally take those ideas and put them with the appropriate scene cards. Some of the idea cards never found a

use—some were stuck on scenes but not used. I just couldn't make them work.

Then I would work my way through the script in my mind—making a final card for each scene or sequence. Eventually I would wind up with a set of cards which would take me through the movie.

At the ripe old age of twenty-four, writer-director John Singleton has already been nominated for two Academy Awards.

I keep a journal and write in it about what's going on right now and how it pertains to the film. Eventually I transfer it to three-by-five cards. Every scene has a card. Each time I write about it or talk about it, it changes. It really has a life of its own.

I come up with new ideas for dialogue and dialects. I write ideas for the style of the film, or the style of the scene. Timewise I may write three hours one day and ten minutes the next. It all depends. If I'm bored with what I'm writing I won't write. I try to keep rewrites to a minimum. I want every word that's there to have passion behind it. I can't write just for the sake of doing it.

Interestingly, it is the right title that acts as Singleton's primary catalyst. During the late 1980s he was a screenwriting student at the University of Southern California during a period in Hollywood when high-concept films such as *Twins* and *The Terminator* were all the rage. Though his films are decidedly different from those projects, he did learn what he calls "an accepted show business notion, a Barnum and Bailey thing" about immediate and direct movie titles.

"*Jaws*, for example, you know what it's about. I think of a title first and then what goes with it. Like *Poetic Justice*. A woman named Justice who writes poetry. *Boyz N the Hood*. It says what it is."

While writers often begin with their own ideas, many of the industry's most successful screenwriters are hired guns, brought in to create a hundred pages or more from a single concept. For Babaloo Mandel and Lowell Ganz, "almost nothing is ever completely generated by the two of us. Generally somebody drops a what-if on us. A lot of them come from Imagine Films."

Their office at Imagine is on the twenty-third floor of a formidable Century City skyscraper where they share a breathtaking view of Los Angeles with director Ron Howard and producer Brian Grazer, whose own offices are nearby. "We run with about 5 percent of the ideas. We have a drawer full of about seven or eight scripts that we've been paid for that haven't been produced." Despite the frustration that goes along with the job, it's a record most screenwriters would envy. Mandel and Ganz tend to speak as one voice:

> Usually the idea starts with a sentence. With *City Slickers* it was "What if three yuppie-type guys who have wives and families in New York go on one of those fantasy cattle drives?" Or Ron Howard might say "I'd like to do a movie about being a dad" and that became *Parenthood*. For *Splash*, Brian Grazer's idea was simply "What if a guy falls in love with a mermaid?"

Research: It's All in the Details

Whether the story is about a modern-day mermaid or the merry men of olde England, the process usually incorporates research. And there always seem to be a few unexpected twists

and turns along the way. Pen Densham's take on Robin
Hood's adventures is illustrative of how the writer's mind
combines the story ideas and research that result in a completed script. "I started off with one line, which was 'Robin
Hood à la *Raiders*' [*of the Lost Ark*], and that sat in my
computer bank for five years."

> Then one day I said, "Maybe I should start in an Arab
> prison, which would be a big twist because you wouldn't
> know where you were, you might think you're in Iran
> today." And then we suddenly go back and realize it's a
> thousand years ago.
> I always wanted to do something which would make a
> statement about the problems of the Protestants and Cath-
> olics in Ireland, it's like the problems of Arabs and the
> Jews, which is how to try and put two religions together in
> a cooperative way.

It was at this point that Densham began to research the
cultural and political milieu that eventually found its way to
the screen.

> I read about the Arabs in *Timetables of History* and found
> that there were Arab doctors at the Court of Germany.
> Arabs were doing brain operations, they understood as-
> trological navigation, so I kept making these notes, I
> started to get these little islands of what I wanted to do.
> I wanted the forces of values and religion and ethics to
> go up against black magic. I wanted Robin to be a sensible
> hero looking for spiritual development and the sheriff was
> his doppelgänger trying to get spiritual development in
> sensual terms, carnality, ritual.

Any story set in a world unfamiliar to the writer presents special research challenges. Mandel/Ganz found themselves in no-man's land after being assigned to do the story of the reunion of a women's baseball team that became the hit film *A League of Their Own*.

We read articles from *Life* and other sources. A woman had done a thesis on the women who had played in the league. We went to the reunion in Cooperstown of the original women players and interviewed them for a couple of days.

What they encountered was a problem that has plagued all interviewers who must reconstruct history from the experiences of their interviewees.

It was very difficult because the women only wanted to answer questions or reminisce from the perspective that they had already done it. But we were trying to find the transformation. We had to get these women to go back forty-five years, to when they were really very different people, because the league had changed them in very fundamental ways and we wanted to know where they had begun.

We asked a lot of questions—basically feeling questions. "You're this terrific ballplayer and how did you view yourself? How did other people view you? Did you feel acceptance? Did they make you feel odd? Did you feel fine? Freaky? How frightening was it? Was it what you expected?"

Every project presents its own unique research problems. For *Children of a Lesser God*, writer Hesper Anderson began with a play by Mark Medoff, but realized she would need to know much more about what it was like to be deaf. "I spent about four weeks learning sign language, and spent several weeks at a deaf school and with the deaf community in L.A. I couldn't write Sarah without knowing sign language, without knowing what it looked like."

It's hard to imagine a more difficult research process than that necessitated by Oliver Stone's *JFK*. Ideally, research springs from a passion for telling a story that the writer feels must be told.

> The grist is in real life. To take from real life. The umbilical cord is to other people. I spent a lot of time with Jim Garrison. Jim talks in a certain way and he gets your juices flowing. I try not to impose my own view from the outside. I really like to take it from the inside. With *JFK* I was very attached. I work as a professional—but *I feel it*.

Structure: Building the Perfect Beast

Once the concept is clear and research under way, most writers turn their attention to structuring the story—seeking out a natural beginning, middle, and end. All mention three-act structure as their basic building block, though the degree of emphasis and use of other nuances varies from writer to writer.

"Story is structure" is one of screenwriting's most enduring clichés, and not without reason. Many of the most successful writers say that story structure is the single most important function of the writing process, one that will ultimately determine the success or failure of the script and of the film itself.

Whether the project is a fantasy such as *Splash* or a historical drama such as *A League of Their Own*, Ganz and Mandel explain that the structure must be in place early on.

> We have a plan before we start writing. It goes from premise (idea), to character arc (change and growth), to story arc—the beginning, middle, and end. We always think in terms of the three-act structure. Act breaks to us are thrusts.
>
> We do spend a lot of time on introductions. We're very patient with them. Our first acts might be long, maybe thirty to thirty-five minutes, but hopefully it's been fun along the way. For us, the second act takes up about 50 percent of the movie. The third acts are short, ideally about twenty minutes long.

Robin Hood's Pen Densham sees screenplay structure in what he calls "geographical" terms. It's as if the writer begins work in a desolate wilderness and, by developing the story, finds a way to tame it.

> You write in layers. When you write a script, you first write the geography. You map out the story. Then you go back and write some more and chisel out a gravel road. Then you pave it and start putting in your freeways. The various roads will allow you to get to these places and you're going to spend a lot of time there. You continually add more details and focus your story.

For Hesper Anderson screenwriting may be an art, but structure is more a matter of craft.

> Craft is easy, art is difficult. Craft has to be digested. I learned craft through three years of working in episodic

television. You need to learn craft until it becomes second nature. Find the opening scene. Set up the scene. Know where you're headed. Shape the story. Build to the action crisis at the end of act two, which leads to a realization by the main character that automatically leads to the end.

In *Children of a Lesser God*, this important realization scene occurs when Sarah finally "talks," really just an inarticulate kind of noise, which prompts her to go home and lead James to sit under water, so he can imagine what it's like to be deaf. And this eventually leads to their reconciliation.

For Frank Pierson, one key to story structure can be found at the end of the first act. "In building the structure of the story, the first-act climax is usually an intense scene in which the nature of the main character is fully revealed, either to the audience or himself or both. It's a scene that changes the direction of the story and sets up the nature of the conflict."

Pierson reveals how this theory applies to one of his most ambitious and successful projects.

In *Cool Hand Luke*, Luke is on a collision course with Dragline, the convict leader. The first-act climax is a fight scene in which Dragline, who is infinitely stronger, beats Luke to pulp. Luke will not stay down; he keeps getting up to face more blows.

Finally Dragline quits, thus forfeiting the fight. In the end, Luke's will is stronger. Though beaten to a pulp he is a grinning winner. . . . This is the turning point at which Luke changes from an unknown and disturbing element to a man with a name and an unwanted position of leadership, and the story changes direction.

Bill Kelley's *Witness* provides another oft-cited model of screenplay structure. In this case the first and second acts have individual rhythms that are devoted to distinctly different purposes.

> I have my three-act structure. I write a little description, two or three sentences. Then I envision the script as a series of sequences. The director doesn't think in terms of scene but sequence. Each scene has to carry the story forward and proceed from the scenes before it and then lead into the scenes following it. So I anticipate the director's use of sequence.
>
> Usually the first act will fall rather nicely into three sequences. In *Witness* the first sequence is everything leading up to the arrival in Philadelphia. The second sequence starts with Samuel seeing the murder and goes through the shooting of John Book. The third sequence is the escape and drive back to the farm and includes the scenes up to John's ability to start walking around.
>
> Then you go into the second act, the idyll in the middle at the Amish farm. We see them falling in love, heavy on subtext. It gives you a chance to relish what you've learned and let it sink in. This idyll includes the barn raising, which I see as the fulcrum of the story, and ends with their kiss followed by the arrival of the bad cops.

In fact, the deliberate pace of the second act contributed so significantly to the success of the film that Kelley tends to use it in most of his projects. "I see a screenplay now with the beginning of the second act of the movie slowing down after three fast-paced sequences. I'm going to slow it down and really get to know the characters and really define motivation."

At the same time Kelley stresses the structure of each individual scene. "The scene still must be beautifully done, it must rise and have its three parts just like an act." Story structure remains a vital issue at every stage of a screenplay's evolution.

Comedy Structure: A Funny Thing Happened . . .

Comedy can present special structural problems. David Zucker learned this the hard way after producing *Airplane!* with his brother Jerry Zucker and Jim Abrahams. It's a movie that still makes many all-time funniest film lists.

> After *Airplane!* came out, we took the wrong lessons from it because everybody thought it was so funny. So when we did *Top Secret*, which combined two genres, World War II spy movies and Elvis movies, we satirized them but without a cohesive plot and without characters who had motivations and clear intentions. We didn't pay any attention to character arcs.

Looking back on the box-office failure of *Top Secret*, Zucker contends that its problems stemmed from the methods he and his partners used while constructing the story.

> We focused too much on the jokes. We'd make notes on all the scenes, and write down all the jokes and sometimes we'd put them on cards so that we could apportion them; this is a love-story joke, or a second-act joke. The pitfall of doing it that way is that you start falling in love with certain

jokes and you start to shoehorn the plot so that it can encompass the joke.

Today Zucker begins each new project with an initial emphasis on story and character. Yet there is always an elusive balance to be achieved between the jokes and the story.

The plot and structure are the most important parts of our films, it's not the jokes. We start by saying "Who's the villain?" That's what the plot is riding on.

At the same time, there's a certain pace to these satires and you don't want to go too long without a joke. We figure about three jokes a page because it's satire. It's much easier to keep an audience laughing once they've started than to start them laughing all over again.

There's a certain grace period at the beginning of the movie. People are eager to laugh, but if you let them down, the audience kind of settles back and you've lost their trust.

Ruthless People is one of those rare scripts that is as admired for its story structure as for its comedic elements. Zucker says it provided a working laboratory where he and his collaborators were able to combine comedy with what they were learning about plot and character.

Dale Launer wrote the script, and it was almost there. We did know that there were going to be three acts in this— there would be a beginning, middle, and an end. Every character was going to have an arc and a payoff. Everybody was going to have a definite want at the beginning. Everything was somehow going to get resolved or satisfied at the end.

But even after doing the movie, we still ended up cutting one whole fifteen-minute sequence which was superfluous to the main plot. So we never stopped learning all through *Ruthless People*.

When writing comedy, Ganz and Mandel also tend to start with the needs of the characters and the actors who play them.

We look at character motivation, what will make the character do the next thing, not the joke. Our attitude is, they're just jokes, we'll write another one. If it doesn't help the scene, we cut the joke. I've seen writers fight for a joke, even when the actor isn't comfortable with the joke. In that case, throw it out and write another joke!

Whether comedy or drama, the primary task of the screenwriter tends to be the structuring of the story. Once the structure or "spine" of the story emerges, it's time to focus on the characters who will inhabit that story and what they will learn along the way.

The Driver's Seat: Character Versus Story

If you were to spend an average day inside the development offices of a major Hollywood studio, the two terms you might hear most often are "story driven" and "character driven." This unique shorthand signals a perceived dichotomy in feature films.

A script is said to be story driven if it relies primarily on a high-concept plot, one that implies action and conflict and can be readily gleaned from a brief synopsis, such as: "A kid is inadvertently left at home while his parents go on vacation. He has to fend off the crooks and save the day." (*Home Alone*)

On the other hand, a script is said to be character driven if its appeal relies primarily on the development of the characters and the changes that their personalities undergo during the film. For example: "A housewife learns to become more independent as she listens to the stories of an aging woman in a rest home." (*Fried Green Tomatoes*)

Character-driven stories are generally perceived to be "softer" and less marketable than more action-oriented story-driven projects. Yet a careful examination of the very best Hollywood films defies this type of categorization. Is *Ruthless People* about the characters or the story? *Witness, Thelma and Louise,* and *The Crying Game* include some memorable action sequences, yet clearly they are mostly about what the main characters learn along the way.

The point is that classic Hollywood films defy categorization because they combine story and character elements into a single, seamless, and memorable theatrical experience.

Creating Unforgettable Characters

Bill Kelley demands that character and story elements work together and offers his own method for getting in touch with one's fictional progeny.

Every scene must reveal character and push the story forward. . . . You know the heart of your story and you've already decided who your characters are. When you come down the stairs the next morning, you empty your mind and listen to your silence, and those characters will speak

to you. If you have done your homework, done your
character studies on index cards or whatever you do, then
they will speak to you.

You've got to walk their ground and let it seep into
your shoes, into your soul. You have to be there and be
quiet, half a day—or whatever it takes. What I want in
the end is a work of art that's living, one that throbs with
life.

Pen Densham is always on the lookout for how his characters
will travel down the paths of the story.

I write down clusters of thoughts about what they're
thinking, then they start to speak in their own language. At
the same time you have to think about the purpose of the
story. With *Robin Hood*, the character of Robin is learning
about sacrifice and human understanding as he is going
through the adventure.

Many writers begin by discovering who and what their characters are all about. Ganz and Mandel are quick to explain,
"Our stories are always character driven. We begin with
the protagonist, asking what kind of people would make
this thing happen? Hopefully the events are character
driven."

They also feel the process can be expedited if the writer
has some basic knowledge of psychology and a healthy curi-
osity about people as well.

It's helpful to be the kind of person who grew up having a
sort of penchant for examining people. You do imitations
of people. It helps if you can honestly say, "This is the kind
of thing that makes me act stupid." Then when our charac-

ters are at their worst or their silliest, we can honestly say,
"We get like that."

We try to write characters that we can identify with
even when we're not admiring them. And of course we're
really big on finding the main characters' voices.

Finding those voices—hearing them—comes about in a number of ways. Writer-director Ron Shelton's *Bull Durham* is
considered by many to be Hollywood's definitive baseball
film. "I won't start a script until I have my characters' voices.
I'll spend weeks or months, but it won't happen until I can
hear how they talk, and what they are going to say."

Crash Davis is *Bull Durham*'s perennial minor league
catcher. His first line is "Hi, I'm the player to be named later."
Shelton says, "As soon as I heard his opening line, I knew I
had him." He explains that in baseball terms, Crash was
always the unnamed player thrown in to sweeten a trade. He
was never the main player. And his entire character grew out
of that one line.

Frank Pierson tries to find something in his characters that
he can relate to his own personality.

There are those who begin a film by constructing a plot
and then try to find characters whose conflict will cause
that plot (and no other) to happen.

I prefer to begin with a character whose drives touch
some unconscious aspect of myself, and then proceed to
work out a story that dramatizes this character's dilemma,
by finding complementary characters whose drives are in
conflict.

You have to feel a deep sympathy and alliance, a har-
mony with the character. The best writing is done when
one can literally feel the body rhythms of the character,

when one can walk and move and dream like the character. It is a kinesthetic empathy, experienced not in the
brain but in the bones and muscles.

Masculine, Feminine, or Human?

With his own neatly trimmed white beard, burly Bill Kelley looks a bit like a modern-day Hollywood Hemingway. It
seems logical to probe him about how he creates memorable
male characters such as John Book of *Witness*. "I start with the
ideal man. Dignity is a very big key to me for the male character. I have to find what a man thinks of dignity, this is the man
who is my hero. And he has to have something of an intellect.
And then I dress him down. What are his faults? What are his
weaknesses?"

Highly regarded for her ability to create complex, independent female characters such as Sarah in *Children of a
Lesser God*, Hesper Anderson says, "I dig deep, I feel everything. I live everything." As she pauses for a moment, you can
almost see the characters flashing before her eyes.

In writing, I become all of the characters. It's dreamtime.
Time to get inside the character. You lay the groundwork
and hope it kicks in. Then a miracle happens, you wake
up, get in the shower, and suddenly your characters take
on a life of their own, they start talking, moving around.
They've taken over. They come alive and they won't shut
up. I become exhausted by them.

Getting It on the Page

Overcoming exhaustion is but one of many obstacles a
writer faces. Once a structured story line is complete and the
characters are speaking, it's time to get down to the business of
"getting it on the page." All writers have their own approach.
For many, getting started is the hardest part. Lawrence Kasdan found a certain comfort level grew out of his card collec-
tion method. "They were an enormous help for me to get over
the big hurdle, which is to start. Once I started I was usually
fine—but the trick was to start."

Bill Kelley describes the process as "Part madness, part
craft, and a very big part is stamina. I'll work ten or twelve
hours a day and it will seem like two hours. You make it
happen by getting your ass in the chair and beginning."

Writer-director Barry Levinson reveals, "I play music
whenever I write. It becomes a little insane. I'll just play the
same thing over and over again. When I was writing *Diner* I
used to play Peter Townshend's *Empty Glasses.*"

Pen Densham's approach might best be described as "taking no prisoners." "Writing is trench warfare. You take it
trench by trench until you've finally won the battle. What you
keep hoping for when you start to type that first line is that
there will be an atomic bomb and it will be over quickly!" He
laughs. "I've never been able to do that. But I have found that
I can win a couple of trenches along the way."

Short of an atomic bomb, there seems to be no easy way to
get through the excruciating task of completing a script. Perhaps that is one of the reasons why some of the most successful
Hollywood writers work so quickly.

Writer-director Ron Shelton's sports-related films have
raised the genre to new heights. If you passed him on the

street you would probably say he looks like the ex-ballplayer that he, in fact, is. Tall and rugged, the term blue collar somehow suits him. "I generally spend a lot of time mulling, then I write fast. For *White Men Can't Jump*, I started writing on September twentieth. By the afternoon of the twenty-first I had thirty-seven pages; all of them wound up on the screen."

He stops for a moment and smiles a painful smile. "Then the next three weeks . . . nothing. Not one line!" Like a minor league catcher recalling his glory days, Shelton confides, "I used to be able to write two or three scripts at once. Not now."

Ganz and Mandel have been through the process so many times they can describe their routine effortlessly:

> We usually talk it through for weeks before we actually start writing, working five days a week. If we're really prepared, once we start writing, it should not take more than two months for a first draft.
>
> We come in at ten or ten-thirty in the morning. We read the previous days' pages. If they don't make us nauseous, we move on. We try to get up a head of steam about lunchtime, talking about what that day's scene is, talk it through for a half hour or an hour. Eat lunch, and then write until four or four-thirty and go home. We average about a scene a day, sometimes two. The rewriting, however, takes about a year!

Sticking to a set schedule seems to work for many writers. Kasdan recalls a time before his first sale—when he was working full time in an advertising job he loathed and feeling very guilty every moment that he wasn't writing.

At that point my wife saved me by saying, "You've got to stop it. You've got to have certain times when you know you are supposed to write and other times when you are free because your free time is very valuable." We had a little boy at that time—our first son. And it saved my sanity.

Shortly after that he did sell his first script, *The Bodyguard*, although it took fifteen years to get produced. Like so many writers, Kasdan also struggles with his own natural inclination to "avoid" writing, even during the hours he sets aside for it. What he finally discovered was a lesson that all writers can take to heart.

It took me many years to realize that the time that I "wasted" reading the trades and reading the newspaper and walking the halls at Fox or Warner Brothers . . . I thought it was all wasted time and I felt bad about it. But eventually I would start to write—whether it was twelve-thirty or four, and I would usually get a pretty good amount of work done, whether it was two or four or six hours. I finally realized that the walking around and reading time was part of it.

I'm not a machine. I had to learn to accept my own rhythms. As long as the stuff came out I was all right. In fact, I wrote very fast. I started keeping track of how long it actually took me to write a script and it wasn't very long. Three months was plenty.

Hesper Anderson alternates between features and television movies. She feels that the type of projects she takes on help dictate her schedule. "I take three or four months to write most of my scripts. I can only do about two projects a year because of the research and emotional depth that I find necessary."

No Pain, No Gain (No Script!)

It takes courage to create—and a willingness to go deep into the truth. Bill Kelley describes the writer's process as "a dredging up of almost all you are, dredging self out of it and trying to get it into another character. You've got to write the awful heart of the matter."

"It helps to have had pain in your life," says Pen Densham. "I think that creativity is an evolutionary survival trait, but it also creates worry and stress. I think people write to discover things in themselves. They may not be conscious of it, but it's a therapeutic process."

Kelley agrees. "I've never known a good writer who didn't feel struggle and pain, whether he'd met it or put himself to it through adventures or testing himself. Hemingway would say, 'If you haven't got anything to write about, try hanging yourself. If you succeed, your troubles are over, if you don't, you've got something to write about.' "

The best writers feel a responsibility to their art and to their audience. "Writing is holy," says Kelley.

We are keepers of the flame. We sit down at our dulcimer and try to steal a little fire from heaven. We are keepers of the word—we must know the word, the proper word. We must know what words mean, and we must know if there's a better word. And we are keepers of the gate, we see darkness and we try to light a candle. We try to be proper citizens of what we occupy.

David Zucker says simply, "We are responsible for what we're putting on the screen and what we're saying. And remember, you may get a successful movie with a bad script, but you'll never get a good movie."

From Script to Theme: What's It All About?

How do great scripts differ from those that are merely well written? Every classic script is about ideas. It has something to say—about life, about the human condition, about the writer's own insights into "what it's all about."

Most writers find that they explore the same themes over and over, even though their stories may be about very diverse subjects. For Ganz and Mandel, the ideas always seem to become entwined with their own interests and personal passions.

Our lead characters are almost always men our age, like in *City Slickers* or *Parenthood*. None of our male characters are traditionally heroic men. They're underconfident nice men. Like us!

We try to find themes that deal with people's anxieties and worries but we always have room for optimism. We are saying that it's hard to be a person, hard just to live, hard to be regular. We're cynical and pessimistic and neurotic and we're worried and we're frightened but we get through our own lives by just hanging on and saying "There's a way somehow."

For Hesper Anderson, a central theme involves communication and the fear of intimacy that sometimes goes along with it.

In *Children of a Lesser God* deafness to me was symbolic of the communication barriers between people. It was an exaggerated form of all the problems in communication that everybody has. That's the thing that gave the film a universal appeal, because it wasn't about deafness, but about the problems that everybody has, particularly in intimate relationships.

Bill Kelley once studied for the priesthood, and his concerns tend to grow out of a lifetime study of theology and philosophy. "I'm drawn back to the same themes again and again. About facing moral imperatives, about reaching for that extra dimension."

The question of theme is a vexing one for Lawrence Kasdan. Twice he resists sharing his own thoughts about "what it all means." Like many artists, he feels the interpretive issues are best left to those who experience the art, not those who create it. But as the question surfaces a third time, he finally gives in with a sigh.

Okay, I think all of my movies are about the struggle between ideal and desire. That is really what's going on in all of these movies.

The people of my generation embodied in the Bill Hurt character in *Body Heat* had sort of slid through life very easily. When confronted with the real world, they found that things were very difficult. And their desires were not always being met. In order to make the big score, it was sometimes necessary to bend the rules. *Body Heat* is set in a melodramatic form but the issue is the same— what are you willing to do to fulfill your desires, no matter what conflict they bring you into with your ideals?

In *The Big Chill* it's much more explicit but the issue is the same. The characters are remembering a time of total liberation where every desire was acted upon and gratified. They are looking back from a time in which all kinds of societal pressures and conventions are forcing them to conform. So the question is—can we lead an honorable life, not just because of the pressures from society but because of the internal pressures of our own desires? This is the issue for me every day of my life.

Kasdan continues unraveling the close-knit threads that weave through a body of work that many feel is the best that Hollywood has offered over the last decade.

A friend of mine did an analysis of *Grand Canyon*. He said it was about the tension between responsibility and liberation—if we equate liberation with following our desires and responsibility with being the family man and member of society.

Grand Canyon is about other things too, but I believe there is a subtext which is that a man who is very responsible is operating in a world that is chaotic and frightening. The experience he has when his car breaks down opens a window for him to another world where chaos reigns.

It's all about ideals, desires, and trying to control a universe which is terribly frightening and random. As random as a bus ending your life.

Rewriting: Making the Good Script Great

With story structure in place, characters well defined, and theme woven throughout, the initial wave of pain and anguish is over. The first draft of the script is complete.

However, the great script rarely appears right away. Once the first draft is complete, there are the inevitable rewrites. For a number of reasons this is the point where the collaborative nature of filmmaking begins to come into play.

No matter how good the writer is, it is difficult to be objective about one's own work. Producers and directors may read the script and find that the story is not as clear as the writer thinks it is. Perhaps a secondary character may appear to be more interesting than the protagonist. Maybe the comedy isn't funny or the action-adventure story lacks action and adventure.

Ideally, rewriting is a process of new discoveries for the writer. With the initial draft completed, the writer may now feel more confident and move to strengthen or sharpen a character. Perhaps a new theme has emerged during the writing process that needs to be expanded. Or maybe it's time to be a bit more outrageous by adding comic elements or to reach for deeper emotional layers during the dramatic scenes. More often than not, the painful rewriting process will yield a script with more depth and greater insight.

Not surprisingly, much of the rewriting will revolve around the nature of the project and who is involved. For Ganz and Mandel there is always someone waiting.

Usually there's somebody to whom we're submitting it—
Billy Crystal (*City Slickers*), Penny Marshall (*A League of*

Their Own), or Brian Grazer and Ron Howard (*Splash*).
They're the first people to see it and they'll have changes to
make. That will lead to a second and third draft.

Then we do a reading of the script, asking favors of
actor friends. This generates a lot of self-imposed rewriting. In preproduction, we get ideas from watching actors
read for parts. The director will come in with ideas, or
the stars. And if it's being rehearsed for a couple of weeks
before it's filmed, that generates some rewriting.

Given enough time, writers working closely with an actor or
director eventually arrive at a shared vision. "For *City
Slickers* we sat for a month with Billy Crystal and went over
the script line by line," says Ganz. "By the time the production started, he was like a writer on the set. He was our eyes
and ears. We felt totally secure that he had the exact same
vision we had."

Maintaining the original vision is somewhat easier if the
writer is also the director. Given the complexity of his scripts,
it is not surprising that Lawrence Kasdan works quite differently from most screenwriters.

I will write a scene and write it until I feel very good about
it. The reality is that I work very hard on the first draft.
Some people find it much more productive to speed
through a first draft, so they have something to work on.
The thing that is terrifying to them is the *unwritten* screenplay.

It was never that way for me. I wanted to like everything that I had left behind. When I started to direct,
the first draft was very much the movie that was going
to be made and it has remained that way. Obviously
there are deletions and changes, and hopefully they

will improve the movie, but I believe in the original impulse.

In practice, unless you are Lawrence Kasdan, it rarely works this way. Writing and rewriting a script for a big studio feature is filled with the kind of frustration that Hollywood legends are made of. Pen Densham, coming from Canada and a documentary tradition, was left aghast as he gradually discovered how the Hollywood system worked.

A script is a piece of papier-mâché and everyone else is going to come along and shape it. They'll mold it a little bit one way because Jack Nicholson wants to be in it and pat it flat again because Arnold Schwarzenegger wants to do it and then pump it up this way and bring in the comedy writer because Bruce Willis wants to do it. Then when that doesn't work, they throw it away.

Scripts are like chips, pieces of a roulette game. You throw them down on the numbers and you hope they're going to come up. And you try to accumulate enough numbers coming up so you get to make the movie.

Given all of this, the writer must remember that the act of scriptwriting, like any kind of writing that comes from the heart, must provide its own reward. John Singleton would always put his teachers on notice. "When I was in school I couldn't work on a screenplay that I didn't have my heart in. I would tell my instructors, 'I'm not writing this for you, I'm writing it for me.' "

Pen Densham says that screenwriting carries with it certain basic lessons in "investment theory."

You have to get your pleasure out of the act of writing it and creating it because if you invest too much in the act of wanting it to be your child, you're going to feel very hurt more times than you'll feel wonderful.

Still, you've got to feel about the act of creating a script as if you had created a child. The thing is you are not going to be the only person that helps it grow up.

Collaboration: Nothing is Easy

Whether the screenplay is close to its initial form or has been rewritten dozens of times, eventually the moment arrives when it must begin its journey to the screen. For the writer, even the writer-director, it means letting go, and that can be painful.

Describing this phenomenon in the *Wisconsin Screenwriters Newsletter*, writer Tom Eberhardt laments, "You should understand scriptwriting is like giving birth, then having the baby stolen by a bunch of dirty gypsies, and then seeing this thing on the street corner years later."

In a scene from Billy Wilder's classic *Sunset Boulevard*, fictional screenwriter Dan Gillis offers this observation on the rewriting process.

> GILLIS: The last one I wrote was about Okies in the dust bowl. You'd never know though because by the time it reached the screen the whole thing played on a torpedo boat.

Screenwriters have espoused such sentiments since movies began. And the truth is that many times, the script will not be

well cared for by its foster parents. Yet the fundamental function of the screenplay is not as a piece of literature, but as a
guide for the work to follow.

A poem, novel, short story, or magazine article is complete
or nearly complete when the writer's work is done. In contrast,
when a screenplay is finished, the real business is just beginning.

A script must serve many masters and accomplish many
purposes. Frank Pierson explains that most writers really
don't understand the very nature of what they have
created.

> The screenplay, before it is anything else, is a technical
> document. It is a different document for every person
> reading it. To the producer it is a story that he weighs for
> audience appeal (or if he's really good, simply as to
> whether he likes it or not). To the director it is a progres-
> sion of images and scenes in a dance rhythm that he or she
> may want to dance to.
>
> To the designer it is a list of locations and sets; to the
> wardrobe people it is a list of costumes; to the prop man a
> list of props; to the actor a list of lines to learn; to the
> assistant director a schedule; to the transportation captain
> a list of cars, trucks, maps, and times.
>
> Assuming they are trained professionals, each of these
> technical people is astonishingly good at figuring out what
> is needed from the slightest clues offered by stage direc-
> tions or the logic of the scenes. You are writing for all these
> people, but mostly they aren't reading anything except
> what pertains to them. They read the screenplay like a flea
> lives on a dog, without caring much what the whole dog
> looks like.

Ultimately the value of any script always comes back to its role as the plan or blueprint for the film. Densham's advice is deceptively simple.

> As a writer you need to tell a story that makes you cry, laugh, feel. You have to validate every step of it. Every element has to have a purpose—the choice of the characters, the choice of the actors, the choice of the music, camera, editing—all must be purposeful.
>
> It's the script that provides the magic that brings together a group of people, and it all comes from the imagination of the writer. That's the purpose of a script. In a sense, it's a magic carpet, where everybody that you need will climb on board that idea or dream and bring it to reality on the screen.

Frank Pierson's final comments reflect his vision of what the very best scripts must accomplish as they offer various possibilities in the context of the collaborative process.

> It is the writer's job to force the director and actor out of merely reproducing a text and into finding themselves in it, thereby allowing some possibility of creating art. The text is meant to be and must be constructed to be interpreted. This is the true meaning of collaborative art.

The collaborative art. Those words keep coming back. When all is said and done, this is what makes the best film writing unique. In the original script the words are the writer's own, as much an original vision as any form of writing. A year or two or ten years later, the lights will go down in a theater somewhere and the audience will finally hear that first line of dialogue. What happens in between is a collaborative experience like no other; a wondrous collision of art and commerce, a maddening high-stakes poker game played with pictures that "move" and mountains made of the money that keeps changing hands as the vision makes its perilous journey from script to screen.

C L O S E - U P

TOM SCHULMAN, *DEAD POETS SOCIETY*

I first got the idea that became *Dead Poets Society* when I was in acting school. We had an incredibly volcanic teacher who would talk about theater, acting, and movies and how relevant those things were to our lives. Every night after he'd speak we'd all go out for drinks and we'd say, "We've got to do that, we've got to form a theater that means something about life and happiness and love and politics." We were all imbued with this sense of purpose.

I thought it would be exciting to write a script about a theater school and about a teacher or director. But it just didn't work. There was no text to it. Acting can be a very self-involved profession, and I couldn't say what I wanted to say that way. So I started thinking back on my dad and an English teacher I had in high school who taught poetry and had the same kind of passion for it my father had.

My father loved poetry. He was a big fan of Tennyson, and *The Rubáiyát of Omar Khayyám*—things he had learned in his school days. So I was aware that poetry had wisdom and that a poet could be accessible.

I went to a high school that was modeled on a British academy so I knew what the school should be like. It would be set in the late 1950s, and there would be this atmosphere of repression where the parents would try to get their children to become businessmen, doctors, professionals. Part of the idea would be about pursuing your dream no matter what.

Hearing the Voices

I've always been fascinated with iconoclastic people—the mad prophet, the person who has an odd or different view of life—and with teachers who forced me to question. I worked on the Keating character for a long time. I tried to find a voice for him. I would just write anything that came to my mind, and look at it and think, "What is this all about? What is he trying to say? What's this voice in me about?"

When I first started to write Keating there were no students, just this man talking to this faceless crowd of people, trying to teach them how important ideas were. I wrote the first draft like that and I read it and I threw it away because it was so embarrassing. I felt I couldn't write it. I wasn't up to it. But a year later I said, "I've got to do that story."

Then I started thinking about who the students were going to be. I knew each would have his own individual arc and would be affected by this teacher. So I really worked backward, starting with kids who were in this lockstep kind of mentality, each with their own back story. But essentially they were flowers ready to bloom, and the teacher would encourage each to bloom in a different way.

One boy would fall in love. The shy kid Todd would come out of his shell. Neil was the student who went too far. He was a residue of the notion of doing the story in an acting school—

but Neil is the one who seizes upon acting. Remember, in that day and age acting wasn't even considered a real profession at all. Anyway, each of these kids would find a way to exemplify the theme the teacher was expressing, which was about creativity and conformity.

Something Special

What happens is that as you write, you're going through a transformation yourself so the growth of the main character parallels the growth in your own life. I always felt Keating was a character I had inside of me. I felt like I had all these things I wanted to say. And I was also like Todd. I was the shy kid in school. I hardly ever raised my hand. After a certain point in high school I just closed up.

As a writer, I was always hoping I could write a script that was so brilliant that someone would read it and never have to meet me. I wouldn't have to sit in a meeting and talk because I was so shy. In writing this movie I struggled with those issues.

It's difficult to write a withdrawn character because he never says anything. He's always hanging around, mute. But Todd, nevertheless, remained the main character in the movie.

He was the one who stood up and led the charge in the end. I was very careful in the script to inform the reader that Todd was the main character. I would constantly focus on where Todd was in the scene, what he was doing, or not doing. In the end this was visualized in the movie with close-ups, et cetera, and I think the key moments were there.

By the time I finished *Dead Poets Society* I really felt I had an idea of what I was doing as a writer. I felt I could at least express my ideas clearly on the page. I had years to work on craft without anybody watching me. Of course, I still wasn't sure it would sell.

Going Through Changes

When it did sell to Disney's Touchstone Pictures, there were some changes in the rewriting. Originally there was an intercut between Neil's suicide and a last meeting of the Dead Poets Society that took place after the play.

That last meeting was cut. One of the biggest changes was the ending. Originally Keating had Hodgkin's disease and [director] Peter Weir wanted to cut this. I found out about it when Jeffrey Katzenberg, the head of Disney, called:

"There's one script change."

"What is it?"

"The end."

I was stunned. Finally I said, "The standing-on-the-desk part? He wants to lose the desk part!"

He said, "I don't know, I'm not sure. I don't think it's about that at all. He doesn't think Keating should be dying."

Peter's explanation for it, which I finally came to embrace, was that it was unfair for a teacher, one who knows he's dying, to lead these kids into battle when he knows he doesn't have to suffer the consequences himself. It also diminishes what the boys standing up on the desk at the end means. It's easy to stand up for someone who is dying, but when the boys stand up for someone who's just like everybody else, we know they're standing up for the ideas that person believes in.

And at the end of the day I also agreed with Peter because when I originally laid out the story in outline, Keating was not dying. As organic as it may have seemed to the story, I had not added it until I actually wrote page eighty. I added it because I thought, I need a reason for Keating being this way. So I put in the Hodgkin's disease.

Peter told me, "It's amazing how easy it's going to be to

take this out—a simple cut of about five pages." When Robin Williams came in Peter Weir told him we had to lose the Hodgkin's disease and cancer. And Robin said, "Good idea."

And I thought, Okay.

There were some other changes. There was the scene where they rip out the pages of the book and before that there was a preface to the book that this boy reads. In the original draft, I used this poem: "The little toy dog is covered with dust, But sturdy and staunch he stands." Both Peter and I found the poem mawkish, but Peter felt some people might like it, so he said, "Let's see if we can come up with something better here."

And that's when we came up with the graph idea—where Robin draws it on the board. I remember Peter called one day and said, "I found it. What to substitute. It's in a book here." And he faxed pages that suggested a kind of mathematical way to rate poetry, so we used it.

We also worked on Neil's father, trying to soften him, to make him more accessible and understanding. At one point we went too far in that direction. He became too soft. We felt this man had to believe he was doing the best thing for his son. That his son was about to make a big mistake and he was going to stop it no matter what. He shouldn't think of himself as a villain; still, the consequences followed his actions.

Peter Weir's golden rule is no repetition if possible. Which can be difficult. As a writer you're trying to make a point. There's a tendency to want to hit these things on the head and make sure the audience gets it. Peter really goes the other way. He trusts the audience with subtlety. Which is one of the reasons he's a great director.

The whole process on this script was pretty much an ideal situation—the collaboration with [producer] Steven Haft and

Robin and Peter was great. It may never go this smoothly for me again.

The Struggle

The more I'm involved in this industry, the more I see the struggle between the commercial versus the personal project. Whenever I speak to writers I'm always encouraging them to write about things they care about and things they know. This certainly goes against the norm of modern movies, because most Hollywood movies are about high concepts and fantasics. But even some of those films have personal things that the audience is getting that may be deep.

I do believe if you write about things you feel deeply, you're bound to touch people. The only time we don't touch others is when we're absolutely disconnected from the things inside of us, when we're writing about nothing.

You have to come up with something that's a resonant theme, something that connects, and it has to be clear. I know that people go to see movies and they think, "I can do a script—that looks easy." So they take a stab at writing. But they often don't write about personal issues and the system doesn't encourage them to dig deep. That's the problem.

You have to really dig and suffer. The more you dig and connect with those key revelatory moments in your life, the better you write. The key to good writing is to write something where you really know the situation. Choose the assignments that really speak to you.

Of course, no matter what, writing is still a struggle. It doesn't get any easier no matter how many times you do it. You go into the room by yourself and you turn the computer on and the struggle remains the same.

2
the
producer
and the
long
run

The producer is like the conductor of an orchestra. Maybe he can't play every instrument, but he knows what every instrument should sound like.

—*Richard Zanuck*

Directors, actors, editors, and composers all have well-defined tasks. The producer is another story, and the proliferation of titles such as associate producer and executive producer in recent years hasn't helped.

Hollywood's most successful producers have grown used to explaining their jobs to those outside the industry. And the definitions tend to vary from producer to producer. Richard Zanuck's *Driving Miss Daisy* is a recent addition to a growing list of classic films that includes *Cocoon, Jaws,* and *The Sting*.

People outside of Hollywood and New York don't really
have a clear idea of what a producer is or what he does. It's
sort of tragic in a way that this important function doesn't
have a clearer image. Most people think a producer is the
person who puts up the money, which is wrong. If you're
smart you never put up the money yourself!

David Puttnam is widely respected for the quality of the films
he brings to the screen and renowned for his controversial
stint as the head of Columbia Studios. He explains the role of
the producer in a crisp British accent: "A producer is a mara-
thon runner who plods along, believing against all reasonable
hope that at some point he or she is going to go through the
tape and actually win!"

Coming from the man who produced *Chariots of Fire*, it
seems an apt metaphor. The producer's long run begins with
an idea that must be moved from script to screen. The rare
victory comes years later, when audiences find a film they love
and a new classic is born. Accomplishing this feat means going
uphill. "You have to take the long view and keep going. You've
got to have patience," says Puttnam.

"There's a kind of perfectionism; you can't be too easily
satisfied. You've got to keep trying to make everything better.
The script can be better. The cinematography can be better.
The music can be better. You must strive for an improved
product at all times."

From the time the starting gun is fired, Puttnam is thinking
about the people out there in the dark.

From Day One the important thing is that you represent
the audience—not necessarily everyone out there—but
the audience that the movie is being aimed at. If it's a

broad-based-appeal film, then those are the interests you
represent. If it's a movie with narrower appeal, then you
have to represent that interest.

Kathleen Kennedy's first producer credit came on *E.T. The
Extra-Terrestrial*, the all-time box-office champion. Since then
she has racked up an unprecedented string of hits, including
*Jurassic Park, Alive, Back to the Future, Indiana Jones and the
Temple of Doom*, and *Who Framed Roger Rabbit?*, "I think the
role of the producer is defined by what the movie requires,"
she explains.

Each picture is different. It may involve a number of
people, a lot of relationships. Or it may be something you
generate from a single idea or a book you optioned and
you have to decide who you want to become involved. All
of that dictates what my role will be.

Richard Zanuck literally grew up on the Fox lot where his
famous father, Darryl F. Zanuck, reigned as one of the last of
the old-time studio heads. Now in his fifties, Richard has the
benefit of a lifetime spent getting movies made.

Ideally, you're the first one on the project, even before
the writer—before anybody else. Maybe you don't have
the original idea of the story—but you will read a
book or see a play and say, "This would make a terrific
film."
    Take *Cocoon*, for example. It came to us as a manuscript
for a book that the writer couldn't get published. He
wanted our advice. What became the picture was only one
small segment of it, but we saw the idea in there. Ironically,

after the picture was a hit, he went back and rewrote the
book to conform to the movie.

Cocoon director Ron Howard joined producer Brian Grazer
to form Imagine Entertainment in 1982. Among Imagine's
more notable films are *A League of Their Own, Parenthood,*
and *Splash.* Grazer defines the producer as "the person who
must remember what the central vision and goal of the movie
is, and to try to be fiscally and creatively responsible for
that."

All of this speaks to the many roles that a producer might
play in bringing a project from script to screen. "There are so
many ways of being a producer," says Zanuck.

> There is the agent-style producer who plugs in the deal.
> The other extreme is what we do, which is shepherd the
> film from inception all the way to completion and beyond.
> In the end everyone else has gone off to do other things,
> but we're still out there in Tokyo or somewhere talking
> about the picture and selling it.

Kennedy says the producer is often the only one on the project
"who is part of the entire creative process. The director might
not come aboard until the script is completed and the financing is in place. In some cases the casting may also be complete.
The producer is often involved long before and after the
actual process of making the film."

The complete producer's role and its relationship to the
film brings to mind a famous line from *Citizen Kane.* After
Kane's death, his business manager explains to a reporter that
he was there "From *before* the beginning, young fellow, and
now it's *after* the end."

The First Decision

Noted for his ability to bring difficult but exceptional material to the screen, Zanuck says the producer must begin with a personal commitment, one that can never be taken lightly.

> The first decision, to get involved, is the most critical one in the entire process, because every decision that you make from that point on can't save you if the first one is wrong. No matter how many stars you put in it—you can get the best director in the world—if the subject is something that people don't want to see, you may make a brilliant movie out of it, but nobody will come to see it.

But what *do* people want to see? Brian Grazer says, "I like warm-spirited movies that have a theme, that are optimistic, with movie stars. You do a concept movie with movie stars, you have a pretty good chance it's going to make money. The movie is definable. You can set up your marketing according to an expectation."

"I never think of the marketplace," says Gale Anne Hurd, producer of *The Terminator*. "If you sit there and are always thinking about 'How will this play in Peoria?' you aren't serving the movie, you're serving the package. I don't think you can serve two masters. A film takes on its own life and you have to be serving that."

Richard Zanuck's career has been spent producing films that *seemed* to have limited audience appeal. Interestingly, this is precisely what he seeks as he makes the crucial first decision.

> I think the key to it is that it isn't a mainstream idea. These projects have a better chance because people get tired of

seeing the same thing, of not having choices. They want something different. Maybe they'll go like cattle to see the latest Schwarzenegger film, but we've proven that there is also a market for pictures that would seemingly have no audience appeal.

You can't just make an ordinary picture—you have to make an *extraordinary* picture. Find a subject that is exceptional and people are going to be attracted to it because it is unique. I'm actually playing it "safe" in a way by picking subjects that are not mainstream. It doesn't always work. *Rush* was a failure. *Driving Miss Daisy* was a resounding hit. There's always a risk.

Once the producer has found the right idea and has committed to it, the long run begins. "The first decision is, this would make a great movie," says Zanuck. The second decision is: Who will write it?

The Script: Working with the Writer

Ideally, producers could find a ready-to-shoot script that they could take to the studios. In reality this rarely occurs. Debbie Robins carved out a career producing successful television movies and moved into studio features with the release of *Calendar Girl*, starring Jason Priestly.

The hardest part is finding the script. Nothing is ever perfect, you never find something that is ready to shoot. What you find is something that is close, has a core, elements, where you think, This could be developed into something spectacular.

Having read so many disappointing scripts, Robins knows
there is always the temptation to approach the next one
with trepidation. This is exactly the attitude that she tries to
avoid.

> The important thing is to pick up everything and read it
> *wanting* to like it. I think part of what has happened in this
> town is that people are reading material and wanting to say
> "No, let's get it off the desk and go on."
>
> My livelihood, my talent, is finding material that I
> love, that I can nurture. It can happen in very different
> ways. You can find a script where the next step would be
> to start attaching talent. You can find one where the next
> step is to get the money in place because you will need it
> to attract the level of acting or directing talent that you
> want. There's so many different ways to put a picture
> together.

Robins advises first-time producers to forget about the marketplace, trust their own instincts, and test their willingness to
persevere.

> My rule of thumb is "Can I live with this for five years?"
> Do I love this story enough that I can wake up every day
> and have people tell me, "Nah, sorry, next," and I can say,
> "I *still* love it!" You have to have a very positive attitude
> and believe that you're going to make it happen regardless
> of the obstacles thrown in front of you.
>
> To do this you have to find the right screenplay. Forget
> about tailoring it to an actor, don't jump into an idea of a
> script because you think it's commercial. What's commer-

cial is always changing. Do it because you say, "I love this story."

Like Zanuck, she sees the "latest box-office trend" as a trap for producers and writers alike.

> I see talented writers who notice that *The Hand That Rocks the Cradle* has been a success. So they run home and try to write it, not because they love it or have any heart in it, but because it's going to sell.
>
> And six months later they have written a derivative genre script and now it's yesterday's news. What they end up with is a derivative piece of nothing. It doesn't have their love in it.

Once the script has been completed, it becomes the producer's duty to protect the original vision as the project moves toward production. It's no secret that the preproduction and production processes can take a toll on that vision and on the script itself. Puttnam explains this in terms of a "geometric progression" that he sees as an inevitable part of the collaborative nature of filmmaking.

> You have to look at it from a geometric point of view. If you start with one idea, be it from the director, writer, or producer, that idea gets seen through a number of prisms. And each time it gets seen, it's 5 percent off.
>
> When the director comes in it's 95 percent of what it was, then the cinematographer comes, now it's 90 percent. By the time you've involved everybody the original idea has gone through a prism and it's likely to be 60 or 65 percent of the original notion. A script is a very

vulnerable, frail object. It can't sustain that type of distortion.

As the producer of films such as *Midnight Express* and *The Mission*, Puttnam is renowned for his view that the script is the single most important tool in the filmmaking process. Not surprisingly, he tends to be very protective of what's on the page. "The truth of the matter is that the only reason you are all together making the film is because of that screenplay. You have to remain true to the original vision."

Writer Wrong?

Inevitably on some projects, there comes a time when the original writer needs to be replaced. Often this undesirable duty falls to the producer. Ed Feldman's first producing credit came in the 1972 with *What's the Matter with Helen?* starring Debbie Reynolds and Shelley Winters. He's worked twice with director Peter Weir, on *Witness* and *Green Card*.

I've always tried to stick with the original writer as long I could. It's a funny relationship because it always begins with disappointment. The first draft is never perfect. It's a tough thing to come in and have a lot of people who can't write tell you what to do. You have to have the patience to stick with the writer. I've had very few double writing credits on my films.

Debbie Robins echoes these sentiments, noting that replacing a writer is among the most burdensome decisions any producer has to make.

It's not an easy decision, particularly if you're talking about a writer who has initiated the script. I think you have to just keep trying till it becomes so evident that they're either tapped out or you're just not able to get your communication on the page.

Eventually it becomes frustrating for both sides. Sometimes the most humane thing to do is to go to another writer. I will probably try to stick with the original writer for too long. But I would rather do that than feel like I was rushed into the wrong decision.

Feldman has worked with dozens of writers over the years. "The writer always feels oppressed," he says with a smile. "But early on, he always forgets to tell you he's the only one who gets paid! He gets his money first. It's a business of uncertainty. If a producer makes $10,000 during a two-year development process, that's a big payday. That comes to about a dollar an hour."

Indeed, the long development phase calls for a unique kind of producer endurance. David Puttnam reveals that there is often "a staggering amount of time in development doing research. It used to take me less, but now it's about three years total. With *The Killing Fields* there was two years of research before a page of script was ever written."

Preproduction: A Penny Saved . . .

Theoretically, the preproduction period affords the producer the opportunity to "map out" the shoot on a day-by-day basis. According to Debbie Robins, the most obvious benefits

are financial. "They always say preproduction is where the
movie is made financially and fiscally. And that's the truth."

Once you get your first assistant director on board, you
come up with the shooting schedule. And you work very
closely to try and figure it out. Are you shooting in the
right sequence? Where are you going to shoot? How many
days is the studio giving you? Is it possible?

Keeping production costs down often depends on strategic
advance planning in preproduction. This is particularly true
for special effects films. "We shot *Terminator* for $6.4 million,"
says Gale Anne Hurd. "We had every visual-effect sequence in
the whole film storyboarded. We knew exactly what elements
we needed to see for the shot."

David Puttnam adds a final preproduction caveat to the
studio executives who seem increasingly intent on compress-
ing the time it takes to make a big-budget feature film.

You can save yourself a fortune in production if you spend
enough money in preproduction. The problem is the studios discourage you from spending the money. But it's
really pennywise, pound foolish.

The Vision Team

Producers agree that the most critical decisions made
during preproduction involve the assembling of a hundred or
more people and molding them into a cohesive production
team capable of realizing the script's most powerful potential.
Most often this begins by choosing the writer and director.
"I try never to enter into a production with a writer or

director where there is not a shared vision of the completed
work," says Puttnam. At the same time he stresses the need for
the producer to protect directors once they have been brought
on board. "The collaboration with the director can be difficult. I don't mind having a row, but directors have to have
some assurances that their films are not going to be arbitrarily
messed around with. Still, they better be able to intellectually
defend every decision."

"The worst experience would be to turn over a project to a
director who doesn't share your vision," says Gale Anne
Hurd. "At some point, the best producer has to let go and let
the director take over. The worst is when the director's work is
not as good as what I could have done myself—and I'm not a
director!"

Brian Grazer says it's easy to leave directors alone when
they are doing a great job. "But there have been some movies
where I've felt that the director was off course, that his goals
had changed."

> You can tell if the tone of the film has changed. If we set
> out to make a comedy, but the actor's choices are dark,
> detached, then I have to say something to the director. It's
> not the actor's fault, you go to the person who's guiding it.
> I'm there to remind everyone of what that common
> vision is.

Richard Zanuck begins by meeting potential writers to get a
sense of how they see the film.

> I never talk anybody into anything. There isn't anything
> you can do as a producer to get the collective vision going.
> You have to find other people who have the same enthusi-
> astic reaction to the material. You take a writer based on

his previous work and things that you feel he's done that are similar. Then after talking to him you know if you are on the same wavelength.

Zanuck employs similar criteria in the selection of the director.

Again, there's no point in talking a director into doing something that he doesn't quite believe in, because it's going to be a disaster.

Every good director has gone through this process. His or her agent says, "You've been making great films and they got good reviews but now you need to break through with a big commercial picture. I've got this picture with a big star attached and your price will go up and you'll go to a whole different level." Every director who has done that has fallen on his ass because he's going in for the wrong reason.

Whenever someone says, "I don't think this is as sad or as funny as you do, Dick," I start to wonder if I have the right person for the job. You need that connection from everybody—editor, composer, et cetera, though perhaps to a lesser degree. The two key people are obviously the writer and the director.

"If you have a good script, you cast it right, and you get a good director—that's 90 percent," says Brian Grazer. "The good director will hire good department heads so the producer just has to stay out of the way. Of course, I will collaborate in these decisions, but directors make the call. You don't want be in the director's face."

The director will bring in the production designer who

will hire the crew of people who will build the sets. The cinematographer will head up a group responsible for the lighting and "look" of each scene.

For Kathleen Kennedy, there is always a sense of how every collaborator will mesh with the others. "It's a bit like casting, but frankly you don't always have time to explore alternatives. You meet with people, you make a determination based on skill, and you throw them together and hope everyone will get along."

> What happens is over the years you look at movies and see people's work and you begin to identify with certain people who have clear artistic abilities that lend themselves to specific types of movies. Sometimes people tend to want to work with the same people all the time. Over the years we've worked with a variety of people and tend to try and find people who are aptly suited to the specific project at hand.

For those attempting to break into big-budget features, the selection process is a frustrating one. Yet it is difficult to envision how it might be otherwise. Debbie Robins points out that:

> The top filmmakers work with the same people over and over again, because once you find people whom you can trust, you don't ever go to someone else. You might say that's not fair, how do new people get into the business? I say, as a producer, I get up to bat so few times and it's so intense. There's millions of dollars on the line. Yes, I'd love to have the luxury to train everybody. But I can't.

For Richard Zanuck it always comes back to selecting the right people—those who can "stay on track."

Even with the right people, this isn't the furniture business or the car business. You have a lot of personalities and a lot of egos, so many factors at play.

It's easy to go astray and very tough to carry the vision through completely every inch of the way, to make it all work. There's economic pressures, there's time pressures, and there are always personality conflicts when you put so many people together. Everyone works for the common cause but it is an ego-driven business, there's a lot of pushing and shoving going on.

Catch a Shining Star

Much of the "pushing and shoving" in today's big-budget features comes from the stars, whose vulnerable images seem to rise and fall with the fortunes of each film in which they appear. Brian Grazer believes in the star system—and in the special something that each star brings to a project. "These people are very gifted. The reason they are stars is because they do a magic that other people can't do. They're a little superhuman. So I try to help them maximize their genius."

If you work with movie stars, you have to be attentive to their needs. They are their own businesses. Arnold Schwarzenegger is ... who knows?—a half-a-billion-dollar business. So you want to do things to help him maximize his skills on and off the set. If you can help

make him feel good and have a good attitude, that's
important.

Gale Anne Hurd agrees. "My job is to make sure that the stars
have every tool, every element they need to perform as well as
possible. When I worked with John Lithgow in *Raising Cain*, I
helped find someone to coach him for the Norwegian accent. I
made certain that he had the right place to stay, that he was
happy with his wardrobe, happy with his hair and makeup—
so that he could be free to act."

David Puttnam acknowledges the importance of stars but
insists that the needs of the project come first.

What I try and do is find stars who see the material I am
offering them as ways of making the same point that I am
trying to make. You make sure that everybody is firing the
bullet out of the same gun and aiming at the same target.
I've been very fortunate with people like Glenn Close and
Robin Williams in this regard.

A star who wants to be in a film but has his own career
agenda for wanting to be in it is clearly going to distort that
movie. It can't be otherwise.

At the same time Puttnam acknowledges that many producers
must temper these ideals with the reality of getting the film
made. For better or worse, big-budget features are increasingly star dependent.

Now, it may well be that the producer is desperate for
money and bringing in this or that star is the only way to
get the picture made. It would be stupid to pretend that
this isn't a perfectly reasonable thing to take into account

when you are making a movie. But then you have to live with the consequences. The movie isn't going to be what you wanted it to be and you're going to spend the rest of your life apologizing for it.

My experience allows me the conceit of believing that it is the movie that counts, not the star. Clearly if you make a great movie with a major star you're going to do that much better. But experience has proved that you can have the greatest star in the world but if the film is no good, no one is going to come and see it.

Puttnam identifies a crucial but little discussed downside to the collaboration process that has spelled disaster for many a well-intentioned project.

There's a fear factor involved here because everybody is terrified of having a relationship go bad, because it's a business of relationships. They would rather the film go down the drain than for the relationship to go bad.

It might be a relationship with a star, a director, or a studio. In these situations the relationship is protected but the price you pay is the project.

Puttnam contends that in times of collaborative conflict, "the one thing that is often sacrificed is the material, when in fact that should be the glue that holds it all together."

Other People's Money

If the material is the glue that holds it all together, the money is the grease that keeps it moving down the track. With the cost of the average studio picture hovering at $30 million, the producer spends a lot of time worrying about where it all comes from—and where it all goes.

Gale Anne Hurd learned her fiscal responsibility lessons by working with Roger Corman, the master of low-budget action films. "We did the most complex, ambitious projects in the world for no money."

By the time I was doing *The Terminator* I knew enough to make sure that the film was not so overly ambitious that we wouldn't be able to stay within a small budget. The biggest problem with special-effects films is that the writer and director don't know what's possible or how much things will cost. They don't take cost factors into consideration when they're devising scenes. So it's up to the producer to research expenses, just as carefully as we might research a historical period film.

As the costs of films have escalated, so have the inevitable consequences. "In 1972 we made *Save the Tiger* for $1.2 million," says Ed Feldman. "Jack Lemmon worked for scale."

The studios used to take more chances. More movies were being made. Today it's $30 million. It's a corporate decision. Thirty million will buy a building downtown and it'll stand there for 100 years. But a $30 million movie can die on one Friday night! The technology is such that after the

8:00 P.M. show on Friday night you know what the picture
will do. They don't even give you a chance to go to sleep
and savor it. It's scary.

All of this means that raising money for feature films is increasingly difficult for every producer, no matter what her or his
track record.

Debbie Robins is fresh from her first major feature, and it
brought her a new appreciation for the tremendous amounts
of money involved.

It's chaos. I mean, people forget you're trying to raise
millions of dollars. Why on earth should that be easy?
That's true with any business endeavor.

Calendar Girl is referred to as a "little movie," and it
cost $11.2 million. Once when I was frustrated, I stopped
and counted up the money I've spent as a producer. I
couldn't believe it. I've spent over $25 million of other
people's money. On movies! But next to the Joel Silvers of
the world I'm small change. These people are working on
$50 million pictures.

Kathleen Kennedy says that such staggering amounts require a
pragmatic approach. "It's not in my wallet. I never see it. I
don't sign a lot of checks myself. Because you are not literally
counting out dollar bills, it becomes a concept. You feel a
certain responsibility, of course, but I can't say that it makes
me particularly nervous."

Since feature films are one of America's most successful
exports, producers have increasingly turned to overseas fund-
ing sources, exchanging foreign distribution rights in advance
for production money. Yet Robins points out that these
methods have their own pitfalls.

There is a tremendous amount of money that can be raised internationally through presales at the Cannes or Mifed film markets. That's a whole different way to go. If you're trying to raise your money independently, a lot of what you do today is go to the foreign market.

But then you have to have talent attached. You have to have some kind of package. You need a good foreign sales representative, but you still need a domestic deal. You can't get away from domestic distribution.

The Bridge Over Troubled Waters

With cast and crew chosen and the money in place, the film gathers momentum as it moves into production. Now it's time for the producer's communication skills to come to the forefront. Every film encounters problems along the way, and it will fall to the producer to make sure everything keeps running smoothly.

Ed Feldman explains, "Part of the producer's role is keeping everybody happy. You try to keep everything moving along in a straight line. Make sure the script doesn't run away from you. Keep everyone focused on what the movie is about. That's what the producer is, he's a manager. Some producers are not mediators, they're agitators. That's not my style."

Brian Grazer agrees. "If you can gain the trust of the important principals on the movie—the actors, writer, directors— and they believe that your intentions toward the movie are pure, and that you will never lie to them, it creates a synergy."

I think of myself as a gracious host all the time. My job is to try to make everybody feel comfortable. As a result, I make sure that meetings are held where everybody is comfortable, where bonding is going to be maximized. I try to make sure there's not a dark cloud on the set. You have to make people feel good. That's just proper human etiquette.

Is it possible to be *too* accommodating? David Puttnam says that ideally the producer becomes the "unthreatening voice of reason."

The studio or financial source is the threatening voice of reason by definition. The audience, if left to their worst devices, can be the threatening voice of reason. You have to be the unthreatening voice of reason.

Sometimes 75 percent of the job is to be a peace-maker, to calm everyone down. One of the reasons that so many poor films get made is that the producer has to spend all his time putting out fires. In that case you end up with ashes, a film that is nobody's. It's this kind of creature that has crept through the undergrowth—it's characterless.

But there is also that 25 percent of the job that usually gets done very clumsily. That's when you have to be very tough. That is when you must be unpopular and unpleas-ant for the good of the film. The film has to be more important than the immediate ego concerns. And that applies to the writer, the director, everybody. Sometimes the producer has to play the heavy.

Debbie Robins has found that the hardest part of the pro-ducer's job comes when those oft-cited "artistic and creative differences" cannot be reconciled.

The most horrible thing in the world is to fire somebody. I have learned over the years that if something is wrong in the beginning, just take care of it. Otherwise it just gets worse and the tension builds. It's crueler to that person if you keep them on and have to ride them for five months or whatever. The best thing for everyone is to just cut your losses right away.

When trouble breaks out on a set and firing someone is not an option, the producer must find a way to reconcile those "creative differences" in a way that is acceptable to everyone. "During the shooting phase your primary job is to troubleshoot," says Kathleen Kennedy.

If you see that something is going wrong or about to go wrong, the producer is the one that has to come in and fix it. You have to have strong people skills. You have to figure out how to be the perfect diplomat. If you've got people at opposite ends of the spectrum, you often don't have the time to go through hours of problem solving. It has to be resolved quickly and efficiently.

She also notes that the producer must maintain a certain sensitivity to the nature of a film-in-progress.

Once principal photography begins, the producer steps back and sees where the movie is going. A film is an organic, living, breathing thing. It's not just defined by what's on paper, it continues to change. The creative process continues throughout and out of that comes sometimes the best ideas. But there needs to be someone who maintains a cohesive vision, a focus on the entire picture and not just the individual elements.

Like so many movie collaborators, the producer must rely on instinctive skills that can't really be taught.

I think it's intuitive. The people that I run across that are most effective don't really know how they do it or why they do it well. They are just instinctively able to function within this pressure-packed environment. They actually enjoy it. They get along well with people. That's a huge part of it. Communication is always the key.

Richard Zanuck says the role of the producer might change dozens of times each day. "Sometimes you have to be a mediator, sometimes a psychiatrist. There are times when you are a ruthless boss—you have to be 'Doctor No.' Sometimes you have to be all of those things. Every day presents new problems and different situations. You have to be a lot of different people."

Producers on Board!

The degree of producer involvement on the set varies. Hands-on types like Debbie Robins are there from morning until night. Or night until morning.

If it's days, you start at seven and you shoot for twelve hours. After that it's overtime for everyone so you don't like to do that, which is not to say that you don't. Night shoot times vary according to what time of year it is. A lot of times you get home at five or six on Sunday morning. You don't really have a weekend, and the crew will show up at seven Monday morning and you've got to be ready for them. It's always something!

"I try to be on the set every day," says Ed Feldman. "I enjoy the set. It's terrific. Somebody gives you a lot of money to play movie-making! You're also passing out a lot of money. You want to make sure it's being utilized."

Since the set is often thought of as the director's domain, some conflicts are inevitable. But Robins sees her duties as complementing those of the director in very specific ways.

Directors have so many things on their mind, you can't ask them to be concerned about the caterer or the crafts service, or the teamsters, or the production assistants. Quite honestly, they have a big burden, they've got to pull off that scene. The producer has other responsibilities. It's my responsibility to know those security guards who are standing up there for twelve hours every day. I need to know their names and give them a hello, to keep everybody happy.

For Kathleen Kennedy, the shoot affords the producer the opportunity to step back and see the big picture, while the director focuses intently on the task at hand.

Directors have to go into the tunnel, they have to become very narrowly focused on what they are trying to accomplish on a daily basis. If producers are to be of value during the shoot, they have to realize the movie becomes the director's picture now.

Kennedy's collaboration with Steven Spielberg exemplifies what she feels are the best aspects of the producer-director relationship. "He's the one who is the best executor. I can put forth all sorts of ideas, but he's the one who has to maintain the point of view. There's only so far any producer can go before the movie needs to be directed and made, so to have the director as your primary collaborator completes the process in a very satisfying way. Unlike television, film is a director's medium. The producer ultimately services the vision of the director."

Kennedy explains that she and Spielberg often work on several projects simultaneously. "It's not only the movie we are shooting but everything that we're doing that overlaps into it. Steven and I can be sitting in between shots, discussing four other pictures."

On the set, Ed Feldman likes to concentrate on the actors. "I believe part of the producer's job is to keep the actors happy. You become like a social director. I think it's a question of personality. It's one of my strengths. I like people."

The level of Gale Anne Hurd's involvement on the set tends to vary. "It depends on the project, since every set creates a different set of problems and demands. On *The Abyss*, I was also the line producer. That taught me a valuable lesson—to insist on delegating. It allows me to have a greater creative rapport with actors, director, and writer, as opposed to worrying about how much every minute of filming is costing. Ideally, I'll be a troubleshooter. I'll stop by the set every day but I don't usually stay."

Richard Zanuck sees it differently. "I've never had a line producer because that's what I do. I'm there every minute of every day. I have to be there and be on top of everything."

You have to know costs, time, have a clear idea about everything that's happening. Decisions are made every day on the set, particularly if it's outside. These decisions affect money and the look of the picture.

You watch everything and everybody. Just being there promotes a certain awareness and alertness. With a lot of people, if the teacher is out of class the kids raise hell.

The producer is like the conductor of an orchestra. Maybe he can't play every instrument, but he knows what every instrument should sound like. To keep people on their toes, you've got to know everything you can about every facet of the process. There's a lot of tricks you learn that can be used to help a picture, and to bring it in on time and on budget.

Postproduction and Studio Relations

With the shoot complete, the film moves into postproduction. The producer may work with the director through the editing and composing stages, but Debbie Robins explains that this is most often a time of letting go.

When you hit postproduction, it is the director, editor, and composer to whom you must lovingly hand over the picture. All you can do is say "Now go shape it and when you're ready, show it to me." So it's really a process of letting go and doing other things, then coming back in.

"You go through a love-hate relationship with every film you work on," says Gale Anne Hurd. "It's like starting a new relationship. At times you think it's the best thing you've ever done and you don't see any flaws."

She pauses for a moment and smiles. "Then, after the rough cut, you have your first big argument. You see every blemish. You realize all the compromises that you made along the line. Why didn't I go for the extra take or that extra effect? You think it's awful. It's the worst thing that's ever been done. 'How did I ever delude myself into thinking this is any good?' Eventually your attitude comes out somewhere in between."

One of the things a producer does during this time is deal with the studio. Invariably pressures mount as the film nears completion. The producer works to make sure there is enough time and budget to complete the movie successfully. Acting as a buffer between the studio and the creative team, the producer must, once again, keep everyone happy.

Ed Feldman explains what is required. "You have to have a strong heart to be a producer. There has to be someone who is focused on the whole movie. That's what they're paying you for. I came up through the ranks, which I think really helped me in this career. I started as a press kit writer in New York. I know the business very well and I know the business of the business as well. So I can see things from the studio's point of view."

If studio movie-making is the collision of art and commerce, the producer is always the one at ground zero. Dealing with the studios is a process that has changed remarkably over the years, according to Richard Zanuck, a highly decorated veteran of the studio wars.

It's so different now—the composition at the top of the studios has a different mentality. It's lawyers and businessmen and agents. In the days of my father and the Jack

Warners—these guys were showmen, real Barnum and
Bailey types, picture-makers. Now the personalities are
corporate. It isn't wrong per se, it's just different, and
it affects how pictures get made and what pictures get
made. These days there are too many chefs. Every studio
has ten would-be Irving Thalbergs in the wings sending notes in. They're not riding on their gut instincts.
They went to law school, not motion picture school.
So they have to have the marketing research to bolster
themselves.

There is no question that marketing research plays an increasingly larger role in studio decision making at every level. Some
producers are comfortable with this; Zanuck is not one of
them.

They do all this market research—none of which I do, I
never have. You can't poll people about what they will
like. They don't know. You can't figure out what 50 million
people will want to see. This isn't an election. It's a movie.
All I can do is figure that if I like it, maybe someone else
will too.

The key is to make something *different*. If you ask the
audience after they've seen it, they will tell you they want it
again. But that's a trap. You have to go find something else.

Audiences have a craving to find new things. Sure they
want to be told what to see, but they also want to discover
things on their own. They look for new openings, new
horizons, new subjects.

How does the producer discover those things? Zanuck combines gut instinct with a sense of why the audience goes to the
movies in the first place.

I'm looking for things that touch you one way or the other, that move you. Maybe a movie can scare you—like *Jaws*— or it can make you laugh or cry. Those are the things that audiences respond to.

I'm fifty-seven years old. The core audience for movies today is what, fifteen to twenty-five? Am I going to try and guess what they want? I'll never know what a fifteen-year-old will think is funny. I've got to go with what I think is funny. Maybe I'll fail, but all I've got is my own feelings and instincts.

Such instincts come into play most prominently as the film nears completion and is tested on preview audiences. The studio looks at audience test scores and works with the producer and director to release a film with the best box-office potential. Needless to say, this is hardly an exact science. Every picture has its own dilemmas. As Zanuck prepared *Driving Miss Daisy* for its first studio screening, he knew a certain strategy had to be employed.

They wanted to see it in a projection room, but I didn't want them to see it that way. They had gone in thinking this was a *Masterpiece Theater*–type project, but I had screened it privately for audiences. I knew with the right audience it would go through the roof. So I made sure they saw it with the right audience. They were startled. They didn't realize the picture would produce that kind of response. After that they really got behind it.

David Puttnam reveals that during his stint as head of Columbia, "I always tried to see the film with an audience, not at a private screening. It's a much more real and telling experience." Puttnam's reign at Columbia taught him a number of lessons about the nature of the producer-studio relationship.

> I was a bad choice to head a studio. I don't think I was the
> right person for the job. My entire career has been spent
> selling ideas and getting things made. Being on the other
> side of the desk means throwing all those instincts into
> reverse. With producers, in those crucial moments, I
> would attempt to be the person that I would want to be
> working with if I were on their side of the fence.

The confrontational nature of the producer-studio relationship doesn't always have to be a bad thing for the movie, according to Ed Feldman. Like every producer, Feldman has had his share of problems during the "studio run" when top studio executives see the film they have bought for the first time. But there are exceptions.

> One of the best I've seen at that crucial moment is [Disney's] Jeffrey Katzenberg. Right or wrong, he knows what
> he bought. And remember that's his own moment of truth.
> He has to make the decision: Are we going to spend $5
> million or $15 million to promote the picture? Are we
> going to reshoot? He always comes in with a lot of good
> ideas. He understands the movie process very well.

To Market, to Market . . .

Having secured studio approval, the film is scheduled for release. The degree of studio support for any film usually translates to the number of screens that are secured for its opening weekend. A potential blockbuster might be scheduled for two thousand or more screens, while others may open in a dozen theaters. While the producer awaits the verdict of the audience, he or she often has a pretty good notion of how the film will fare. Yet there are always surprises.

Kathleen Kennedy recalls that "when we made *E.T.*, the marketing people told us it was being perceived as a children's film—so we couldn't open in more than six hundred theaters."

> Then we screened the movie and it screened off the map, and we started getting lots of calls to put the picture in more theaters. But, with the rare exception like *The Crying Game*, that just doesn't happen anymore. For the most part the studio decides how many theaters the picture is going to open in, based on the results of sophisticated national market research studies.

Is it possible to predict how a film will do? Ed Feldman says, "Since I came out of the marketing end of the business, I believe that you can make and sell almost anything if you just give them hope in the final reel." But some tasks are more daunting than others.

> It's hard to succeed with a dark movie. You look at a film like *Husbands and Wives*, which I think is an outstanding movie, but it's a grim view of married life. I walked out of that picture pretty depressed. And it's a comedy!

The death of a key character at the end of *My Girl* posed a similar problem for Brian Grazer. "I didn't think it was going to be that successful. I thought it was too soft, that it would open well and fall off," he says. "Instead it opened huge and kept going. I learned that kids, as well as adults, want to experience that crying emotion. We managed to generate some controversy with the bee-sting scene, and we skewed it in the direction that worked for us."

The Revenue Game

In today's multimedia environment, revenues flow not only from a film's domestic and international box-office grosses, but from numerous ancillary sources including home video, product placement, merchandising, and promotional vehicles.

Product placement (showing specific brand names on screen) is becoming increasingly frequent, but it remains a relatively small part of the financial picture. Debbie Robins says it's "not much, you can't hang your hat on it. It can help a little but nothing substantial. Still, if you're a good producer, you'll go after all of that. Saving a dollar for me is just as relevant as saving $10,000. You have to have that attitude."

Merchandising is another matter. From *E.T.* to *Jurassic Park*, Kathleen Kennedy's films have almost always involved major merchandising contracts.

It depends on the movie and what the movie dictates. With a film like *Jurassic Park*, it involved a massive amount of licensing contracts and promotional deal negotiations. The artwork used to sell the movie had to be incorporated into various promotional campaigns. There were point-of-purchase displays to review for merchandising and publishing purposes.

You need to define what the logos are going to be early on. Marketing has become such a sophisticated element of the filmmaking process, it needs to be consistent throughout all aspects of the campaign. The images you choose become the identity of the film through the media. All of this must be in place long before the picture is released. *Batman* was a perfect example. If you can come up with a strong symbol early on that is identifiable with the movie, it can become a tremendous calling card.

Just before *Jurassic Park* was released, the press was full of reports that the $60 million film was being supplemented with $65 million in promotional funds. But those figures can be deceiving, says Kennedy. "That money is not being spent by the marketing department at Universal. Rather it is the total amount being generated by companies that are involved in selling the picture."

At the End of the Day

From material concept to merchandising contract, the producers are often the only collaborators who oversee the film for the full length of its long run. In fact, it can be argued that with video and television exposure, the long run never really ends. Ed Feldman says all of this places an extra burden on the producer.

You have to be careful of what you do these days because it doesn't go away. It's great to see your name on a picture, but if it's a bomb you don't want to see it too often. Your picture is going to play forever. *Save the Tiger* was 1972 and it still plays on television. And it's still a very important movie.

On the other hand, a long time ago I produced a cult skiing film called *Hot Dog: The Movie*. Maybe not my best work. But I still get revenues from it every year and

send out checks to the people involved. And people still
watch it.

Gale Anne Hurd learned an interesting lesson regarding the
long-term impact of films while traveling in Micronesia.

> I was on a boat and I happened to visit islands that are
> rarely visited by tourists. These people fish out of dugout
> canoes. But they had this one generator that they would
> power up a few times each month to provide electricity for
> a TV and a VCR.
>
> When I found out they had all seen *Terminator 2* it was
> terrifying. I didn't want to invade their culture with some-
> thing that would impact them the way it did. Here were
> these peaceful people living in paradise, but with no run-
> ning water, indoor plumbing, or telephones. And they had
> all become fans of Arnold Schwarzenegger and urban,
> action-oriented entertainment.
>
> At that moment I realized that whatever you may think
> your responsibility is, it's overwhelming. It changed my
> perspective on the influence that I have as a producer.
> There are very few places left in the world that will not be
> impacted by films.

For better or worse, the producer's legacy can be found in the
films that bear their name. Like writers, directors, and all
other film collaborators, this is what they will leave behind,
forever. "The ultimate satisfaction is putting the finished
movie up on the screen and being able to watch the audience
respond," says Kennedy. "Very few people get to have a job
where you create something that generates immediate feedback. That's quite unique, and that's what's addictive about
this business."

To achieve this and get any film produced requires a certain mindset, and invariably it takes a toll. At the end of the day, is it worth it? Debbie Robins pauses for a moment.

> I've had to really find my self-esteem within. Because very few people tell you you're doing a good job or encourage you in any way. It's the real world. It's high-stakes money, power, and politics, and everybody is pretty much in it for themselves. It is a very narcissistic world.
>
> It's a business that likes to exclude people, not include them. I don't think there's anything gentle about the way business is done. So I've had to really learn how to process a lot of disappointment, a lot of insecurities in myself. You can't depend on anybody else.
>
> The studio doesn't care if I'm up or down. All they care about is does the movie make money. Of course, when you do hit that moment and you produce the $100 million picture—then all of sudden, everyone is calling you up and telling you that you're brilliant. If that ever happens to me I'd like to think I could handle it because of what I've been through.

In the producer's day-to-day world, there is little time for such reflection, but the most caring and successful producers have thought long and hard about what it all means. And each of them has an agenda of his or her own.

"I won't do any pictures where women are debased," says Ed Feldman. "I find it appalling in this business today— graphic depictions of rape at knifepoint—there are people sitting out there in a dark room watching and you're responsible for that." He leans over his desk for emphasis. "All these high-minded depictions about how life doesn't imitate art. I

don't buy it. I think we are very responsible for what we put
out there. You have to be very careful."

Such sentiments are sure to spark a debate among filmmakers, and David Puttnam would like to see more of it.

I used to talk quite a bit about the need for debate. It still
hasn't happened. I find it staggering that such illustrious
organizations as the Motion Picture Academy or the
American Film Institute have no ongoing format for debate or the clash of ideas on what cinema is and what its
role in society should be. By not having those debates,
we're allowing the media and the Dan Quayles of the
world to do it for us.

Whether it's the liberals or the conservatives that are
attacking us—we should be ahead of them about values.
We should be taking the lead in that debate, and not
merely responding to it.

For his part, Richard Zanuck worries most about the films that
the audience never gets to see.

There's a lot of pictures that never get made because
people don't have the courage to make them. A lot of the
pictures I've been associated with have had very tough
battles to get made.

There's a real audience out there starved for these
pictures. When one sneaks through, people respond by
saying "Finally, there's a picture that we want to go see!"
Cocoon proved it. *Driving Miss Daisy* proved it. We get the
most heartwarming letters from people all over the world.

What is a producer? What should a producer be? "In fact, we
are paid seducers." David Puttnam laughs. "Our job is to

seduce audiences, but to seduce them in ways which I believe are user-friendly, as opposed to ways in which it can be damaging."

I want to make films which don't attempt to pretend that the world is a simple place—because that's one of the things I find most damaging about many of today's pictures. They're selling the audience a bill of goods because they pretend that the problems of our society are not complex and that the application of brute force by two buddies on the police force can solve them all.

Life doesn't always provide easy resolutions. But in the movies, if you are clever, you can offer up apparent resolutions. At the end of *The Killing Fields* the boys do get together, but no one is pretending that the problems of Southeast Asia are solved.

For the best film producers, the stakes are high; yet it's not about money but something of far greater value. "Yes, life is complex," Puttnam concludes, "but at the same time it is also worth living. I want to show people that if you actually apply yourself, you *can* make a difference. That's what it's really all about."

C L O S E - U P

STEVEN HAFT, *DEAD POETS SOCIETY*

I got the *Dead Poets Society* script as a writing sample. I had an idea for a movie that I ultimately never developed. And I heard about this guy Tom Schulman who had this dead-something script. So I read it and I thought it was great. It was literate and about something.

Tom's agent, Jeremy Zimmer, told me it had been out twice and everybody had passed on it. So from an agent's standpoint, it was, literally, a dead script. But it hadn't been around to the smaller companies, so on the strength of that bit of possible life, I optioned it.

Tom and I had a number of meetings about where we were going to go with it and shared some thoughts about the issues involved. We started sending it around and, of course, we were turned down by a great many places. On the other hand, when I tried to "package" it, actors that we gave it to loved it and fans began to develop among various talent agents. Eventually we had one small company interested, but they wanted Tom to rewrite it to focus less on the poetry and more on the kids' antics. About that time I began preproduction on *Mr. North* in Rhode Island.

That was when I received a phone call from Jeffrey Katzenberg at Disney, saying that he was aware that there was another company bidding on the right to develop it. He asked whether I was in a position to immediately terminate my negotiations with the other company and give him four days in which to consider the project. At that time they would either pass on it again or give us a firm production commitment for $4 million. After a bit of negotiation I said "fine."

Unlike the other executives who had passed on it, Jeffrey had actually read the script. That was the difference. Story editors had done coverage on earlier versions. I'm sure lower-level executives had read it, but it had never gotten to someone like Jeffrey. And keep in mind that Jeffrey is somebody who went to private school. This is a world he knew. It meant something to him.

The Kanew Period

Tom and I, we were elated when Disney told us they wanted to do it. Jeff Kanew (*Tough Guys*) was recommended by Katzenberg to direct. Things went pretty smoothly for a while but we couldn't get everyone to agree on who would play Keating. Disney told us to keep moving forward anyway. We scouted for locations. We were all set to go. Then Kanew and I got a call to meet with Katzenberg. I had a sinking feeling.

We went up to Jeffrey's office. I remember him talking about what a great effort Kanew had made on this film, what a terrific cast he had assembled, the locations were great, all the hard work he had put in with Tom Schulman and so on. But Jeff knew what they really wanted. This whole preamble went on for seven or eight minutes. Finally Kanew says, "Let's get on with it, I feel like I'm having my back rubbed until I die." So Katzenberg says, "Regrettably, we want to move on and redevelop this picture with another director." Only at that time, nobody knew who that director was. We protested.

Kanew really had put his heart and soul into this. This would be the most important movie he had ever made. It meant a great deal to him, and losing it was devastating. I got on the phone and asked Katzenberg to reconsider. I felt he wasn't being fair to Kanew. He said, "What's fair?" Two nights later he called back and agreed to give Kanew and me a chance to set it up elsewhere. We had ten days but we were only free to offer the script with the two actors that had approved Kanew: Alec Baldwin and Liam Neeson. During that period we went to every major studio, mini-major, every large financing source. We had some video of the school, the boys, the script, and the two possible actors. At the end of ten days, nobody would make the film.

So the rights reverted back to Disney. Jeff and I received

some bits of abandonment money and Katzenberg said, "We'll give it a rest, then we'll start again after the first of the year." This was about December sometime. After all that time and effort *Dead Poets Society* was dead in winter. That was the low point. I went home to New York, figuring it was all over.

The Hoffman Period

About a month and a half went by, and I got a call from Katzenberg saying he wanted to start up again. Dustin Hoffman's agents had been in touch with Disney saying that he was looking for something to direct and now that Kanew was out, how about *Dead Poets Society*? Katzenberg said fine. I remember Dustin called me from L.A. and said, "I know you're involved in this, I'd like you to stay involved." There were general kinds of breakfast meetings, Dustin and his people, Tom and myself. That was followed by a series of meetings between Dustin and Tom.

Tom went through a couple of drafts with Dustin, no major changes. While this was going on, Disney was trying to finalize the deal with Hoffman. It was proving to be difficult. The problem was not financial. If I remember correctly, Dustin's deal was going to be $200,000 as an actor for the Keating role and Director's Guild scale. But he'd also get a large piece of the gross. It was a good vehicle for him to direct since there were so many scenes where Keating wasn't on camera.

The problem was certain commitments with regard to delivery. Dustin has a history of getting in and out of a project and he's a perfectionist, maybe the ultimate perfectionist in town. One could imagine a fairly long process of getting the script right, a long production process, and an extended post as well. Disney was trying to structure the deal around certain penalties for late delivery at various stages. And that's where it fell apart.

The two sides became embattled and Disney finally gave him an ultimatum: Dustin has to close this deal by the end of the week or Disney would take the picture elsewhere. Friday came and went. Dustin didn't sign.

The Williams Period

The next week I get a call from Jeffrey saying "We're moving on, I'm going to see Robin Williams for dinner on Saturday night and give him the script." Williams had been approached earlier and there had been a long process to see whether a marriage could be made between Williams and Kanew. It couldn't.

Around that time Robin's managers were sort of reevaluating his choices because other than *Good Morning, Vietnam*, he had made a number of pictures in a row which hadn't been successful. Hard to believe it now. So it was presented to him at this dinner on Saturday and by Monday morning Robin Williams was attached to the movie.

All hell broke loose at CAA [Creative Artists Agency] because I don't think Dustin took Katzenberg's ultimatum seriously. And they are both Mike Ovitz's clients. It took Dustin a good long time to accept the fact that the ship had sailed. Robin and Dustin are good friends as well, so it was complicated.

It's hard to imagine what that film might have been like with Hoffman directing and starring. Maybe it would have been a little more didactic. Robin was an inspiration, Dustin would have been a teacher. Dustin's inclination would have been to teach these lessons whereas, given Robin's personality, he lived them. Obviously Dustin is a brilliant enough actor to teach them in a way that wouldn't turn you off. But I think his inclination would have been to lecture rather than take a lighter approach.

Peter Weir was given the script shortly thereafter. He was the first choice although other directors did read the script while we were waiting for him to respond from Australia. Quite a few turned it down. Finally Peter committed and we went back into production, a full year after the aborted Kanew attempt.

On Location

The ironic thing is, after all we went through to get into production, it's impossible to imagine a better experience than the one we actually had. We were all in this cold little town in Delaware. There was one good restaurant. We were working with a West Coast crew on an East Coast location so it was too complicated to send people home.

For Thanksgiving we had dinner at a church we converted into a dining room. We all spent Christmas together. The New Year's party was at the production manager's house. Everybody showed up. It was a friendly set, a dedicated group of people. Everyone made an effort to deal with each other as individuals. We were all on a first-name basis. It gelled in a very personal sense. Everyone who was a part of the movie knew it was special.

What made it special? It was a movie that had something to say. In take after take you've got a hundred members of the crew, standing around listening to somebody saying "Seize the day, take time to listen and feel things and think lofty thoughts." We all became indoctrinated. It became like a mantra. I don't think anyone was immune to it. Peter was fond of saying that "the teamsters cried at dailies." It was true.

I'll never forget shooting the scene where Robin goes into the classroom after Bobby Leonard's character [Neil] kills himself. He sits in front of the desk and looks at Bobby's books that are left behind, and he starts to cry. You look around the set and everyone in the room is crying. The crew would be thinking: I've shot crying scenes before, I'm a cameraman, or whatever. But you look around the room and there isn't anybody who isn't crying. I'm not saying you would find too many copies of Keats under people's pillows at night. We were all drinking beer and going bowling, living our lives in a fairly normal fashion, but you couldn't help but listen to the message and ultimately to absorb it as well.

Peter Weir: The Moral Force

Peter Weir's direction was a big part of it too. He's incredibly bright and forces everybody to stretch in an intellectual sense. He has a knack for casting people who are fairly close to the characters they are playing. In the end the boys really merged into the characters that they were playing. The uniforms, the setting all drew us in as if it were a play, as if it were all happening live.

It was interesting to watch Peter and Robin work together. Every scene would be shot first with Robin doing the script word for word, very reined in. It was like—give yourself to Peter and just read the script. So maybe there would be several takes like that. And then Peter would have him go "balls to the wall," just go with the scene any way he wanted to do it. Then they'd confer and maybe take a little from each and shoot it a third way.

In editing, you could never put the first two together in any fashion, because Robin wasn't looking the same way, or standing in the same part of the room, or even saying anywhere near

the same lines. But you could put together the second and
third or the first and the third. And the third way, the merged
version, ended up on the screen a lot of the time.

It's hard to imagine any assembled group of people in
which Peter Weir would not be the smartest person in the
room. And he has a very comprehensive worldview, a very firm
set of values. His ability to see the larger message, to create the
compelling metaphor for the work he does is incredibly inspiring. In a way the best films take you into a world larger than
yourself, weightier than your own life. Peter is able to bring
that experience to the people around him during the making
of a film. If you ask any of the boys or Robin, they'll say that he
was our Keating.

Peter doesn't just direct a film, he presides over it. Let me
put it this way: If Peter were a world leader, he would be more
like a pope than a president. He's a moral and intellectual
force, someone who looks on filmmaking as a personal calling
and not just a job. And it makes you feel like you're part of
something loftier just to be around him while he's doing it.

The Disney people kind of recognized this. For all one
hears about how invasive Disney is in the process of filmmaking, that was not the case on Poets. They never tried to force
anything on us; they really left it to Peter.

Disney and Marketing

There was this one problem about the title. Disney registered two other titles, *The Unforgettable Mr. Keating* and *Keating's Way*. Peter, Robin, and I laughed about those titles until
we found out that some of the marketing people were serious
about the change. We loved our title but we recognized it might
turn some people off. Mostly we were not going to have it
homogenized into something meaningless without a fight.

Disney knew how we felt. In the end we were able to prevail but only because Jeff Katzenberg and Bob Levin couldn't come up with a better title. At lower levels I am sure meetings were held and entire campaigns devised around *Unforgettable* and *Keating's Way*. But Disney has become the best marketing company in the industry by making smart choices in the end.

Finally it was time for the test screenings. I thought we'd made a picture for adults, a picture about poetry, and I had my own doubts about how big the audience was for it. The last thing I wanted was a test screening that showed that people weren't excited about this movie. That would have demoralized the postproduction process. We got the marketing people to agree to stock the audience heavily with adults. We figured that type of audience could provide us with some intelligent comment on what worked and what didn't. We didn't want to pack that first audience with the usual core fifteen- to twenty-four-year-olds, who we assumed would be less interested in a period piece about poetry. They agreed to hold a screening for teens later with a separate set of response cards. The first screening went great. The cards came back very strong, 89 percent good or excellent. We were very relieved.

The surprise came a week later. The teen scores had been even higher, 94 percent! We all thought we were making a movie for adults, a kind of nostalgia piece. The film covers a period before sixteen-year-olds were even born. What we hadn't counted on was that sixteen-year-olds like to watch other sixteen-year-olds on the screen. The actors weren't wearing tights and they were speaking English. So it wasn't perceived as this "art" film. And, like everyone else, they loved the story.

Other than the fact that the cars were dated, the whole picture could have played today. Even Disney wasn't sure until that second screening that this picture would play well to young audiences.

The Audience

The movie affected people in powerful ways. Every time I went to a party and someone introduced me as the producer of *Dead Poets*, there would be another story of a person who now it and left a job, or made some serious life change. Peter called me once because these people had come to his home to tell him they gave up this successful business to do what they really wanted to do. I think Peter felt responsible and a little uncomfortable with these confessions.

I can remember the moment when the film's impact really crystallized for me. My wife and I were in New York, walking down the street with Robin and his wife, Marsha. This middle-aged man came up to Robin and simply said, "Thank you," for *Dead Poets*. Robin bowed to him slightly and turned to me and smiled. He told me there was a definite difference in how people approached him about this film versus his other work. Usually people say, "Hey, great film," and so on. And that's fine. But with this picture it was always "Thank you." That's a very gratifying reward for our efforts.

3
the director: from vision to action

Every film has its own life, its own destiny that must be guided. The reason I make films is that films are forever.
—Norman Jewison

Look carefully at Ron Howard and you can still catch a glimpse of Opie, the character that so captivated us on *The Andy Griffith Show*, or Richie Cunningham of *Happy Days* fame. Mayberry is a distant memory, but Howard's experiences as an actor left an indelible mark. He begins by explaining how they helped shape his decision to become a director.

As a kid I loved hanging around with the actors, but I also loved hanging around with the crew, and it didn't take me long to discover that the director was the one who got to play with everyone. That's what I feel like. There's something very electrifying, energizing, and very rewarding about being at the center of all these creative discussions.

The collaborative spark, that electric energy that drives a classic film from script to screen, is a series of creative discussions. At the center of virtually all of them is the director, the one person who functions as a kind of living touchstone around which all other creative decisions swirl.

What is a director? An architect? A bricklayer laying brick upon brick? These descriptions fall short of the mark because what is being built is more volatile than stable, more fluid than secure. Roland Joffe's first feature was *The Killing Fields*. "Being a director is like playing on a multilayered, multidimensional chessboard, except that the chess pieces decide to move themselves."

But do they? Director Norman Jewison (*Moonstruck, Agnes of God*) has a contrasting theory. "The most important thing is to manipulate. Some people call it communication or inspiration. I call it manipulation. The director is constantly manipulating people, whether the actor, camera person, sound, lighting, composer, writer. They're trying to manipulate everyone to conform to their interpretation, their vision."

The director is first and foremost a storyteller. In an *Esquire* interview Robert Redford confides, "I never even think of myself as a director when I'm directing. I think of what I'm trying to say."

And the director is also a team captain, forming the troops into a cohesive squad. Ron Shelton (*Bull Durham, White Men Can't Jump*) agrees that the director's ego must never get in the way of what's best for the picture. Instead, he thinks in terms of the egos of his collaborators. "You don't want to crush the egos. You want to max the egos. You want them to be all they want to be, yet it's a team game."

According to director Martha Coolidge (*Rambling Rose, Lost in Yonkers*), "Any director needs a strong male and a strong female side, an ability to move the film along with a nurturing side." Amy Heckerling (*Look Who's Talking*) agrees. "You have to know about painting, music, literature, and costumes, but most of all, you gotta have heart."

So What Do They Want?

In the beginning there is the word. Hollywood is full of scribes trying to create the write stuff, scripts that will attract the attention of top directors. Contrary to popular belief, there are a *lot* of well-written scripts out there. This fact alone does not guarantee that they will find their way to the screen. Barry Levinson (*Diner, Rain Man*) explains this rather contradictory process in terms of the personal challenges a script provides.

> I'll read some scripts and say, "This is a good script but I already know it, and I don't know what else to do, it's all just there." I've got to find something that ultimately challenges me to the point where I don't know if I can make it work.

Coming off the surreal environment of *Toys*, Levinson found himself preparing a film set in modern-day Los Angeles. This posed a formidable challenge.

> When you make a period movie or a surrealistic movie, you can control your environment totally. For me as a director, the hardest thing is a present-day movie that's shot in Los Angeles. It's hard to see it any way except the way it is.

Is there a magic formula for attracting a top director to a script? Sometimes it seems that there are as many answers as there are directors. For those whose success has given them a large measure of freedom in choosing the projects they pursue, interest in a script can stem from a set of values and experiences that stretch as far back as childhood.

Martha Coolidge read the script for *Rambling Rose* and was struck by a visual description that connected her to a personal memory.

> You're always looking for a metaphor that is extremely visual and dramatic so that it becomes a picture and not just words on the page. In the script there was an image of sunlight coming through the window in a kitchen, this vivid light hits the fruit on the kitchen table.
>
> And I realized that Rose brought love and light into that family. The metaphor came out of the writing but the visual image gave birth to the design of the entire film, the way the cinematographer lit it, the production designer's color scheme, everything else.
>
> The image was just like a memory that I have of my grandmother's house. I actually made a documentary about my grandmother which has a lot of things in common with *Rambling Rose*. So there was this connection to my feelings about my grandmother's house.

Ron Shelton comes from a background of talkers and storytellers. "I have a hard time giving up the games of childhood," he admits. The rules of those games are a part of what attracts him to sports stories.

> To me rules are a sign of civilization. You must assign rules to things or there is no sense of order. If you're a fisherman

you can go take a big net to where the fish are and scoop them in. But that's not fishing. Fishing is about ties and worms and bits of string. It's ritual and religion, a way of making sense of things. Stories are about that as well, they're just a way of sorting out and making sense of things.

Oliver Stone remembers his own childhood and how it led him to the kinds of projects (*Heaven and Earth*, *JFK*, *Platoon*) that have become his trademark.

My father always talked politics and ideas at the table. I grew up in that tradition of talking and writing and discussing ideas. So, many of my movies are issue oriented. I try to show the cause and effect of the world around me. The 1960s are paying off now, they're not past history; it's Buddhist time where all the issues are cycling.

Norman Jewison is another director whose enthusiasm is driven by the social terrain that a story explores, and his conviction that "films are forever."

First of all, it has to be a good story, but I'm looking for an idea behind the writing—political or emotional or a thrust of truth. Somewhere along the line, hopefully the film is going to affect thinking, your concept of life. It's the idea behind a work of art that perhaps makes the work of art enduring.

For Roland Joffe, the challenge of transforming real events into feature films yields the most enduring art of all.

I love taking a true event and saying "what was it like to be inside it?" *The Mission* came from a true-life story, *Killing*

Fields from a magazine article, *City of Joy* from a book. I like to put myself in a situation where you're confronted by the fact that it is true, it is real. I try to make it like a life experience, to give it the same volatility as life, and some people are very uncomfortable with that.

Director John Singleton says he is trying to give voice to stories that have not appeared on film before and remain true to his own experience. "I'm a black male living in America. I have to draw on that to make films," he says. "It's all I know. It's not that I am trying to change the world, but good film work will always find its way into the culture. You put the movie out, then it's on its own."

Boyz N the Hood was a street fairy tale. It was a story that a lot of people have lived, it was a lot like their own lives. So they rallied behind it. They felt, Hey, that's my story, that's my experience. And they don't see that story on the screen very often.

Of course not every classic film is driven by the burning need to make a social statement. But most explore some aspect of human behavior that is "real" in the sense that it resonates within the director and the audience as well. Ron Shelton describes it a quest for "honest moments." Like Stone, he can trace it back to his roots.

I'm interested in doing films about real human behavior. Even a pratfall is an honest moment if it's earned and it's utterly dishonest if it's not earned. My mother used to say, "Give people their dignity and you'll be amazed how many times they rise to the occasion." She treated everyone the same, and I'm sure some of that rubbed off on me. I start

by embracing the characters because I identify with
them."

Creating an unforgettable character in a script can be the key
to winning the heart of a director because so many directors
begin by considering how the character's journey through the
story will ultimately affect the audience. For Ron Howard this
is the single most important consideration.

> Everything is changing all the time. If you're trying to
> maintain the status quo, you're probably going backward.
> I think there is some sort of force within us to be better
> people. We have it within our power to actually phase out
> certain behaviors, such as violence, and create viable alter-
> natives.

Directors like Howard tend to seek out material that will
confirm their own worldview. More often than not this involves an attempt to carefully select the kind of stories that will
have a lasting and positive impact on the audience.

With his penchant for hard-hitting real-life stories, Roland
Joffe sees the differences between life as it is and life "as it
should be" as a source of persistent inspiration. "To me, life is
very volatile, chaotic, complex. There is an immense difference between the world that people want to inhabit and the
world that we do inhabit. And that fascinates me."

What conclusions are possible regarding the kind of script
likely to attract a top director? In the end, patterns begin to
emerge. Roland Joffe, Oliver Stone, John Singleton, and Norman Jewison tend to seek out the difficult political and social
truths. Barry Levinson searches for scripts and stories that
challenge him to make them work. Martha Coolidge seeks
visual metaphors. Ron Howard prefers projects that are life-

affirming. Ron Shelton tries to find the honest moments. And everyone wants "a good story" with "strong character development." Put these reasons all together and they offer a good overview into the kinds of scripts that are likely to attract the industry's most respected and successful directors.

Research: Getting Inside the Material World

Once the director has settled on a project, the development process goes into high gear. Since the story may be based on a book, real-life event, existing script, or some combination of them, research is usually required to get inside the material.

It's hard to imagine a more formidable research job than that employed in the making of *JFK*. For Oliver Stone, it was the herculean task of gathering written, film, and video material from hundreds of public and private sources and then weaving them together into various story lines.

In *JFK*, there are four threads—the Garrison story; the Oswald history, which comes from a combination of public sources and *Crossfire*, the Jim Marrs book; there's the reenactment in Dealy Plaza, which is based on Marrs plus public sources and witnesses that I talked with. The fourth part of the screenplay is essentially the Mr. X story—the Fletcher Prouty story, which he told me when I interviewed him in Washington.

Getting inside the story often requires a kind of "method direction" as the director goes into the field to share in the lives of those who are to be portrayed on the screen. For *Backdraft*, Ron Howard began by getting a taste of what it was like to be a firefighter. "The writer had been a firefighter. And I spent some time with the firefighters. I spent a night in a fire house, went out on some runs with them. During our rehearsal period, we had half days dedicated to a kind of boot camp, a fire training school for the actors."

When filming overseas, the director must learn enough about the other culture to present it honestly on the screen. This can present special problems. In these situations Roland Joffe is not one to cut corners.

For *City of Joy* I went to Calcutta several times over four years, traveling on a bus, staying in villages. Most people see the India of the gurus, or the India of the Taj Mahal, but that isn't the truth about India. The truth is the teeming immensity of the struggle of life.

Martha Coolidge says "good research is very critical" and explains how it often leads her to important information she uses in her films. In a crucial scene in *Rambling Rose*, a sinister doctor suggests to the rest of the family that Rose's sexually charged nature could be surgically "taken care of" without her knowledge.

I found out that ovariectomies and clitorectomies were commonly done in the 1930s. They were doing a lot of experimental psychological surgeries. That related to the attempted "castration," so to speak, of Rose. To say nothing of the contemporary metaphor of a woman's right to her own body.

I learned as a documentary filmmaker that in reality, in the truth, you find much greater and more interesting images and a variety of details than you ever would find in something that you made up.

The best research is that which yields a true vision of the arena in which the story takes place. Ideally this means going beyond the cultural clichés to create a dynamic and insightful script that will result in an honest movie.

Shaping the Script

As research nears completion, there is generally a need to reshape the script to get it ready for production. Virtually all directors will provide input at this point. Sometimes this results in major changes. In the original *Dead Poets Society* script the Robin Williams character was dying. In *Alien* the Sigourney Weaver character was a man.

Then there are minor revisions that may involve changing locations, seasons, or transforming a scene on a bus to one on a train. Some directors will do rewrites themselves, becoming a co-writer on the script. Others spend hours working with the writer to achieve clarity in the story and richer emotional nuances in the characters.

During this crucial period, Oliver Stone likes to work directly with the other writers. At the same time he maintains a discreet but discernible distance.

> I co-write the script but I believe in sitting there alone. I never work in the same room unless it's an audio experience, like with Richard Boyle in *Salvador.* He told me stories, but I basically shaped them . . . dramatized them. With Ron Kovic [*Born on the Fourth of July*] mostly he talked. He talked. I shaped.
>
> I often overwrite, almost deliberately. I'd rather shoot more and shoot a little more intensely and overdo it and look to come back in the editing.

For Norman Jewison the art of revision begins with a series of notes.

I make a lot of little notes about how something should be said or what that person is feeling right at this point. I'm constantly reading the scenes and performing them. I read the scenes out loud, and I play some parts and the writer plays the other parts.

With any luck, the process eventually begins to reveal the essence of the story. Like a sculptor slowly chiseling an obstinate piece of stone, Jewison "romances" that stone by seeking out the distinct emotions inherent in each scene.

I'm looking for the secret of the revelation of human emotions. I'm looking for comedy, the humor that's in life. Every day I laugh, almost every day I'm brought to tears. Laughter and tears are two very basic emotions that must be there in every single story and in almost every scene. It's the yin and the yang because there's something constantly touching us and pulling at us.

Keeping the emotional content of the story uppermost in mind, Jewison shapes the script into its final form.

I work with the writer to make the script as revealing as possible through honest behavior. The transitions from one scene to another must be absolutely seamless so that the story flows with a certain rhythm and an ease. This is the art of screenwriting.

Nina Foch's extensive résumé includes work as an actress, director, and consultant. One of the most respected voices in

Hollywood, she says the beats of the story should lead naturally to the director's visual ideas. These in turn should yield a
kind of story clarity that speaks to the ancient role of all
storytellers.

Every beat has to be broken down to learn the style of the
scene, how you want it shot, where the camera should be.
You must see the clear needs of the script, what is in the
way and what needs to be fixed.
    You need to know the moral of the story. And you
want to be able to tell it in three sentences . . . the plain
simple story as it would be told by a shepherd in the hills
gossiping, so it has an absolute clarity.

"Every Picture Tells a Story"

As the script nears production, the director begins to "see
the movie" in visual terms. At this crucial juncture the art of
directing comes to the forefront. The very best directors will
make creative visual choices that enhance the script and
breathe life into the story. Ron Howard explains:

By the time I'm committed, I'm already starting to make
little notes, little visual ideas in the margins. Generally that
first round of ideas gets thrown out. They can be as simple
as drawing a line along three-quarters of a page of dialogue
between two characters and saying "this should be a two-
shot because it's overlapping." Or "it would be great if all
this played in a full-figure shot because it's important to let
the audience know that these people are part of a world
and to show them that world as part of the background."
    The location might be written "backyard—day" and

we ultimately might find that the scene would play better
in the subway at night. It might be something as simple as
"I need a powerful image here." I might not know what
it is.

The search for images is unrelenting. Ridley Scott's work in
Alien established him as a Hollywood director with a definite
visual style. You can glimpse his background as a painter as he
describes the process. "You need to keep an overall image in
mind. I think in terms of light, visuals, sound, texture."

The ability to think in pictures and intuitively sense when a
shot will work is something that all the best directors seem to
possess. As Scott describes the now-famous opening title sequence from *Thelma and Louise*, you begin to see how the
process works.

> I had no idea how to start the movie. So while I was in
> Utah, I was standing on this perfect road which went to a
> mountain and somehow the whole thing represented free-
> dom. So I banged off a six-minute shot knowing that
> somewhere I'd use it. And I ended up using it on the
> opening titles.

Sometimes a single image might serve as a metaphor for an
entire story. Roland Joffe found one for *City of Joy*. "The
rickshaw is a central metaphor for the whole movie. It's the
freedom of work and the enslavement of a burden, it's power,
but under the power of others. It contains all the complexities
and paradoxes of India. Notice it is also a kind of family
member, they take it inside with them when they sleep."

Whether it's a visual image for the entire film or for a single
scene, each decision must be thought through carefully, with
an eye toward building layers of meaning in the film.

In *Bugsy*, Barry Levinson's imaginative use of a blank screen shrouds the two central characters who appear as shadows. This visual device, used in their first love scene, provides one of the film's most memorable moments and offers a kind of visual commentary on the "Hollywood syndrome."

> Bugsy and Virginia Hill wanted to be movie stars. He had a screen test made. He saw himself as a leading man. So here were these two people who wanted to be movie stars that never made it. I thought it would be interesting for these two lovers to end up on the wrong side of the screen, to play it as silhouettes behind a blank screen and end up as a negative rather than a positive.

A different kind of visual predicament faced Ron Howard in *Backdraft* when he decided to go with four major fire sequences. How to keep from being redundant?

> I wanted each of them to evoke a little different sort of feeling or reaction from the audience. Visually, I didn't want us to be repeating ourselves in the fire, so I tried to come up with four different styles.
> The first fire, which the child observes at the beginning, we did as a more dreamlike fire, from a child's point of view. The second, as the fire character begins to evolve and grow, we turned into combat footage. We have a rookie firefighter and we stay pretty much with him, and it's a sense of how hellish, how violent, how chaotic, and how terrifying the whole experience could be.
> Our next major fire sequence is the haunted fire, the supernatural. Doors breathing. Firefighters would talk about the fire as a creature, an opponent. We shot this with

a Steadicam, a lot like *Alien*. Where was the fire going to
pop up? Lights flickering, that sequence was more like a
thriller, a monster.

The last had little camera movement. When it was
moving, the movement was broad and sweeping. That
sequence was shot more traditionally, more operatic. More
like a western, a mythical confrontation.

Myth and Meaning

Envisioning mythical confrontations and finding appropriate visual metaphors for them is at the heart of the directing
process. Ridley Scott reveals that with *Thelma and Louise:*

> The mythical dimension really begins on Louise [Susan
> Sarandon] as she sits outside while Thelma [Geena Davis]
> is robbing a store. And she looks at an elderly woman
> who's staring back at her. It was a moment where she
> decides to make up and then decides not to and throws the
> lipstick away.
>
> And there's a moment when she looks at the woman
> who is staring back at her through the window and that to
> me is a way of saying "You better make a decision about
> your life before it passes." And then Thelma comes out
> from robbing the store and says "Drive" and from that
> moment on they pass over, they cross the line, they leave
> their old reality behind.

As a director who built his reputation on action pictures, Scott
is acutely aware of the pitfalls of the genre. "I think dynamics
are not car chases or people shooting each other but story and

emotional dynamics, the exchange of information." Of course, it all begins with the script, but it's the director who needs to find the image, build it, clarify it, and give it form.

> You can take a great script and just shoot it. *Thelma* was an excellent script, as good as you're liable to get. But the choice becomes "What do you want an audience to feel at the end of it?" Do you want to take this script as a straight-ahead story and treat it as a docudrama, or feel marginally mystical at the end of it, since these characters become two mystical figures in a way?

Many contend that the decision to go with the mystical ending transformed the film from a well-executed genre piece to a groundbreaking masterpiece. Scott modestly concedes, "The journey of these two characters became a slightly more elevated experience than just two girls in a car being pursued by the law."

Hear It Now: The Inflections of Film

A director's decisions involve an intuitive process that seeks out the basic rhythms in each scene and story. This process applies to the characters as well as to the film as a whole.

Norman Jewison sees, senses, and *hears* the rhythms. "Certain films have a slow lyrical style, others a more staccato rhythm. *Moonstruck* is an opera: Loretta [Cher] is the lyric soprano, Cosmo [Vincent Gardenia] the bass, Ronny [Nicholas Cage] is the tenor, Johnny [Danny Aiello] is the baritone, and the mother [Olympia Dukakis] is the contralto."

John Singleton focuses extensively on the language of his characters, what they say and how they say it. His gritty visual style provides a perfect match for the stories he wants to tell.

> The whole thing about black cinema—about films produced by black people for a black core audience—is that you must do it in the language of the culture. You don't try to water it down any more than you would try to water down Japanese culture if you were producing films for a Japanese core audience.
>
> If you get it right, it comes out like strong coffee and it keeps you awake. If you water down the language with cream and sugar, it won't have the same effect.
>
> My films are not about people I have seen or have met. They are about people I *know*. My characters say things that ordinary people say, exactly as they would say them. Sometimes they're funny. Sometimes they're dramatic. But mostly they are *real*.

Getting in touch with the reality of each script invariably involves listening carefully for the inflections inherent in them. It's almost as if they have a life of their own, and it becomes the director's job to "tune in." Oliver Stone explains:

> I've always found that I have different rhythms for each film. And it has dictated the pace of my life, the tone of my life, the editing room, the music, it becomes like an acting job. You live inside that rhythm—that wheel—for that year or two years or whatever it takes. Every film has its music. A visual rhythm.

See It Now: Story on Board

A director seeking to bring a script to life may employ any one of a number of techniques. The most common and practical way of visualizing a script is storyboarding. Often created by an artist working with the director, the storyboard is a hand-drawn frame that shows what the camera will shoot. These can be anything from Ridley Scott's stick figures (see figure 3.1) to fully rendered drawings (see figure 3.2). For directors like Scott who have artistic ability, storyboarding is crucial. His drawings are commonly referred to as "Ridleygrams" by his collaborators, and the mere mention of them never fails to bring a smile.

> I always storyboard. I mostly know where the story is, but I'm looking in there for something for me because I believe that every director has his own performance apart from the actors. The Ridleygrams help me feel the scene, I know what it ought to be like.
>
> It's like an absorption process. It's a playing around with the visuals. I'm testing the water before I shoot. It's my area of absolute concentration because I'm drawing an image which may take me one or two minutes to draw.
>
> In a way, I'm like the writer who has writer's block. They start tapping the keys and things start to emerge. When I draw, I'm thinking on two or three different levels. I'm thinking about who those characters are. I'm thinking about the light. I'm thinking about the music and what the scene will mean at this point in the story. How far along the transformational line are they? Have

they started to elevate yet or are they still normal human beings?

In Scott's films the storyboards also serve a practical purpose as he seeks to communicate his vision to the rest of the collaborators.

When I walk onto the set, the Ridleygram is printed and handed to everyone who's working on the scene so everybody knows where they're headed and what they're going to do. And while I'm shooting, other departments can be preparing as well.

Not every director storyboards. David Zucker says that storyboarding helps most during complex action sequences that must be shot from many angles in order to look authentic. Lawrence Kasdan rarely storyboards. For Ron Howard the process has served as a metaphor for his own development as a director.

I can't draw so I used to resist storyboarding. Like so many other things in my evolution as a director, I've learned to give away more to get more in return.

In the beginning, the first time I worked with storyboard artists, I listed every shot in advance and sat with them and made them draw what was in my mind. I used to think other directors were taking the lazy way out—handing storyboard artists the script, having a conversation with them, and then letting them go off and draw.

But for the first pass through it, it can be very rewarding to reap the benefits of this person's imagination because they're visually oriented or they wouldn't be artists. All of the fires in *Backdraft* were storyboarded (see figure 3.3).

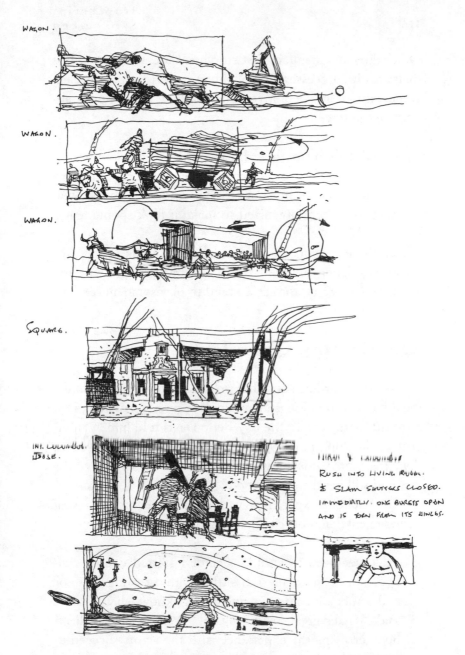

Ridley Scott's "Ridleygrams," such as these from *1492: Conquest of Paradise,* help guide the crew through each scene.

Other directors maintain that storyboarding actually inhibits
their creative processes. Ron Shelton prefers to approach each
scene without any definitive notion of how it will finally appear on the screen.

> I don't like to storyboard. I like to go to the set wanting
> something to happen. I like to make discoveries. I believe
> in a lot of prep, but not storyboarding. Of course, you
> have to be very organized to make it look spontaneous.

Oliver Stone concurs. "I don't storyboard. I talk to the production designer. We share notes. But my films grow on the
set. When we go on the set we tend to play some more."

The Casting Quandary

As storyboarding and other preproduction tasks continue,
the director's attention is increasingly focused on casting. Ron
Howard fondly recalls the day Bette Davis told him "95 percent of directing is the script and the casting. Once you've
done that, the rest is knowing how to stay the hell out of the
way and still get the movie shot."

Ron Shelton's experiences with the audition process reveal
a fundamental and oft-cited casting quandary.

> I'd never been in auditions until I started casting *Bull
> Durham*. So suddenly I'm sitting with a casting director
> and actors are coming in and I don't know what to say. I
> said, "That's great, read it again." Pretty soon I realized
> how terrifying the experience is. If the actors succeed in
> passing that terror, then they have the real terror, now
> they're onstage and in front of the camera.

SCENE 1

EXTERIOR. PORCH AND GROUNDS OF RURAL SOUTHERN HOME.
LATE 1930's. AFTERNOON. A CAR APPROACHES HOUSE.

1) <u>VIS:</u> Begin tracking shot of car along porch as car turns around bend in road. End shot as car stops in front of porch steps.

2) <u>VIS:</u> Cut to <u>extreme close up</u> (ECU) of woman.

3) <u>VIS:</u> Pull back to <u>close up</u> (CU) of woman in front of car.

4) <u>VIS:</u> Continue to pull back to <u>medium shot</u> (MS) or <u>American Shot</u> of woman and girl.

5) <u>VIS:</u> Continue pull back to over-the-shoulder shot (OTS) of woman and girl, framed by figures on porch.

Examples of storyboard technique created especially for *From Script to Screen* by Lee Storey.

For *White Men Can't Jump* we read over three-hundred guys. Ten of them were great basketball players. I'd look at them in the outer office flirting with the secretary, nervous energy, couldn't sit down, up and down. Then they'd come in and they'd be just deadly, dull. Something happened when they walked through that door, they *had* the part out there. I would call them back, some of them four times, trying to figure out how to get "out there" in here, trying to help them get rid of that baggage.

Part of Martha Coolidge's reputation has been built on discovering young "unknown" actors. She often conducts casting workshops. "It's a critical, painful, but very creative part of the business," she explains. "For me it's very rare to see an actor and think that they could never play the part. It's like most actors have the part when they walk in the door, but they lose it in the reading." How does she know when she has found the right person?

Acting talent has to do with a subtext that goes on in the individual that the camera will see. It's often connected with a kind of power that is quite frightening. Some people come in the room and scare me because they are so real or so different or so quiet or angry, these are really good signs.

Another paradox involves how much the actor needs to fit the director's operational vision of the character. Norman Jewison begins with the physical characteristics.

I'm looking for the actor that has the same sound and look and body language—height, weight, age—all those things

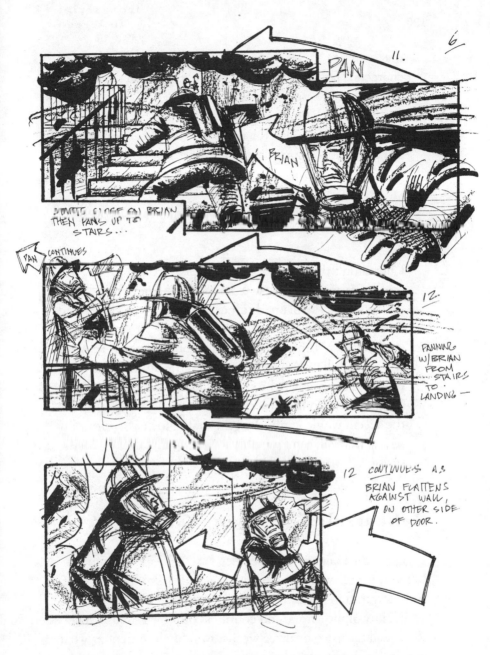

Storyboard sequences can be especially useful for big action scenes such as these from Ron Howard's *Backdraft*.

that you see in your mind. I've been living with these characters for so long. I know them better than the actor at this point because I've lived with them.

At the same time on occasion an actor will come in and he may not look right for the part but he will give something to the character, a dimension that I hadn't even considered. And it will jolt me and then swing me over.

With *Moonstruck*, Jewison ran into a major casting problem immediately.

Cher didn't think she could play the part of Loretta. She said, "I'm not from New York. I don't know how to do that accent." I explained to her that she was a singer and all accents and dialects are rhythmic.

I put her with an Italian lady from Brooklyn to work with her [Julie Bovasso, who played the aunt]. And I told Cher she was going to be surrounded by people from New York, and surrounded with the reality of that sound, that the accent would come. And the dialogue in *Moonstruck* is so real that you can't possibly go wrong if you stay with the script.

Rehearsal: The Trying Game

Once the major roles have been cast, rehearsals can begin. In today's Hollywood, there is increasingly less rehearsal time, and its duration varies according to director preference, the availability of the actors, and countless other variables. Generally it will take two or three weeks. Ron Shelton defines what he tries to accomplish during this time.

We spent two weeks rehearsing for *White Men Can't Jump*. We rehearse in a room and tape off the floors of the sets that we know. I tell the actor, "I know nothing about blocking. Here's the chair, here's the wall, let's just block it from scratch." The blocking comes out of rehearsal.

I encourage input from actors. "If you don't believe your line of dialogue, let's find a line of dialogue you do believe in." I wrote this character, I know more about this character than anyone, but I want the actor to surprise me. I rewrite the scenes during rehearsals. If we play out a scene and I don't believe it, I'll say I don't believe it, and we'll change it. Or if an actor says, "I don't know how to say that," I'll work with him and we'll change the lines.

Like Shelton, Norman Jewison sees rehearsal as an opportunity to get to know his actors and to establish the boundaries of the collaboration. "I love rehearsal. It's very important that you meet and talk about the character. You tell the actors how you see the character. If they disagree with you then you allow them to prove it."

Of course, every story and location presents special challenges. Often these can be resolved as the rehearsal process evolves. Ron Shelton's films provide a good example.

For *White Men* and *Bull Durham*, we had a basketball and a baseball camp that was run by professionals. They would work out all morning, and then we'd rehearse all afternoon. All the plays were choreographed. I gave the actors the play book and they had to learn the plays. Ten to twelve hours a day on asphalt. Over and over. The trick is to make it look unchoreographed.

Oliver Stone is a firm believer in the process. "We rehearse a lot. We rehearse wherever the base is for a week or so, and then on location. And then we rehearse the day of the scene—when we start a new scene."

Roland Joffe uses rehearsal to his advantage by juxtaposing scenes to get the most out of his actors. The emotionally potent *City of Joy* provided many such opportunities.

> I rehearse for several weeks, and improvise the scene before the scene I'm shooting, so that the actor comes into the scene with all the feelings, all the events he just went through. When Max [Patrick Swayze] enters the city he's just been through the scene with the lepers, and he can barely get the words out. That was real, because he's carrying all those feelings into the scene.

Some directors take their cast on location so they can experience the environment in which they will work. Stone set up a kind of boot camp for *Platoon*. Francis Ford Coppola took his cast to the Philippines for *Apocalypse Now*, a long rehearsal for a legendary shoot that ran more than two hundred days.

It should be noted that not all directors require or even desire rehearsal time. Some prefer to bring the actors to the set and rehearse just before shooting while others simply opt to shoot it all, hoping to catch something unique as the actors play a scene for the first time.

Spontaneity is always an issue. Ron Shelton adds a final note of caution. "One more thing about rehearsal, when I feel it's about there, I quit. I always get nervous when we nail it in rehearsal. I'd rather leave it slightly unrealized until we shoot."

Lights, Camera, Action!

With rehearsals complete, the lengthy preproduction process finally comes to a close. At long last the time has come to actually shoot the film.

Permits are issued and an armada of hundreds moves into place. Catering trucks roll, wardrobe assistants scramble to dress everyone for the first day's scenes, and dozens of production assistants sporting walkie talkies seem to appear out of nowhere.

In the midst of the chaos the director of photography (cinematographer) works closely with the director to set up each scene. Their collaboration will result in a visual interpretation of the script that will ultimately determine the success or failure of the film.

Veteran director Robert Wise, an Academy Award winner for *The Sound of Music* and *West Side Story*, has probably been through this process as often as anyone in Hollywood. He stresses preparation and flexibility.

Although you have worked out much of the blocking in your mind in the office and may have storyboarded many of the scenes, you don't want to lock yourself in to those shots. Frequently when you're on the set with your actors, you'll find new things you can't anticipate in your office.

In the simplest terms, it begins with a single question: Where to place the camera? The director has a number of options. The camera can pan back and forth or up and down. It can also move, as with a hand-held camera or Steadicam. The cinematographer can follow the actor, or dolly.

Most directors begin with a master shot, where everyone is

included in one take. Then the scene is shot again and again as
the camera moves in to focus on medium shots, two-shots, or
close-ups. During the editing process each take will be
screened and creative decisions made regarding which will
appear in the final version.

Asked what the director needs to keep in mind during
production, Wise begins with his own thoughts about the
master shots.

> You will probably be shooting some master scenes that go
> on for several pages. The whole scene is done with the
> camera in one place. You'll need to have a fairly wide shot
> to show the entire scene. Of course, even while keeping
> the camera on a stable tripod, you can still tighten a little
> bit, pan back and forth, or move up and down.

While there will always be debate about the *best* possible place
to put the camera, there is a consensus on the worst place.
Wise quotes John Ford, who once told him, "An eye-level
camera is a dull camera." He explains that the scene is always
more dynamic if it's lower or sometimes higher than eye level.

Occasionally the image is captured by using more than one
camera. Wise and Robbins did not storyboard the intricate
dance sequences in *West Side Story* but opted instead to use
three cameras. "Of course," Wise says with a wistful sigh, "we
also had three months of rehearsal."

Next comes "coverage." The director will cover the scene
by shooting it over and over again from various angles and
perspectives.

> You need plenty of coverage so you have a number of
> shots to choose from. You have two-shots and close-ups
> and over-the-shoulder shots in order to have a lot of

choices so you can build the scene rhythmically and dramatically.

You want to have enough coverage in case you need to fix a scene in editing. When the film is previewed to an audience, maybe there's a laugh line that doesn't work or a line you have to remove. You might decide to use the over-the-shoulder shot so you can dub in a different line.

Despite all of the technical considerations, the director must never forget what the process is really all about.

The most important thing is the scene itself. Get that scene up there. Get it building. Get it playing. You still always start with the emotional moments—with the actors in the scene. But you're also thinking of how the scene will look within the frame.

I want the image to fill the whole screen. If you add space on the side, you lose the dynamism of your composition. So if I have three people in the scene, perhaps shooting them in a medium shot from the waist up, they'll fill the entire frame—no air on the side.

Remember all those Hollywood spoofs where the would-be director holds up two hands to make a box, as if looking through a camera lens? ("That's fabulous!") In fact, David Zucker points out that the framing process is crucial when shooting comedy. "Comedy happens in the frame. You need to be very exact about what is within the frame, not only making sure that the frame shows the whole joke, but also being aware of the depth of the image."

In *The Naked Gun 2½: The Smell of Fear*, Leslie Nielsen and Priscilla Presley make love on a bed while the traditional fireplace flickers in the background. Look carefully and you'll see a skewer of meat and vegetables slowly turning above it. Zucker explains: "What's going on in the background of a shot might be just as important and as funny as the joke in the foreground. Sometimes the best joke might be in the background."

The Moving Camera: What Is It Looking For?

Now that the camera is in place, the next question is: Will it move during the shot? Wise recalls legendary director John Ford's simple philosophy. "He didn't like to move the camera. He liked to move the actors."

In a way, the eye of the camera represents the eyes of the audience. To keep the natural look of a scene, Wise stays away from too much movement.

> I don't like to overdo it. Sometimes people take the camera 360 degrees, which makes you conscious of the camera. Try to make the moves fit the action so you're not conscious of the camera moving. The audience should be as unconscious of the filmmaking process as possible.

Zucker resents the trend toward epic shots that call attention to themselves. "I don't move the camera unless it's natural to. I'm not proud of great camera moves. They're only great if they help tell a story. If you have to move the camera because the script is boring, you're in trouble."

Recent technological breakthroughs have made it more tempting than ever to keep the camera moving. Most notable is the invention of the Steadicam. Wise explains:

The Steadicam is a camera with weights around it to, literally, keep it steady. It's operated by one person, rather than a camera crew, and it gives the operator flexibility to move the camera and to follow the actor in difficult-to-get-to places.

In the past, if you wanted to move the camera, you had to hold it as steady as possible, which could be difficult, or you laid down dolly tracks and moved the camera on those tracks. But the dolly tracks couldn't go everywhere, so you were limited. The director has more options now.

One of the most memorable uses of the Steadicam in recent years was in Martin Scorsese's *Goodfellas*. The long, breathtaking shot follows the main mob character (Ray Liotta) as he walks down the street and into the side door of the Copacabana restaurant. We journey with him through the kitchen as waiters swirl around, then into the dining room where a table is set up awaiting his arrival. He's seated, and Henny Youngman comes onstage and tells a joke—all in one long shot!

Michael Ballhaus's cinematography in the scene helps convey Liotta's sense of power and prestige as he is greeted by those he encounters along the way.

A similar approach came at the beginning of *The Player* as the camera moves slowly across a movie lot, catching various producers, writers, and executives pitching projects, gossiping about who's in and out, making lunch plans, and opening their mail.

Such examples illustrate how camera movement can be essential to the story and theme of a film. Roland Joffe opted for movement in the very first shot of *City of Joy*.

The camera begins low, as if seeing it from a child's viewpoint, and then begins to move. You hear sounds of a train and singing and the clack of machinery, and the camera then moves up to end up above.

I like to use the camera to get close in, and sometimes as if looking through a window, from the distant to the close, and then back.

Landmark camera movement came in *Gone With the Wind* during the scene in which Scarlett is surrounded by dying men at the train station. As the camera moves relentlessly back and up and the frame widens, we get an increasingly devastating view of the horrors of war. By the time the long shot is over, a tattered Confederate flag is seen in the foreground and we understand why she runs away, devastated.

Recalling one of his most memorable moving shots, Ron Howard reveals that he had the audience's point of view uppermost in mind.

The last shot of *Far and Away* was the first shot that I had thought about for the entire film, and it was while we were still writing. I had been fascinated by out-of-body experiences. I knew that the person who has died is able to see his body from the top of the room.

I hadn't seen that shot in a movie. So we used a moving crane shot, starting low on Tom Cruise, and then quickly moving high. The wide lens on the camera also made it feel like you were really going up there.

At this point the audience is convinced that the Cruise character is about to die. Howard explains with a mischievous grin, "I thought it would be great to push the audience right to the edge of thinking that we were actually not going to allow a happy ending."

Problems, Problems

Any director—no matter how powerful—sometimes finds the cameras at the mercy of actors who simply won't take direction. Amy Heckerling discovered this while shooting *Look Who's Talking.*

> The hardest shot was always of the baby sleeping. The baby wouldn't fall asleep with all the commotion on the set. So we'd have the entire crew working with their shoes off in the dark, so the baby would stay asleep as we set up the shot.
>
> For the newborn baby, when we wanted it to cry, I'd snap my finger on the bottom of his foot. The nurses do this to check the baby's reactions and to make sure the baby is okay.
>
> We could do that with a baby, but if we had an animal on the set, we wouldn't be able to do that. According to animal rights rules, you can't make a rat upset!

By the time she got around to shooting the sequel, Heckerling had picked up a few tricks.

> We used five different babies, representing different ages. In *Look Who's Talking Too* the toddler, who was about two years old, was very responsive, very intelligent.
>
> There's a whole montage where he has to be jealous of his sister, and I was able to talk him through the shot by having him mimic me—to look angry, jealous, or to be thinking mean thoughts, or to say "I hate her." I'd be making the faces and he'd be looking at me and imitating them. He had a wonderful sense of how to react.

After working with real babies, plastic replicas would seem to
be easy. "Not so," says Heckerling. Like any props or special
effects sequences, these had problems all their own.

> We constructed this puppet—the baby inside the
> womb—but the baby kept breaking down.
>   The plastics and the materials weren't lasting the way
> they should, and there were all these different moving
> parts on the puppet's face: expressions—one eyebrow,
> the other eyebrow looked the other way, twist the mouth.
> During the course of any reaction there's a lot of mus-
> cles that get used and usually they wouldn't all work
> together.
>   Each part was controlled by a different puppeteer.
> They all had to be timed so it might take a few days to set
> up the shot, and we might need to have twenty-five to fifty
> takes of every movement.

Shooting on location is always an adventure and always presents special problems of its own. There's unpredictable
weather, those planes that keep thundering overhead, and the
unnerving ability of a camera to draw a crowd. Nothing prepared Roland Joffe for what he discovered while shooting *City
of Joy*.

> The real problem of shooting in India are the crowds.
> Indians are very curious people, and when you're shooting
> on the street, they will come up to the camera, sometimes
> even stand in front of the camera, except, instead of two
> people doing that, you have *two thousand*!

Ready on the Set?

In the midst of the chaos that is the shoot, the director attempts to establish a set where creativity can flourish. Nina Foch sees this task as crucial to the success of any film. So much is riding on the director that she or he must be in a position to inspire the other collaborators.

> I believe that it is not possible to work in a condition of discord. I don't care what you feel, you say to yourself, "I'm going to create joy today."
>
> No matter what the problems you have elsewhere, they will stay right there if you say to yourself, I will feel joy. . . . It's in this condition that you can play the darkest scenes, you can get the best out of your people and the best out of yourself.

Of course, every director has a slightly different approach. In the end, the "tone" of every set is determined to a great extent by the director's personality. Amy Heckerling admits.

> I'm not the kind of person that gets everybody to sing camp songs or fly paper airplanes. I'm pretty quiet, and insofar as I set the tone, it's like I'm not a leader-type person.
>
> I like actors a lot, and people feel that, and feel like I'm really happy they are there. They are always free to try something and be silly. They need to be comfortable and not feel like somebody is going to be bothering them and judging them, particularly if they're messing up. Even if I'm not this band-leader type—I want it to be a comfortable place for them.

Oliver Stone says, "I try to feel myself in the shoes of the actors, to feel what they are going through and understand and support them. Because they do need emotional and moral support."

Asked about working with actors, Norman Jewison echoes these sentiments and responds with an obvious and genuine warmth that radiates outward as he speaks.

> You have to be totally *simpatico* with your actors. I feel closer to the actor than I do to any other aspect of the film. You really have to like each other, depend on each other, trust each other. The actors must feel that I will protect them, that I am their best friend, that all I want is for them to be wonderful in that role.

Actors: The Number One Storytelling Tool

The actor is the most vulnerable person on the set, and it's up to the director to bring out a great performance in the midst of the actor's uncertainties and insecurities. As Jewison sees it:

> If there's a problem with the actor, I'll take him or her aside. But if you've had enough rehearsal before you shoot, a lot of the problems will have already emerged.
>
> Sometimes it's a wrong line or a problem of behavior or understanding or conflict. It's a matter of talking it out. The last resort is giving a line reading, although I have done it.
>
> There have been times I cleared the set of the crew and closed the picture down and took everybody through a

scene and kept working at it until the right rhythms were
there and until I was satisfied.

Ron Howard often draws on his own acting experiences to
achieve those elusive "happy days" on the set. Not surprisingly, he sees a lot of parallels between the two professions.

The process of directing and acting is quite similar. The
actors are looking for the honesty in a scene, some breakthrough that is going to allow them to play the scene in
order to tell the story.
    Like the director, they have to be aware of tone,
rhythm, the desired result. Is this a comedy? Laugh line?
Are people supposed to be crying? Good, creative actors
find ways to make that dialogue into something a little
more than just straightforward.
    Directors pretty much have to do the same thing. It's a
great advantage to be able to talk to actors. They still are
the number-one storytelling tool. You can shoot it wrong,
you can have lousy sets and crappy lighting, but if the
writing is good and the acting is good, chances are the
whole scene will still be effective.

Howard gazes out the window to the city below as he considers what he is saying.

My theory is, if you know where you're supposed to be
going with a scene and each character's course within
that scene, if the actors can find their own way to get
there, they will accomplish what they're supposed to
accomplish.
    Sometimes the only thing an actor needs from a direc-
tor is "nothing"—to be left alone. Otherwise you impose a

lot of ideas on the actors and you're not allowing them the
freedom to create.

Some actors want to be given a line reading, they want
to be given a result. Other actors freeze up when you start
talking about a result. You have to be able to talk to the
actors, and they'll make the adjustment.

Knowing what actors need in order to accomplish their best
work is, of course, easier said than done. According to Nina
Foch, there are times when creative conflict can lead to artistic
success.

In the first week, often there is a fight of some sort. A
power play. It can be over a chair, or the way a collar is, it
can be over the most foolish thing and it must be won by
the director. That doesn't mean fight, just win. If you win
it, then particularly with the young actor, he feels relaxed,
feels okay. "I have a good father or a good mother."

Ultimately, actors desperately need approval. You talk
to them privately and quietly and want to make damn sure
not to let your compliments become cheap. If you're going
to lie—"oh, how wonderful"—to help somebody, do it
privately. You need to get close to the actor, but only
business close. Whatever you do, don't get emotionally
close to anyone you're working with until after it's over.

Sometimes directors have to be willing to be vulnerable in
order to get the desired result from actors. This might mean
exploring their own emotions in a psychological game of give-
and-take. Foch continues, "The director, when confronted
with an actor who doesn't understand, is now able to confess
some of his or her own baggage. By telling the actor a personal

story, you are accessing the actor's own emotional life. The real message is that we're all in this together and nothing matters but the work."

Getting the best emotional response from an actor can be difficult for everyone involved. But the payoffs can be enormous in terms of what winds up on the screen. Norman Jewison remembers a particularly difficult night while shooting *Moonstruck*:

> The big love scene was shot at three in the morning. Cher did not want to do the scene because it was so cold and she was in a light dress with high heels and no protection from the cold. Actors have a problem when it's cold. They have a problem giving this natural believability to the performance because physically they are so cold that they can't control their body.
>
> So I set up the camera . . . and what happens is she is so cold that she starts to feel totally uncomfortable and tears almost come to her eyes. But because she's so tormented in that scene and can't make up her mind and is moved emotionally, the physical problem ends up working *for* the performance within the scene. By forcing it we got a wonderful performance.

Creative directors constantly seek solutions. The best ones always seem to find them. Another kind of problem was encountered while Ridley Scott was shooting the crucial climax scenes in *Alien*.

> In the last seventeen minutes of *Alien*, there's no dialogue, so it's Sigourney trying to emote without any other actors to play off of. And that's very difficult. So I was always

trying to cook up ways of helping her. I even had three- or four-inch speakers lining the set which I used to play Tomita's "The Planets" for her. And it used to help her because she had everything going rather than doing the whole thing in silence.

In order to make each scene become as real as possible, the director must overcome the fact that the story is being shot out of sequence. Norman Jewison sees the director's vision as the essential tool he uses to get the best from his cast in these situations. "You try to take the actors back to the moment emotionally, they must be quite aware of where they are in the story. The director is making this seamless story in his mind, but he is usually shooting it totally out of context."

While the director labors to make sure everyone on the set achieves his or her best work, it is the actors who invariably receive the lion's share of attention. Ron Howard strives to provide "a set where people interrelate, where people respect the actors and what they're doing." Nina Foch agrees, and offers this final, simple advice to every director. "How do you talk to the actor? With enormous affection and respect."

The Collaborative Art

By the time the shoot nears its final frantic days, chaos often reigns. In this heady environment, the director's intuitive instincts become more important than ever. For Ridley Scott, the set is like a big kitchen where the final results are always unpredictable.

Creating is like a stew. You put it in the oven and it becomes a casserole and you bake it. And frequently you don't really know where you're headed. It's all by instinct and intuition. You can rely on a few logical elements, you know that you're going to move in a certain direction because decisions have to be made and you've got to move on. Because unfortunately filming is all against the clock. So it's a constant battle between commerce and creativity.

Oliver Stone uses a similar analogy:

It's all the same soup. The writing, editing, directing, acting. We're all in it together. Directors are actors to a certain degree. Writers are actors. You act it out on paper.

The fun of movie collaboration is that you really work with a lot of people who are different from you and you learn a lot from them. People you don't like. But you learn to live with them. It teaches you tolerance.

The need for mutual trust, respect, and affection between all the collaborators can be seen in all phases of production. As the shoot nears completion, the struggle between commerce and creativity heightens. Whether soup or stew, the contributions of each and every collaborator along the way will, it is hoped, merge to become one seamless celluloid experience. For Ron Howard, it's a three-step process.

I try to come in every day with a plan that is solid enough to provide a foundation for the movie. That's where it starts.

Next you look for ideas and inspiration from your collaborators: actors, cinematographers, production designers, and others.

Then there is a kind of editing process where I sort through the ideas, weave them together, and apply them to my original overview. You look for things that will embellish on that fundamental point of view and elevate the storytelling quality of the film to help take it to the next level.

Martha Coolidge begins by asking collaborators such as the director of photography and production designer if they have images or ideas that connect with the script.

It's very important that everybody is making the same movie so I want to know if their first instincts are similar to mine, both on a visual and psychological level.

It's a collective vision but it's the *director's* vision. That's the vision that is shared or interpreted by the artists working on the picture.

She emphasizes that at the end of the day, it is the director who must accept responsibility for what winds up on the screen.

It's about choices. You choose the cast, you choose the sets. You decide how to shoot it and which takes to use. You sit in editing and every single frame on that screen is yours, it's up there because you picked it after looking at it hundreds and hundreds of times.

The amount of attention that goes into every shot means that nothing is in there by accident. So you must take responsibility for it, and that includes taking responsibility for what doesn't work. It's painful but it happens.

If films were physics, directors would be the fulcrum, the axis around which all the immutable laws of the universe hum. Ron Howard's journey began in Mayberry, but his evolution as a director has taught him a deep appreciation for the infinite mysteries of collaboration.

The buck does stop with the director, but there are so
many others involved. I think that the sooner we all see the
same movie in our heads, the sooner the collaborative
process works and the film benefits from the valuable
ideas coming from all those different areas of expertise.

Caught up in his own enthusiasm about the spirit of collaboration for a moment, he smiles as he adds a final thought. "You
know, there are a lot of very creative, intelligent people in this
business."

C L O S E - U P

PETER WEIR, *DEAD POETS SOCIETY*

I remember the first time I read *Dead Poets Society*. I was
planning to do *Green Card* with Gérard Depardieu and it had
been delayed a year. Jeff Katzenberg at Disney called me:
    "What are you going to do for the next year?"
    "I'll wait and work on the *Green Card* screenplay and go to
the supermarket."
    "Why don't you make another movie in the meantime?
I've got just the thing for you."
    So he sent me the script to read on the plane on the way
home. I opened the envelope without much enthusiasm, but
the title was intriguing. It didn't give me any idea of what the
thing might be. So I found myself reading. And as soon as I got
the idea that it was a school movie, I wasn't particularly
interested.
    Still, it was well written. And then I found myself being
drawn in by other things. I was very interested in the Keating

character. I was totally engrossed in the story as I reached the last act. But the bottom fell out of it when I saw he really had Hodgkin's disease—the cancer. So *that's* why he said "Seize the day." Who wouldn't?

Then I read beyond that to the ending, which I thought was sensational. So I got back to Australia and thought about it for a while. My agent called and asked what I thought. I thought it was pretty good, but I didn't want to do it. When I called Katzenberg and told him, he didn't understand.

"If you thought it was very impressive, how come you don't want to do it?"

"There's a problem in it for me—the cancer. Cancer is one of those things that says: This is a film that will move you. But stories which have people suffering from cancer or other horrible diseases are really specific. You lose the universality of the theme. And I saw Keating as touching on greater themes."

In the end I don't choose the material, the material chooses me. You get an emotion rather like the way music can affect you. And then you know you are going to do it. With any project, the challenge is to put that initial emotional response that you had at that first reading on the screen.

You can't define the emotion because it's like a ripple through your body. It's like describing how you feel when you hear Mozart—moved. Touched. It's something so strong that it can sustain you for a minimum of twelve months of production and dealing with hundreds of people and practical problems.

The Script that Lives

The script is a living thing. I will be constantly changing things. Most of my scripts are blue, or blue and pink and green. There's really very little of the original white pages left. The original pages to me are only a guide. I keep changing them—it could be visuals, the order of a sequence of a scene, it could be an idea, any of those. I collect pictures and magazine photos, a lot of visual references which are a personal inspiration that carry the film. And these will go in the back of my script. And some of them will get hooked up into individual scenes.

When all is said and done, eventually you get to a place where everything seems fine. It seems like there is nothing else you can possibly do. It's just right. Then a couple of weeks go by and all the experiences, all of your antennae are active, you're extremely intuitive. Talking to the crew, dinner at a restaurant, a man you saw standing at the bus stop, the plane flight over, the stop in Hawaii, all are going through your computer banks and being sorted and translated for anything that might be useful to your story. I think the whole process of directing has to do with this heightened sensitivity that one has during that period of time.

Production

During production, I worked a great deal with the ensemble of seven boys, so they would relate not to me but to each other. I wanted to take the boys back to the way I remembered my friends in the late fifties. Like Tom, I went to a private school. Mine was in Sydney, The Scot's College, and it was much like the school in the script. I was a terrible student, the school was ironbound. I tilted the school in *Dead Poets* to be more like my school. Made it a bit Scottish.

Most of the boys were getting their first major break in a movie with Robin Williams. And there was a tendency, initially, for potential tensions to show because some people had better parts than others. Will they get their close-ups? So I had to create an atmosphere where we worked as a group and they almost lived their characters.

With the boys, we began by getting them into uniform, haircuts. Then I held three or four classes, where I played a teacher. We had desks set up. I told them, "This is an imaginary school and I'm the drama and English teacher and we're going to put on a Christmas show. You have to stay in your character."

Since it was in the 1950s, I gave them a list of words that they couldn't use, such as "keen," or "it was really amazing," or "aaah, yeah . . ." all those broken-up sentences. I had them acting as reindeer and carrying packages, abysmally childish. Throughout the process the boys became younger, sillier, funnier, and lighter.

And Still It Changes . . .

Even during production there are script changes. Tom and I had a disagreement about the first cave meeting. He had the boys pretty much reading poetry straight off. I said, "I don't believe it. I could see most of them going to the cave because they wanted an adventure, not just to read poetry." I finally talked to the boys about it and they said, "Oh, no, we wouldn't read poetry."

So I rang Tom up and told him the boys agreed with me. He said he'd rewrite:

"What do you want?"

"Something upfront, chatting a bit before they get into the poetry, they're triggered by it."

But the rewrite came back and it wasn't right. So I got the boys together and we spent three lunch hours talking about what they would do. Out of it came food, then telling ghost stories, showing the *Playboy* picture.

From Page to Picture

In the original script, Tom says, they leave the precinct of the school and hurry through the adjoining forest and reach the cave. It was probably three lines, and yet I knew it was part of that feeling that led me to doing the picture.

That run to the cave was wonderful. It wasn't just a run to the cave. It's a very particular journey and they're wearing particular clothing, which led to the hooded coats and things. And I was trying to link it all to the secret societies that go back to meeting in caves.

Then I worked with Wendy, my wife, who did the design. I said, "I see these hooded black monks." And she said, "Do we dare line it with red?" We then added an owl. One of the boys looks back, the others don't see it. But it was like running back through time.

Then I added the fog in the scene. I think all filmmakers like fog. There is less information that comes through on the screen. It's closer to black and white. You have more control. Part of the appeal of fog is that it isolates and obscures and it's full of secrets. Oh yes, absolutely. Hooded figures in a fog inside a forest is one of those special moments.

I also added the birds. There were a lot of birds around because of the harvesting of the various crops in the area. They moved like schools of fish. I've never seen so many small birds! They almost formed a shape, and they would swirl and it would look like a question mark.

I'd sometimes stop the car when I saw them on the ground to go and startle them to see how they would move. I said to the main unit cameramen, "Let's get some shots of those birds because I like them." Later I said, "If you see birds on the way to work, you should be late."

So the birds became a motif and they seemed to be full of

hidden meaning. They're like those anonymous kids at the school, everyone is in uniforms, there's no individuality. Keating is sort of naming the birds. It's talking about individuality and finding your own individual voice and so forth. Not swirling and moving with the group.

In editing, we placed the birds next to the image of the boys coming down the stairs, the image of this freedom and flying versus this very contained space. I always thought of the boys like birds, just moving in a group, without individual shape and focus.

Lost in a World

I've always been fascinated with the silent films, and I've lately been looking at half a dozen classics and often sitting with the writer and saying: How could we do this scene without words? With all my films, I'll take them home and play music with them with the sound off and just let the images sort of flicker away.

It doesn't matter how you do it so long as you get results. In my case, I'm particularly susceptible to atmosphere and moods of people that you're harnessing for the good of the picture.

And locations. They do have power and if you're highly sensitized you can pick that up. This is not part of the practical considerations, but there's nothing like a place that suggests things to you. It can be anything from a car park underground to a natural setting, a house.

Or props. If there's a half a dozen knives, there will be one which will photograph better, has more power, one that has a sort of oddity to it. You've got to have a feeling that this would be plausible within the confines of your story. And you've got to feel satisfied about that.

A film takes on a life of its own despite all of what is planned. It has a personality of its own. And you must recognize it early on. That's what dailies are all about. They're about watching for signs of individual personality.

The individual's personal history can be penetrated by the close-up. And suddenly you see another aspect of a character. Perhaps a character has humor or a wry quality or even some disturbing quality which we need to grab more of because it's actually fueling the fire.

You have to remember that the audience is sitting in their seats dreaming and if you can connect with their unconscious, you really have a powerful connection between viewer and screen. You want them to let the stuff come up from their unconscious, provoked by your energies with just enough logic to feel like you know what you're doing and the picture is under control. That's the challenge, to have enough logic without inhibiting the unconscious.

So you're constantly monitoring that line. The true test of it is when you come out of a picture and you can't remember whether it was day or night when you came in. "Where did I put the car?" That is the ultimate. Lost in the world of the film.

4

the actor
and
"the kindness
of
strangers"

You don't just deliver the line. You think about it. You dream about it. You connect with it in very personal ways. If you're successful, you have something to bring to the party.

—Leonard Nimoy

"People think that acting is walking and talking and so they say—'Hey, I could do that!'" Acting teacher Nina Foch laughs. "But acting is very difficult. The best succeed precisely because they make it look so easy. Maybe if you're an actor your whole life long, you might do one or two scenes completely well."

It begins with vulnerability. For actors to do their best work, they must be willing to be totally open, to experiment and allow all that is inside to be exposed. To accomplish this at the highest levels requires tremendous discipline. Actors work with their emotions, their experiences, traumas, feelings, and memories. Bodies and voices become finely tuned instruments that express and convey the character.

Since the actor *is* the instrument, he or she is in a very different position from film's other collaborators. The writer projects an inner life onto a piece of paper, the composer uses notes, the producer has contacts, the director a vision. But actors stand alone. It's not about the work but about *them*. And it's very personal.

Veteran actor Peter Strauss has dominated television movies and miniseries since his performance in the highly acclaimed *Rich Man, Poor Man*. He says a certain trust must develop between actors and their collaborators.

> Ultimately, most actors have to walk on the set like Blanche DuBois in *A Street Car Named Desire* and say, "I have always depended upon the kindness of strangers." Because you may be dressed in the scene, but trust me, you are naked in front of a lot of strangers. And you are ultimately depending upon their kindness.

This is exactly why actors are so vulnerable to criticism. When the critic says "the script doesn't work," the writer says, "Well, it's just a script, it may be part of me but it's not *me*." The actor can't displace the criticism. There's nowhere else for it to go.

The critics have been kind to Mary McDonnell. Her performance as Kevin Costner's co-star in *Dances with Wolves* brought her an Academy Award nomination. Another came for her starring role as a recently disabled ex–soap opera star in *Passion Fish*. Response was also positive to her role as Claire, the "woman who found the baby" in Lawrence Kasdan's *Grand Canyon*.

She feels that the experiences that help the actor or actress perform can be traced to childhood. "I think that most actors had a difficult time growing up because of the level of their emotional response," she says. "They had no control of themselves, and were often seen as overly dramatic or negative. They have these tremendous emotional responses and other people say 'What's the problem?' "

McDonnell points out that actors live in a different world from that of their fellow collaborators.

Actors are part of a certain percentage of people on this planet that have an emotional vocabulary as a primary experience. It's as if their life is experienced emotionally and then that is translated intellectually or conceptually into the performance.

In Search of Magic

Like the best directors and producers, successful actors and actresses must choose from among the many projects available to them. As with the other collaborators, it all begins with the script and, according to Peter Strauss, a certain attitude.

I always try to approach the script with great excitement. I go find a quiet corner and open up a screenplay with three anticipations.

First is the truth. I don't care if the script is funny, sad, black, yellow, about politics, love, death. I want to find the truth. I look for insight in the writing, depth, the courage to go behind closed doors—I want the writer to be daring.

The next thing I want to find is the magic. Why do this movie? Does it shimmer? I want to be transported by the screenplay. To go to the movie, to be in the dark and have magic happen.

Finally, I need to know that every day coming to work will be a challenge. I don't want to be doing reality. I want to go above it, to raise the meter. I look for passion, aliveness, hatred, rage, fear, pain, joy, bigness. I want to feel big, I want to be angry big, feel sad big.

The inherent artistic challenges of any script begin with the actor's initial response. Is it to the story or the character? Edward James Olmos's career (*American Me, Stand and Deliver*) has been characterized by stories that speak to universal truths.

For me the most essential aspect is the story. Character is secondary to the story. I look for the intent, the subtext. I believe that intent equals content and therefore it doesn't matter how intensely buried it is, the intention will inevitably come out.

Mary McDonnell's roles in films by Lawrence Kasdan and John Sayles have afforded her the opportunity to work with two of Hollywood's most renowned storytellers. Not surprisingly, they have also influenced the way she approaches the script.

What I respond to is a good story and then I look at the role. If it's a good story, usually the role is going to be a great one, no matter the size of it. It's a story that has a structure to it that you understand. It involves what I perceive as an honest reflection of the human dilemma. If I read something that I feel is false, it seems to be placing itself out of the realm of humanity.

What gets me charged is being in a situation that connects to the general population. To connect myself to the world is a big part of what drives me. It's important for me to know who those people are in the audience. That we're sharing a common experience.

John Lithgow's distinguished career has included performances in some of Hollywood's most interesting feature projects, including *Terms of Endearment, The World According to Garp, All That Jazz,* and the cult classic *The Adventures of Buckaroo Banzai: Across the 4th Dimension.* As he describes his approach to the script, you begin to understand why those career choices did not happen by accident.

I want a story that grabs me and a character who travels a journey. The action of the story affects the character and he changes, going from one point to another as the story unfolds. Also, the character has to have something new about him that surprises me. It might be the way he uses language or a different look or accent—some surprising behavior that I want to try to pull off.

Graham Greene is best known for his role as the Sioux Indian who befriends Kevin Costner's Lieutenant Dunbar in *Dances with Wolves.* He has his own novel approach to the script, one that begins with an examination of the character he has been asked to play.

I take out all the pages that pertain to my character. I read them first and see if the thread is good. Then I take the rest of the script and read it *sans* my character and see if that thread is good and try to match them up. If I can't understand what the script is about, then I can't make somebody who's watching it understand it.

the actor and
"the kindness of strangers"
151

It's hard to think of another actor in Hollywood who is more renowned for his ability to recognize a great script and a great character than Dustin Hoffman. In an interview on *Larry King Live* he emphasizes the scarcity of really good scripts. "There are probably one or two scripts that I read every year where the structure is sound." And the character?

> With *Hero* I didn't hear the character and I had to talk to the writer for a long time. I said, "I would like to play this guy because I like the way he interacts in terms of the story, the narrative, but I can't say I hear him." And it took me about two or three weeks to find something fresh about the guy for myself.

At the same time, Hoffman reveals that his penchant for finding "something fresh" in the character occasionally prompts him to turn down roles he wished he hadn't.

> I read *Close Encounters of the Third Kind* and I thought, "This is a great script. It's almost a perfect script." But I turned it down because I was naive and I thought, "I don't know how to do this part in a fresh way." Now I know how rare it is to get a really good script with a good director. And even if you don't know what to do with the part, you take it.

This was precisely what happened to Mary McDonnell when she first read *Dances with Wolves*, but getting the script—that was the problem!

> When I first heard about *Dances* I was in New York and my agent called me and said, "You've got to go down to this hotel and read this new Kevin Costner script." I asked

what it was about and she told me it was a cowboy-and-Indian movie. I said, "No way, I'm not interested." She said, "I know, but there's something really special about it."

I asked why I had to go to a hotel to read it and she said, "They're not letting it out." I remember that I had a horrible reaction to that. You can go to the library and get Shakespeare, Shaw, Ibsen, but not this script? Right.

So I went with an attitude and they gave me the script and about fifteen pages into it, it just knocked me out. I was on fire. Kevin had come to New York because he said, "I want a woman, not a girl." He said he wanted somebody older, someone who "had a few lines in her face." As it turned out, that was me!

I also think he was looking for a level of skill necessary for the language. It's rare to have so many challenges in one script because you know there won't be one moment of dissatisfaction or boredom. Just the very act of being asked to pull it off is a gift.

My World and Welcome to It

With the question of artistic challenge settled, most actors begin to reflect on the themes of the script. How will it affect the audience? How does it reconcile with their personal worldview?

Usually the writer will originate a story, or sometimes it begins with a director or a producer. Yet it's the actor whose image will forever be associated with the story. What's more, the performers will spend the rest of their lives being approached by perfect strangers who want to discuss the values and philosophies inherent in the story.

There are few performers who have experienced this phenomenon more frequently over the last twenty-five years than actor-director Leonard Nimoy. Though his feature directing credits include *Three Men and a Baby* and *The Good Mother*, it is his role as Mr. Spock on the *Star Trek* TV and feature film projects that have brought him worldwide recognition.

Whether he is doing a public appearance or shopping at the grocery store, *Star Trek*'s enduring philosophy is always topic A among those who approach him.

> *Star Trek* was certainly entertainment, but time and again people ask me what its longevity and durability are all about. I think part of it is because you can revisit the shows and films and experience new levels.
>
> An eight-year-old will respond to certain visual and audio elements. But that same person at twenty will see something else. They may discover the ecological themes or find something that relates to a novel they just read. It's all about connections, and over the years they add up.

For Edward James Olmos it's "about the clash of cultures— sometimes they clash, sometimes they're bonding, but it's all about culture."

At the Golden Apple Awards Geena Davis exclaimed, "I choose roles that honor women and give them something to root for."

When the Write Stuff Is the Wrong Stuff

Ideally, actors will commit to a good script they can believe in, and they'll go about the job of helping bring it to life. However, as we have seen, the Hollywood filmmaking process often means the script will undergo a number of changes along the way. Whatever the situation, the actor's performance will depend on the script, and very often that script will not be as good as it could be. All experienced actors encounter this problem. John Lithgow reveals how it impacts on the performance.

If the script is not a very good piece of work, you need to struggle to give it some emotional authenticity. Sometimes you do too much to try and puff it up. The hardest roles to play are poorly written or underwritten, where you don't have enough information to create a multidimensional character.

The ones that are effortless to play are well written. *Terms of Endearment* was a perfectly written script. At first glance the scenes seemed prosaic, but you didn't have to do much with them. In the end they were extraordinarily moving because of the good judgment and writing of Jim Brooks.

Nina Foch says certain other problems tend to crop up in scripts, most notably in the dialogue. "What you want from the writer is a storyteller with an ear, one who can hear the way people talk. In addition, the actor can work with the director to cut out the extra lines that don't need to be spoken."

Graham Greene (*Dances with Wolves*) acknowledges that like everyone else, writers have their good days and their bad days.

Sometimes you get a really good script and the dialogue just jumps off the page at you. Other times, it's just syntax. I say to myself, "It definitely must have been ten to five when the writer wrote this!" I like to bring a little humor to most of the roles that I do. Very few writers demand that you say exactly what they've written.

Like most actors, Peter Strauss finds it easier to start with a great script. "I love subtext. I love colors in a character. The more that's there, the less I'm going to have to do."

As for the problem script, Strauss uses an interesting visual metaphor to describe what it can do to the actor's performance.

> It's a nightmare for the actor when the screenplay doesn't work. Sometimes I know in my gut that this scene could be a great dramatic scene and I ain't got the words for my character. And I'm banging my head.
>
> If it's a good skeletal frame, the actor will blossom. If it's a man where his legs are sticking out of his ears, that poor actor is going to be suffering up there. Now, it's the actor's job to know that. The more you dig and demand, the better it's going to come out in the end. My job is to keep fleshing out the character in the direction the writer intended.

Leonard Nimoy points out that there are also times when the actor knows the character better than the writer. This occurs most often on television, but applies increasingly to features, thanks to the sequel phenomenon.

> Sometimes a performance characteristic that I'm not even conscious of sneaks into the character. The writers will pick up on it and ask you to do it again. "You raised your eyebrow when he said this to you. That worked. Let's do that again."
>
> The problem is I didn't know I would be doing it for

the next twenty-five years! It becomes such an identifiable characteristic. Now all of a sudden every seven or eight pages it says "Spock raises an eyebrow." So you have to say to them, "We're going to lose the value of this if we keep using it as a way out of every situation. Let's find something else. Don't make it so cheap."

Scripts and Tips

Whatever the ultimate state of the script, actors must eventually move to try to make the characters their own. This is accomplished by manipulating the script in a variety of ways.

Mary McDonnell likes to know her territory. "In *Matewan* I mapped out the material. It was like a graph that showed the evolution of my character, what might occur when, what she might feel, page by page. Then when we started shooting out of sequence, I could just review my notes."

Leonard Nimoy reveals that "Science fiction calls for a certain kind of theatrical imagination. Sometimes it comes from me, a personal experience that might be applicable. I make notes to myself, or I'll hear about something on radio or TV that's topical, a thematic idea that becomes useful."

Nina Foch recommends that her acting students stay in touch with the totality of the script.

The actor does everything the director does, breaks down the action, the intentions, the props, every little beat in the scene should be broken down.

I advise actors to take their part out of the script. Take the actual pages out and put the rest in a drawer. Then read their pages at least once every day. You need to know what's required of each scene and how to help it be better.

Leonard Nimoy says a successful actor must "bring something to the party."

The best actors bring something to a character. Perhaps it's based on personal experience or the lives of others. They get the best out of what the script has to offer by discovering ways to illuminate the ideas in it. Perhaps it's an attitude, a posture, or a gesture, so the audience can see more than a character and say "I *know* who that is."

You don't just deliver the line. You think about it. You dream about it. You connect with it in very personal ways. If you're successful, you have something to bring to the party.

Research: You *Are* the Details

For Peter Strauss, part of making every character effective and each scene better involves research. Given today's high-pressure production schedules, though, research is a luxury. "An actor who gets to research gets really excited about the opportunity to bring color to his work." He demonstrates how this can involve anything from in-depth character analysis to something as simple as holding a gun.

Every time a weapon is in the script, I'll go out to the valley and practice so I can be comfortable with it in my hand. Most characters who have props in their hands handle them without it being a meaningful event. But when an actor gets an Uzi in his hands, it's a meaningful event!

Today's roles require research. If you get to play an AIDS victim, you've got to spend time learning how an AIDS victim dies. At Northwestern University they taught me that if you're going to play an English king, you need to know English history. I buy that.

Hollywood lore is replete with stories about the extensive research Nick Nolte brings to his roles. While shooting *Farewell to the King*, Nolte transformed his hotel suite in Borneo into a war room worthy of Patton. There were battle charts, arcane historical accounts of Allied objectives in the Pacific theatre, and a frayed copy of the script into which the relevant pages of the adapted novel were inserted for background. Several sources report that director John Milius took one look at the chaos and barked, "What in the hell does any of this have to do with acting?" To which Nolte replied, "Everything!"

For *Down and Out in Beverly Hills*, the actor disappeared for several days into Los Angeles' skid row. While there he drank cheap wine and slept in vacant lots. By the time he appeared at rehearsal, Bette Midler and Richard Dreyfuss were dumbfounded because he literally stank. Of course, that was exactly what the script called for.

Director Paul Mazursky says, "Nick would never be so pretentious as to call himself a method actor. He just does it." In a *Premiere* magazine interview Nolte explains, "Preparing for a role is when I get to indulge. To me an actor's technique is about learning so that he'll survive. Only then can he deal with his insecurity and his fears."

Bio Research

Research becomes increasingly complicated when playing a real-life character. For *Stand and Deliver*, the true story of extraordinary teacher Jaime Escalante, Edward James Olmos

was able to spend time with the entire family. "I talked to
Jaime for hundreds of hours and watched him for hundreds
of hours. I would stay there from early in the morning until
late at night. I would just watch every behavior and ask
questions."

In a *Calendar* interview that coincided with the release of
Hoffa, Jack Nicholson reveals his own methods to writer
Hilary de Vries.

> I look at endless tapes, a lot of books. We also shot in the
> towns that Hoffa worked in, and there are a lot of people
> still living who knew him. I met his son and I talked to the
> prosecuting attorneys in both cases where Hoffa was tried.
>   There are some parts that you say, "I could play this
> and I sort of know how" and then there are some parts,
> and Hoffa is one, where you say . . . "Jesus Christ, look at
> the size of this. It's like a huge mountain." You know you
> will do it but you don't know if you can exactly, because
> you don't know how exactly.

Hoffa was an especially interesting case because, as with *JFK*,
no one really knew what happened in real life. Nicholson
found this somewhat liberating.

> It's not a biography, it's a portrait, and there is a difference.
> Because no one really knows what happened to Hoffa, it
> gives you license to do a lot of guessing with other things
> too. I had a certain amount of license in my job as an actor
> to have an inside interpretation of the guy.

An actor's interpretation of a character can be formulated in
any number of ways. Graham Greene likes to prepare a mental biography that is rich in detail.

I work out the background of my character in my head. Each one is a little different. Is he married? What does he like? What kind of clothes does he wear? Does he even care about clothes? What kind of house or car does he prefer? How much money does he have in the bank? Who are his friends? His allies? Who hates him?

For Edward James Olmos it is a matter of moving "forward into the past," but there are always larger implications.

The past is what we look for in building the story. How far back can we go to develop a bible that allows you to understand what this character's choices have been? What happened to him as a child? How does that permeate itself inside the character?

I think that you must understand the back story before you can move forward. It's like trying to understand yourself as a human being without understanding your past. That's why most of us have to really look at ourselves and our civilization and understand where we come from, so that we can understand what motivates and drives us in the conscious mind today.

Accents: Say What?

Talk with any actors about the challenges they face as they prepare for a role, and sooner or later the subject of language and accents comes up. Often this is accompanied by a sigh, groan, or similar disparaging remark.

Mary McDonnell laughs as she recalls how the meticulous John Sayles gently corrected her fledgling Louisiana speech patterns in *Passion Fish*. "Mary, you're no longer in Louisiana, you just entered North Carolina!"

Regional American accents are something of a specialty for Peter Strauss.

> Language has eccentricity. It has some rules. But stand in a room with fifty Americans, and you have fifty dialects. So there isn't any American dialect. There's just a way of speaking. It's flavor, subtlety.
>
> For the television movie *The Trial* I played a southern sheriff. I had dialect work to do. I did it with videos. I had the film commission send me videos of the newscasters and local talk shows.

The task becomes more difficult as the geography expands. John Lithgow's experience in *Raising Cain* is typical. "I worked with a Norwegian linguistics professor at Stanford and I got his accent. I had him teach me the accent and we sang Norwegian lullabies."

For *Dances with Wolves*, Graham Greene had the most difficult assignment of all: learning an entirely new and unfamiliar language.

> We had to learn the Lakota language. I couldn't retain any of this, it was so foreign. I've learned a number of languages phonetically, but this was completely different. To learn it, I sat in my hotel room for eight hours a day. We had tapes, but they were slowly pronounced, and we had a dialogue coach that was with us and was on our case every second.
>
> It took two weeks to learn all the dialogue, and then I'd work in my hotel room until two in the morning, going through the speeches. Next morning I couldn't remember

any of it! I was nearly in tears. So I'd go back to the beginning and slowly it would come.

Mary McDonnell's role as Kevin Costner's interpreter in *Dances* put extra pressure on her, but also taught her a deep appreciation for the intricacies involved.

There is a real modesty in Lakota speech, there was no aggressive quality to it, rather a kind of musicality. It's gentle, nasal, and economical. When I was learning Lakota, I found myself becoming very nasal. One day Kevin said, "You're starting to sound a little Chinese."

When a scene called for her to switch from Lakota to English "for the first time in twenty years," there were emotional barriers for her character to overcome. What's more, they had to be reflected in just a few halting syllables.

The implications of giving up her primary language are so painful that when Graham Greene's character asks me to translate for Lieutenant Dunbar [Costner] I say, "I don't think I can do this." What I'm really saying is that I don't think I can remember. What I'm feeling is completely emotional, I'm threatened by the possibility of having to go back and retrieve that traumatic memory.

The Inside Trick

Mastering accents, doing research, imagining biographies and back stories—all of these represent an attempt to "get inside" characters and bring them to physical life. There are as many ways to accomplish this combination of mental and physical challenges as there are roles to play. Edward James Olmos defines the two basic theories.

> The English form of study teaches you to go from the outside in. You do the behavior and it starts to seep inside. The Stanislavski method teaches you to go from the inside out. You begin with the feeling and memory, and those feelings begin to affect your behavior.
>
> In other words, some people will turn around and get a limp and then figure out where the limp came from. Other people have to figure out why they have to limp before they can do the limp.

Nina Foch sees the two basic theories increasingly merging into one.

> The fact is, everybody uses both. You see a limp, you steal it, you put it on. By doing it, it begins to become organic. By adopting the outside behavior, it affects the inside.

John Lithgow's experiences in *Ricochet* illustrate the process.

> I developed a limp based on the fact that this character had been shot in the knee early on. The moment he'd been shot was a moment of humiliation and defeat which he carried around with him bitterly for the rest of his life. I thought about the limp. I figured the knee had been frozen up a bit so I put a knee brace on my knee.

Graham Greene found a rather unconventional way to get inside one very unfamiliar character. "I had to play a fifty-six-year-old man who had no teeth, was loud as sin, and had bad posture. I put a slice of bologna in each shoe. I needed something slimy in my shoe to make it work."

John Lithgow has achieved a considerable amount of fame for his ability to get inside characters. He begins with the physical accoutrements that accompany each role.

A lot comes from external trappings. Wardrobe fittings are extremely important. You try out your ideas with the costume designer. I go through a personal process: looking in the mirror, seeing how the clothes are beginning to characterize this person. Then there's the haircut, maybe you grow a beard or wear some peculiar makeup prosthetics, all that plays a part.

When asked to recall his most memorable challenges, Lithgow cites three very different characters and reveals how he brought each to life.

For *Buckaroo Banzai* I was an Italian scientist. Forty years ago his body had been inhabited by a tyrannical evil alien from another dimension. He was *still* inhabited by that alien but he was forty years older. The idea was to figure out how forty years of being inhabited by an alien changed you. I put a lot of thought into this and came up with some very striking physical devices.

Since he fed himself on electricity and sugar, I hit on this idea of red hair as a sort of shock wig, the hair going straight up as if I had been electrified at least once every day of my life.

On another occasion, Lithgow discovered a simple way to get inside the diabolical mind of a tortured killer. "I gave myself a milky contact lens in one eye. This was a bizarre, sadistic horrible character, and I liked giving him a couple of characteristics that made him loathe himself or made him self-conscious."

Finally, there is the challenge of how the actor's own physical identity must be sacrificed to create an unforgettable character. Lithgow learned more about this from George Miller, who directed him in a segment of *Twilight Zone—The Movie*.

Miller wanted me to dye my hair black and I told him I didn't get the point. Then he said, "How about a cold sore on your mouth?" I asked him what he was driving at, and he said he wanted to think of something that would throw me off my image of myself.

That stuck in my mind because now that's always something I look for. It was a gift from him to me. For *Twilight Zone* I ultimately decided to have a three-day growth of beard and my hair was full of grease. I looked very, very haggard, and I wore a black suit and a brown shirt. I certainly was not my image of myself. And it's somehow liberating because it facilitates the whole process of becoming another person.

One of film lore's most famous transformations came when Dustin Hoffman assumed the role of a woman in *Tootsie*. In his *Larry King Live* interview he confesses, "All I can say is that we did seven months of makeup tests, and I really wanted to look as beautiful as possible. But I was shocked when they told me that this was as beautiful as they could make me. I thought Hollywood could do anything!"

"Let's Get Physical"

The physical stamina required to act for hours and hours and do what is physically needed can be considerable. During a shoot the actor might routinely rise as early as four in the morning. Several hours of makeup may be required, hours more may be spent sitting around waiting for the first cue. But when the camera rolls, the actor must be totally there, totally present. It's all right for the director to be a bit tired, or for the costumers to yawn, but the actor must be totally alive.

All of this becomes more complicated when the role calls for the actor or actress to assume a character who is severely disabled. In *Passion Fish*, Mary McDonnell's character May-Alice spent most of the film reconciling herself to an accident that had left her paralyzed from the waist down.

> It was clear to me that I had to start physically. I needed a great deal of upper body strength to do the role in order to pretend that I didn't have it. Because if I had been as weak as May-Alice was, I would have been very sore and run down.
>
> I worked with a trainer to build up my strength so that I could lift myself into my chair and crawl on the floors and do what I needed to do without looking like I was in training. At the Rehab Center, I worked with a therapist and a counselor who was a paraplegic. They put me through rigorous training. It was frustrating but it helped lead me into some of the emotional aspects of the material.

The physical demands of a role may also include developing certain skills that must accompany it. Harrison Ford's use of the bullwhip in the Indiana Jones movies was certainly central to his character. Ford explains how he did it in an interview with *Playboy*.

I do all my own whipping. But it's not a skill I keep up between films. It's a bit like riding a bike. Once you've learned the basics, you remember them, so that you're not lashing yourself about the head and shoulders as you did when you were beginning.

I have bullwhips in various lengths and practice with them on posts and trees. Now it all comes naturally when in action, you know. I must say, though, that it was hard to find somebody to teach me. Amazingly, there aren't that many expert hands with a bullwhip.

Being There

Acting is not just about doing, it's about *being*. It's about making the moment ring true so the audience really believes the actor is the character. For Nina Foch, the "doing" comes from the actor's own ability to completely comprehend what is happening in the character's inner life.

Understanding leads to doing, which leads to emotion. How do they eat? How much do they care about their bodies? Do they wear tight clothes? People who live on Big Macs and beans probably break wind a lot. People who don't take care of themselves are constipated.

I can't even walk through the door unless I have an idea of what I had to do to get to the door. All of this understanding has to occur, to know the preparation for the entrance, or any scene.

Graham Greene explains that "Film is internal. As an actor, internalizing is about listening, relating."

Peter Strauss has to ask the six basic journalism questions: "Why, when, who, where, what, and how? Who am I? What am I? What drives me? Why is my character like this?"

Dustin Hoffman's description of his approach in *Tootsie* strikes a similar chord. "What if I was this woman? What if I looked like this? How would I have been different in terms of my own personality?"

The trick seems to be in developing the ability to transcend the self and the task at hand, the "doing" part, and to become the character, literally, the "being."

Nina Foch teaches her acting students to use their own physical selves to become the character. "You have to know how to use your body and voice as an instrument so you can call on it and use it easily. The actor must learn how to play that instrument. That requires getting rid of your own tension."

"You Must Remember This"

The use of personal memory to convey the appropriate emotion in a scene is a tool that most actors find useful. This is most often accomplished by a journey within. "Everything is inside you," says Foch. "There are only eight emotions: love, loss of love, pleasure, loss of pleasure, fear, grief, rage, and impotent rage."

For Peter Strauss the truth of a performance is one way to measure the actor's ability. "You have the truth in your gut," he reveals. "That's the magic of the good actor versus the bad one. The bad one doesn't know the difference between truth and falseness. The good actor does. And the exceptional actor gets in touch with truth on screen and is unafraid of being in touch with it."

Actors must be fearless when it comes to the delicate issue of dredging up their most painful personal experiences. Before achieving film stardom, Mary McDonnell's career flourished on the stage. It was there that she learned performance and pain often go hand in hand.

All actors possess an ability to project disaster and drama on situations. I remember one time I needed to make an entrance and accomplish a certain emotion on stage. I started to think about something that was very terrible on a personal level, and I had a tremendous emotional response to it and walked out and played the scene beautifully.

But afterward, I was upset with myself for tampering with this. I had to rethink. Do I want to do this my entire life? What are the boundaries in terms of what I'm willing to tamper with on a psychic level? Because as much as I don't think I control anyone's destiny or fate, I do believe that thoughts create energy. So it makes you wonder . . .

Peter Strauss acknowledges the role of pain in these situations. "You always will have the pain. Pain won't go anyplace. You've got pain in the bank. The next step is to achieve openness as a human being. As an artist, you've got to be prepared to explore another person's point of view."

Good actors tend to take a personal experience and somehow let it gleam. I had this discussion with an actress. She was sitting there with her husband. He wanted to know how she managed to be in such pain in the scene. She said, "Well, I imagined that our child was dead." The husband looked at me dumbfounded, disturbed. Finally he said, "That's really sick!" I wasn't sure how to respond. She got very intense and said, "No, that's our gift."

It's a bizarre thing to do but actors do it all the time in order to turn their pain into something positive. They take people they love and kill them, beat them, cut their hands off, make them sick, lose them, divorce them. To some people on the outside looking in, that's neurosis, but to the actor that's a gift.

Can actors afford to be neurotic? The press is full of stories about how this or that actor or actress threw a tantrum on the set. Peter Strauss acknowledges the thin line between emotion and neurosis, but sees a key difference.

There are actors who say "I don't want to go into therapy because if I make myself happy, I won't have any pain to draw from." I used to think that way. It's the most grievous error I ever made.

Ultimately it is when you begin to understand yourself that you are more open and willing to exploring the scene from a whole new perspective.

Rehearsal: The Self-Discovery Channel

As the project nears production, there is usually some rehearsal time. It is during this crucial period that performances begin to gel. John Lithgow explains how the process works.

I want about a week of rehearsal time. First we'll have a cold reading. Then, as a group, we sit down and break the script down scene by scene. We read the scene through once with the assistant director reading every word of the stage directions to remind us about them. And the very reading of the material triggers ideas from the director and actors.

Then we put it on its feet, spending time in a rehearsal room. We've taped down the basic set, which is very elaborate. Beyond that, we set up four or five chairs to represent the interior of a car or bus or restaurant.

It is only after the physical situation is set up, Lithgow maintains, that the real business of rehearsal begins.

Then we discuss what the character is going through and what the scene is about. It's easy to forget little details in one scene that affect events in scenes that occur five or ten minutes later. Just by rehearsing you pick up on those things. Inevitably the shooting schedule is going to jump around. It's only by rehearsing that you keep the sequence of events straight, exactly where you're supposed to be on the time line.

You don't want to overrehearse, but I think it's great to get to the point where you're playing the hell out of a scene even though you may still have a script in your hand.

For the actor, rehearsals are not just about "nailing it" or "figuring it out" but about discovering if there will be chemistry between the actors. Most prefer to keep the rehearsal process quite fluid in order to experiment. Peter Strauss reveals, "To me, rehearsal is where you really discover scenes." Mary McDonnell says the process differs significantly from the common misconceptions about it.

The right people rehearse in a way that's open-ended by nature. It's not about finding the answers and then showing up on the set someday and executing the choice. I respond creatively to a rehearsal situation where you are opening up opportunities, starting to see the myriad aspects. You try to see different things and you start to get comfortable with the idea of experimentation with the other actors.

Often the nature of the material will have an impact on the rehearsal process. McDonnell recalls that for Lawrence Kasdan's *Grand Canyon*, a probing portrait of the nature of contemporary urban life, the cast began by discussing what life in Los Angeles was like for them and how it affected their own daily behavior.

Larry Kasdan's rehearsal processes are filled with exploration. He told us he was excited about directing *Grand Canyon* because he was going to witness everything as a director that he couldn't know about as the writer.

McDonnell contends that the best actors are the ones who aren't afraid to make mistakes, no matter what the stage of the performance. "A very wise director once told me before opening night in the theatre, 'Go out there and make some mistakes. You can make some beautiful mistakes. They're so interesting.' "

Dustin Hoffman points out the fundamental differences between rehearsals for theatre and film.

In the theatre, you have a chance to rehearse every day. You can get out there and find that character over a period of weeks—even during previews, even after you open.

Many times, actors say to each other, "Don't come see me until three months after opening night." You can grow into a part.

You can't do that on film. Sometimes there is no rehearsal time. Once you start shooting, you are trying to find the character, but it's all on film. And if you improve that character too much, it doesn't match at six weeks what you did the first two weeks.

Mary McDonnell had the luxury of a relatively long rehearsal for *Dances with Wolves*, but there was so much to learn.

We rehearsed for three weeks out on the prairie. We would get up in the morning and pile into a van and then they'd put us on horses. Then we went to language class to learn Lakota. Then we would get fit for these costumes. I was being asked to learn very quickly and I started to understand about the adaptations one makes in trying to survive and conform.

So rather than being familiar with everything, I focused on the unfamiliarity and what that made me feel like. And that helped me understand what created this little girl who was without a family. The guilt. The sense of aloneness.

Invariably, actors discover something about themselves as they move through rehearsal. McDonnell fondly remembers the scene where her character passes out and must be carried home across Lieutenant Dunbar's (Kevin Costner) saddle.

I remember when we were rehearsing the little ride that it felt so comforting to have someone take me physically and care for me. My character probably hadn't felt a lot of that.

And I had a sense that she hadn't had a really connected physical life with another person for a long time. So I started imagining what happens to a being even in that unconscious state.

The next time she meets Dunbar consciously, there is obviously something in the unconscious that she doesn't necessarily want to face. She is quite happy with the Indians. But the presence of this man brings up for her a whole level of desire. There's a need for emotional connection that's been denied for a long time. Then it starts to surface when she is around Dunbar, the chemistry begins.

McDonnell is enthusiastic about the discoveries that she makes during rehearsal. "Often I discover some amazing things. I make notes about it." At the same time she stresses a low-key approach because of the ego factor. "I keep it kind of vague. You don't want to pay too much attention to yourself. It's more like: What was the experience? What was the territory we stepped into? It's a stimulation, a reminder."

Ready on the Set: Let the Gains Begin!

With rehearsals complete, the actual filming begins. There are a number of strategies for dealing with the pressure-packed atmosphere of the shoot. John Lithgow relates that if the rehearsal process was successful, the actor has something he can take with him to the set.

You have this memory of having gotten it right at least once before in rehearsal. You've found the essence of the scene. Then you may shoot the scene from four or five different angles and with each angle you may have seven or eight takes. That's forty times you're doing the scene. In addition you may have camera rehearsals and maybe you've run the lines with the other actors. You've had lots of opportunities to get it right.

Once the master scene is complete, you have to cling to that basic version of the scene. You can't start messing around outside of those parameters. But you certainly can fine-tune different inflections, different rhythms, different intentions. And a good director is very watchful. He knows when you're going too far. He has you try it different ways. He gives himself lots of choices.

Actors begin by familiarizing themselves with their surroundings. Graham Greene relates that in a project with the scope of *Dances with Wolves,* even that simple process can require some formidable adjustments.

It required me to literally divorce myself from civilization. I would get into my costume and walk around. Finally it became livable. As an actor you have to get used to that set. You can't walk around stumbling on rough terrain. Whatever is there, you've got to get used to it.

Mary McDonnell tries to pay attention to her own responses as the shoot continues.

You put yourself in the scene and start to pay attention to some of your responses because it leads you to the direct response you're having to the scene. I may have disregarded the fact that every time I played a certain scene I

have my arms folded and I was scratching my face. But
now I pay attention because it helps me understand my
emotional response.

Some scenes are easier to play than others. The problem
always involves how much to trust your own emotional response and how many adjustments need to be made. McDonnell recalls the scene in *Grand Canyon* where she finds the
baby. Many felt it was one of the most powerful scenes in the
film. Even at the script stage it had a direct effect on her.

> I pretty much left that one alone. When I read it I was pretty
> much blown away by the experience of finding this child. I
> had such a strong response reading it. I was in touch with
> all my maternal feelings as soon as I read the scene. They
> came flying to the surface really quickly. I thought, Don't
> even tamper with it, don't get too used to it.

Graham Greene advocates a zenlike concentration coupled
with an ability to relax.

> The only thing that's important to me is the scene at that
> moment. I found that napping between scenes is very
> important. I kick back. Sitting is recharging my batteries
> to get another go at it. You have to ignore everybody else.
> Sometimes it's difficult to focus and concentrate, but it's
> my responsibility.
>   My whole thing is that they are paying me this amount
> of money to do a job. My responsibility is to be there and
> do the job I was hired to do. Not to gripe about why
> there's no banana on the craft service cart. It's not my
> damn business. My business is to stand in front of the lens
> when somebody says "Shoot."

Like Greene, Leonard Nimoy emphasizes a certain work ethic. "You do an honest day's work. You don't do shoddy work. You try to make it better and walk away with a sense of accomplishment." Nimoy explains he learned this during his childhood. "My father was a barber—and there was a sense of completion when he'd snap the apron off the guy and say 'Next!' He'd done a good job of cutting the man's hair."

No matter the state of his haircut, Dustin Hoffman commands a kind of respect on the set that few actors can. He reveals that much of what he learned about the process came from his first film acting job.

> *The Graduate* was my first movie, and it still is one of the richest experiences I've ever had, in terms of a director who was so thoroughly prepared.
>
> One day, apparently I was dogging it a little and Mike Nichols said something to me that stuck with me. He said, "You're never going to get a chance to do this scene again for the rest of your life, and it's going to be there, and you're going to look back on it one day and you're going to say 'I could have done better.'" And I must say, his words stuck with me.

The challenge of maintaining intensity throughout the production is crucial as the same scene is shot over and over again. First the master shot encompasses the entire scene. Then the director moves in for the tighter shots, and finally the close-ups. Graham Greene explains how this translates to the actor's performance.

> You can do anything you want in the master, but you earn your money in the close-up. That's where you have to convey a thought. If you don't have a line and they cut to

you and you're sitting there blank—it just doesn't work. But if you're thinking seriously about what the other actor is saying or doing, maybe he did something really neat in the master. You bank that, you put it away.

Greene's ability is also appreciated by his fellow actors. Mary McDonnell worked with him for many months in *Dances with Wolves*.

A part of the skill involved in movie acting is acting with authority. Graham Greene has an incredible facility that way. There's a learned ability to make a discovery in one lens and know how to reduce the role or exaggerate it for the next lens. In a sense the master shot is like the last rehearsal.

For Dustin Hoffman the peculiar needs of filmmaking lead to a kind of schizophrenia for the actor.

If you're stage trained like I am, even though you are making a movie you really feel like you're rehearsing a play. But when it comes time to have opening night, you've already finished making the movie. And now you want to start to play it, but it's too late. It's over. Movie-making is like rehearsing.

Jack Nicholson contends that the special demands of film require a kind of intensity that is very different from other forms of acting.

Movie acting is harder than stage acting. No one could play Hoffa on stage for three hours. The amount of energy that's telescoped. They'd die.

Also, in film, you have to see your work yourself. In the
theatre, you give a rotten performance, twelve people say
it's great. But in film, the mind knows this—or at least *my*
mind knows, "Ah, I'm going to have to see this." And I've
done a lot of film editing and I know that at a minimum, at
least half of what you do every day on a shoot stinks. It's
the worst that it could be.

Peter Strauss's favorite "Jack story" is illustrative of how
Nicholson approaches filmmaking. It involves the advice he
gave to one of Strauss's friends, actress Mary Steenburgen.

They were working together and one day he said, "Okay,
this time do the scene, and kill the darlings." In other
words, kill the things you know will get you through, the
little grimace, the grin, the tilted head, the raging look, all
the things you do in almost everything you do. These are
the things that reflect your stereotypical but generally
salesworthy moments.

Energy and Synergy:
Collaboration with Other Actors

Since actors rarely work in a vacuum, it's not surprising
that they benefit from their experiences with one another.
What finds its way from script to screen is often the result of
their on-camera collaboration. Leonard Nimoy compares it to
a tennis match.

You begin to interact with other actors to see what kind of
rhythmic exchanges you're going to have. You can only do
a character alone for so long. Then it's time for the tennis

match. You have to know what kind of balls are going to
be hit at you and start thinking about how you are going to
return them.

How is she going to play this scene as your wife? Is she
angry? Is she sad? I've got to see her face, her body, hear
her intonation, so I can respond to that specifically. You
can't bring a rehearsed performance to the set and refuse
to change it. You have to be flexible. Acting is all about
chemistry.

Graham Greene uses the same word to describe the collaboration process.

The director has to make the judgment about how it's
going to work with all these actors together. Sometimes it
doesn't work and you find yourself with another performer who becomes an adversary on the set. Although at
times I've worked with people that I didn't get along with
and it showed on the screen. And it worked! It's *chemistry*.

During the shoot, any number of things can happen, even
though they may not be in the script. The actor needs to be
able to maintain the flexibility to go with them as they occur.
In *Grand Canyon* Mary McDonnell's Claire had one long
scene with Steve Martin that became one of the film's most
memorable moments.

I was surprised at the deepness of the tone of the scene
with Steve. She kind of gets a kick out of him. She dis-
agrees with him on everything and that's okay because
they have a great love for each other.

I had thought of Claire as a sort of contemporary
woman with a clear head about facing the trouble in her

marriage. But as we did it, I discovered this was an opportunity for her to touch those feelings that she'd been afraid of. And when she actually talked it out with the right person, someone who was safe, it just all poured out. Suddenly she was sad, terrified, threatened by the potential loss.

Another kind of synergistic challenge comes from playing a supporting role. Graham Greene says simply, "It can be really tough. Supporting is a big word in my mind. You're boosting that character." He chooses his words carefully. "You can't overact, don't be stupid, don't steal the scene. You can act your face out in your scene, but in someone else's scene, be supportive. There's no shame in being a bit player. It's like they say: There are no small roles, only small actors."

Jack Nicholson has become one of Hollywood's superstars by specializing in supporting roles. In his interview with Hilary de Vries he explains:

Film acting is different from stage acting and when you get just three scenes, which was the case in *A Few Good Men*, you couldn't play through the entire production at the intensity that I played them for two weeks. I was quite spent at the end of those two weeks.

No doubt it was a tumultuous two weeks. The result was his tenth Academy Award nomination, in this case for best supporting actor.

Large roles or small, it all comes back to the way actors function together on the set. Their collaboration can help make the film flourish, if all the elements are right. Dustin Hoffman says simply, "There is a synergy that takes place, and for a moment, you feel like you're in a jazz group."

Collaboration with the Director

During the course of a film, a special relationship forms between the director and the actor. Each is dependent on the other. Each must learn to trust the other. What does the actor need from the director?

Peter Strauss says, "First and foremost, I want a protector of the integrity of my work and a nurturer of courage." For John Lithgow, "A good director helps you move in new directions, makes you feel comfortable, liberates you."

Mary McDonnell explains that "good directors are in touch with their masculine side, they have a sense of balance. They know how to give orders and have a heady sense of the whole picture."

Then they turn around to the actor and have their feminine side—they become a reflector and emotional supporter. It's a remarkable thing to see a director with that kind of balance. You just feel great and want to be there.

Most often actors want a director who will protect them while transforming the set into a space where creativity can flourish. For Peter Strauss, it is the actor's willingness to risk that is at stake.

Actors are only good when they're daring, and if you're afraid to be daring, you're dead. In order to be daring, you have to have a fertile place to work, a place where your work is given a place to fail. You don't want to be ridiculed or frustrated by time elements. You want a director who insulates you and protects you from everyone else on that set.

The notion of being protected on the set is something that
actors mention again and again. Why is this so vital? According to Strauss:

> The actor has to please. He comes through the door, the
> scene calls for him to be in tears and to accost a girl and
> walk out.
>
> Some directors will say, "Let's go, Peter, come
> through the door, just get through the door, I've got to
> get the shot." The director of photography might say,
> "Peter, when you come through the door, get out of that
> light, come in at this light." The costumer says, "Well, I
> wish he would wear his tie closed as opposed to open."
> And the prop person is saying "Do you want a brown
> suitcase, as opposed to a black suitcase?" In that case,
> you're dead.

And how might a good director solve problems like this? Is
there any way the director can help the actor cope with the
chaos on the set? Strauss says:

> Sure. Another director will say, "Okay, I want the props,
> costume, sound, makeup, talk to Peter now, get your
> problem solved. Is everybody happy? Good. Now Peter
> and I are going to work."
>
> The director takes me aside and says, "What do you
> need to get you through that door with tears in your eyes,
> because I'd like to start on a close-up?"
>
> Or he will say, "Look, I need coverage, so I'm going to
> start on a master, don't blow it, take it slowly, we'll work
> up to it. Do you need a minute of quiet backstage? Are you
> capable of doing this? Do you want me to help you?

Would you like to try it and I'll let you know how I feel
about it and what it looks like?"

Another aspect of the director's job is to keep the thread of the
story in mind and to correct the actor if something is out of
sequence or if his or her emotional line doesn't track. Mary
McDonnell has worked with some of the best directors in
Hollywood.

> A good director keeps you in tune with the thread. With
> all four directors I've worked with recently—Larry Kas-
> dan, Kevin Costner, Phil Robinson, and John Sayles—
> each has come up to me at a very important moment and
> said, "I think we lost the thread of something." I wonder
> how they can do that? I only keep track of this one little
> person and they keep track of everyone. I'm blown away
> by what directors have to keep in mind every day.

A good director can make the shoot a great experience for the
actor. Then there are the other kind. Leonard Nimoy says, "I
am most comfortable when I see myself as a workman. I
consider myself a laborer." Working for the director, he tries
to "build" the best possible performance.

> Less-than-competent directors will force actors or ac-
> tresses into unworkable situations. They will ask you to
> deliver a chair with three and a half legs. And when you try
> to point out that it will fall down, they will say, "Just do it."
> So you do it. And sure enough, it falls down.

Nimoy says his background as an actor has certainly influenced him as a director.

I think the biggest edge for actors who become directors is that we understand the actor's problems. We're aware of what the actor's contributions can be. We're not threatened by it, we invite it. You know because you've been there.

Peter Strauss feels that most directors could use a little more understanding when it comes to their actors.

You need a mentor figure who understands the creative process and knows how to nurture it and protect it. And most directors don't know that. They'll know how to move the camera through your nose and around the corner to catch the glimmering sunlight, but they don't know a thing about your dilemmas.

You can sense the frustration in Strauss's voice as he describes what happens so often on the set.

In the end, you're on the set and you're looking around grasping at straws half the time, hoping you'll get some clue that will help you get the emotional content right.

Maybe the actress will be so damn good that the scene is going to work because you're touched by her great ability. And the director might have told you a story at lunch and you think you can use it.

You're on the set and it's a whirlwind of activity based on economics. And you're hopeful. You've gotten your homework done as well as you could to get through this quiz. That's all the time there was. The problem is that it's not the quiz, it's the *final*.

Clothes Encounters: Love and Sex Scenes

A particular kind of trusting collaboration is needed between the director and the actor during love and sex scenes. In the 1990s these film moments have become increasingly explicit in such films such as *Henry and June, Basic Instinct,* and *Sliver.*

Playing a love scene with the likes of Tom Cruise or Sharon Stone certainly sounds appealing. "Not so," says Peter Strauss. "There's always a degree of discomfort. It's uncomfortable for the actors, for the director, and for the crew. Why shouldn't it be? Here we are at our most intimate and we're supposed to forget about these sixty bored technicians standing around watching us. I've done a great number of love scenes and, believe me, actors are rarely oblivious to the world around them."

It is up to the director to reduce that discomfort. Strauss explains that this can be done in a number of ways. "First of all, the director can reduce the number of people in the room who are watching. Secondly, it's important that the director create a trusting place to work so that the performers feel they are being protected. These scenes depend on the professionalism and the sense of humor of the principals involved."

Methods for the creation of a comfort zone can vary from director to director. Nina Foch recounts how director Philip Noyce did it while shooting *Sliver.* "He played a scene nude himself and showed it to the cast in dailies so they could see what would be expected."

Strauss and Foch agree that actor preparation is similar, whether you are doing an eating scene or a love scene. But on-screen lovemaking requires a little more thought. Foch em-

phasizes that there needs to be some attraction to the other
actor, even though it might not exist in reality.

> You have to know what the scene is about, know what you
> want from your partner, and you have to decide why he or
> she is attractive to you. In most cases you are not attracted
> but you have to say to yourself "this will be over within a
> few days. I can find something in this person that's attrac-
> tive for the length of the scene." If you're really playing the
> scene and are clear what you want from that other actor,
> then you have no time to think about the fact that you are
> exposing yourself.

On the other hand, real attraction between performers can
also create a problem. "The ultimate terror for an actor is to
get turned on," says Strauss. "With a man this demands a kind
of mental control that generally would not exist in that kind of
intimate moment." He smiles. "It means that the actor has to
do a little more acting than usual."

> In these situations actors have to protect themselves. You
> should know exactly what's going to be required and it
> should be in your contract. You need to know how inti-
> mate the scene should be, how much will be shown.
> There's also the question of allowing still photos and
> who has photo control. You consistently hear horror sto-
> ries, particularly from actresses who didn't know there
> would be a still photographer or how the camera was going
> to be positioned.

Mental and physical preparation is a good idea for those
intimate scenes. "Have massages, have a facial, be sure that
you are your best self," says Nina Foch. "That's something you

have to do in any picture, but particularly for a nude scene. Know that you've done everything you can, and then forget about it."

Beautiful bodies don't happen by accident. "The body builder and the dentist are always visited before films," says Strauss. "You find actors suddenly showing up at the gym six weeks before their big scene, expecting miracles."

Are there *any* advantages to playing love and sex scenes? Strauss admits to a few. "Hey, I get to be intimate with someone and get away with it. If there's a halfway respectable relationship with the actress, there can be a kind of warmth to the experience. Besides, I'd rather play a scene that says 'he kisses her passionately' than a scene that says 'he rescues the horse from the raging river'!"

Collaboration and the Actor: The Kindness of Strangers

In the best of films, the spirit of collaboration seems to extend outward in every direction. John Lithgow feels the actor can contribute through a willingness to form relationships with as many collaborators as possible.

I try to think of every single person on the set as a collaborator in several ways. Because I come from the theatre, I count on an audience, a feeling that people are watching me. And I always like to treat the crew as my audience and to get them interested in what we're all doing. I try to have a specific personal relationship with every one of them, first because it's more pleasant and also because you're collaborating with them in very specific ways.

If you have a working relationship with the dolly grip,

you can work with him in timing your moves. You can tell him when you're going to pause. If he's dollying along next to you and he gets to know that movement, that can save you a couple of wasted takes. The same thing with the focus puller and camera operator, or gaffer. It helps to have a first-name working relationship.

The spirit of collaboration can even extend from the set into postproduction, to the unseen faces of those whose needs may be anticipated by the actor. Lithgow cites the actor's relationship with the editor as an example.

The editor on *Twilight Zone—The Movie* said he was amazed I had been able to stick with continuity even in the midst of these scenes where I was tumbling through the air, screaming, behaving totally irrationally. I was always still in frame, exactly in focus, and he was able to use almost anything in my performance.

He said, "You have no idea how I've had to save actors' performances who don't pay any attention to continuity." Well, I don't want to ever do anything great that nobody can use because it doesn't cut. And in order to do that you really have to get everybody working with you.

With the shooting over, the long postproduction process begins. It is interesting that so many actors acknowledge that this final stage of the film will determine how their performance will be received. By the time postproduction gets under way, they will be on to the next job. Most often they will not even meet the many men and women whose job it is to make the film work and to make the actor look good in the process. This is why Peter Strauss emphasizes that actors all must ultimately rely on the kindness of strangers.

You are depending upon the kindness of an editor who doesn't know you at all, and may not know how hard you worked for that subtle, subtle nuance. For him, it may be a longer take, and he needs to go to the shorter take. Or he looks at it and doesn't catch that moment that you built your entire film around. He still goes through that footage from his point of view; the composer is looking from his.

Ultimately, everybody's in their own little world and the director is supposed to coordinate all these roles. But he has to deal with the ramifications and repercussions of all those strangers. And, of course, so do you.

Strauss pauses for a moment, reflecting on the difficulty of transforming a classic film from script to screen. All of these strangers, millions of dollars . . . How does it happen? "It's amazing when we make a great movie." He smiles. "It's so easy to make a lousy one."

C L O S E - U P

ROBERT SEAN LEONARD
DEAD POETS SOCIETY

All seven of us boys arrived a week before shooting. We were told that the week was reserved for haircuts and learning how to play soccer. It turned out to be a week of getting to know each other. The first morning we went through the script as it was, and the following mornings were basically improvisations.

Once Peter Weir directed us to get up one by one and give a speech in character. He would do silly things, like he would pretend he was a teacher putting together a Christmas pageant and we were all supposed to be in it. Some of us formed a human sleigh and the rest of us had to be reindeer. Maybe it was silly but it got us in touch with our characters and the feeling of the script. And it also helped us get to know each other.

The Cave Scene

Right away Peter told us that the poetry scene, the first scene of the boys in the cave, would be the hardest scene to pull off in this movie. The audience has to believe that there are seven young guys in this cave that are having a good time reading poetry. They don't want to leave. And Peter said if we could make that scene work, the movie would work.

In the original script, that first cave scene had problems. It was just us reading poetry. One of us had a line like "Isn't this fun?" or "How great." Finally Peter said to us, "I just don't believe it. I don't believe that these guys would sit in a cave at midnight and just read poetry."

And then he said something I'll always remember because it was wonderful. He said, "I don't know what happened that night in the cave, but you all do. That's why I hired you. I met you and I knew from talking to you that you were all there. You know what went on that night and I need you to tell me." So we all went home like fiends and wrote seven different scenes on our own, and we worked together, and improvised a lot of ideas.

Late at night somebody would knock on my door and say, "I have an idea about this," and then we'd discuss it. Then he'd disappear and we'd keep writing. It was incredibly collaborative and fun. We came up with things like the food and the ghost stories and the *Playboy* magazine. We thought of how we would sulk around at school and rag on our teachers.

These were things that we honestly thought would occur.
We'd bring them to Peter and he'd say, "You're right, let's
do it."

Up on the Roof

There was always a kind of freedom. He would take in all
of our ideas, keep some, throw some out, and then have Tom
rewrite scenes. Like in the final version there's the scene where
Ethan [Hawke] and I throw the desk set off the roof. Ethan
and I had done the original version of that scene together for
Peter when we had auditioned. Ethan says, "It's my birthday."
I ask him what he got—was it the same thing his parents got
him last year? And he says yes.

In the original version he goes on about his family and
says, "I used to think that all parents just automatically loved
their children and now I know it's not true. Because my
parents certainly don't love me, or at least not as much as they
love my brother." And then he walks away and I sort of look
after him with concern.

We shot the scene at three in the morning and Peter said,
"I don't think this is right. I think we already know all this.
We're overstating it. The audience knows this by now. It's in
the performance, it doesn't need to be said. I'd rather this
scene be more about friendship than about a confession or
exposition on the boys' problems. I want it to be more active, I
want something to happen."

So he put it in our hands, and we went off and decided to
destroy the desk set. Peter said it was a good idea but he
wanted us to throw it off the roof because we only had three
desk sets to work with. So the three of us wrote the scene on
the spot. Half of it was improvised in front of the camera. It
was great.

Another scene that got changed was where I perform in the play. Originally my character's father walks onstage in the middle of the performance and drags me off in front of all the other actors and the audience. Peter wanted me to complete the performance, to see the people cheering. And that's what we did.

The Big Sleep

My character's suicide was obviously a major scene in the film, and it kind of hung over everything. At the beginning of filming Peter explained, "I want you to put that scene out of your mind, I don't want you playing it like this boy is doomed. I want you to pretend that he goes on to become a doctor or lawyer, there's nothing wrong." He didn't want to give the audience any clues. He wanted it to be one of those cases where everyone says, "My God, he would be the last person I would ever have thought would have done that!" We shot it toward the end of production.

Much of my preparation was subconscious. A lot of it involved the love I felt for all the boys, and for Peter and Robin. I just adored Kurt Smith who played my father. When you're surrounded by people that you're comfortable with and that support you, the difficult scenes become a lot easier.

I did read a lot about teen suicides and quotes from people who had attempted it. I found that a lot of teenage suicides happen because their world is smaller and it's much easier to feel trapped, especially somewhere like that school. They don't know the world beyond the school. Their parents and teachers are their whole universe.

Neil was like a child who had his candy taken away. His father takes acting away and tells him he's going to go to military school, there's no choice in the matter. It's the end of everything he knows and loves.

When you're that young, you don't feel that there are any options. That's where the trapped feeling comes from. No future. And I don't think Neil thinks it out too much. For him it's a romantic, passionate decision.

Working with Robin Williams

There's a scene with Robin in the schoolroom where I lie to him and tell him that my father gave me permission to be in the play. He says, "Did you tell your father? What did he say?" and I say, "It will be fine." The scene was only about five lines and then I was to get up and leave.

But when the camera was on me, instead of letting me leave, Robin repeats the questions again, "Really, you really told him?" In my mind I'm thinking, why aren't we cutting? What's happening here? We're completely off the script and why aren't we cutting? Robin says it again, "Really, you told him what you told me?" And he looks in my eyes, and I'm terrified. I say, "Well, he wasn't happy," and then I mumble something, which I don't think makes any sense, like "He'll be in Chicago, so it won't really matter."

I totally made that up as the camera was rolling. Robin just tortured me. He kept repeating all the questions, and I had to improvise different answers. I'm totally on the spot. And of course it comes across wonderfully that I'm lying.

Peter said, "Cut" and "Perfect," and that was the take that was used. Robin made that scene work, and that was his strength. He's incredible on his feet. We were all very young and impressionable, and I would never have had the nerve to go completely off book with Robin Williams. But it was his

the actor and
"the kindness of strangers"
195

place to do that, since he was the star. And he did. He treated us as equals. He was a joy to work with.

C L O S E - U P

ROBIN WILLIAMS, *DEAD POETS SOCIETY*

It was the script that first attracted me to *Dead Poets Society*. It was quite powerful. The philosophy of Keating was combined with a spirit and an intelligence. There was grace, dignity, and a lot about the creative force. These are all things that are quite near and dear to me.

I agreed with Peter about eliminating Keating's cancer. It gave a whole different thrust. I think that the illness combined with Neil's suicide would have been too much.

To prepare for a role, I use anything that works. With Keating I was combining teachers that I had, there were probably two or three of them in there somewhere. You try and put together people you've known and kind of synthesize them into yourself.

I started with my own beliefs about what is creative, and then those were combined with the poetry. I usually write some notes on the script, scene by scene and overall notes for the whole piece. They are often notes about things to remind me of the different points in the scene. You don't have to knock the socks off of every scene, you just need to know where you are in the whole piece. That's the key.

The Weir Factor

Peter *was* Mr. Keating for me and the boys. Peter was a man who is as inspiring as the character that I was playing. He was doing that on purpose. He would even dress like Keating. When he went shopping for clothes, he bought one set for me and one set for himself. He was an inspiration for me and the boys so that we could be an inspiration in the movie.

During filming he would play music before a scene to get us in the mood to try different things. One of his favorite things to say was "Try something." Which is very freeing. And he would also say, "You don't have to do anything." Peter is so confident that it just allows you to feel safe even when you're doing nothing.

Peter helped me learn that to "let it be" can be quite powerful. You need to realize that stillness and silence are just as powerful as speaking. It's true that one of the more emotional scenes came after Neil's suicide. Here's a boy that's committed suicide, one of my students, but as an actor, you have to find the right level of response. Too much is sentimental, you need just the right amount. You're looking for the perfect tone, you need to have something in mind, but it also has to fit within the context.

Preparing for this type of response, you use things you have in your mind but you never want to talk about them. You don't want to give away all the magic. As Jack Nicholson says, "It's a secret that no one knows."

Sometimes you're tapping into your own experience, and other times you find different things that put you into the scene. You may be thinking about something that's very personal for you, but you don't tap into something if you haven't learned to deal with it. If you're tapping into a recent painful memory, you're not going to be able to handle it as an actor. It becomes some kind of method madness.

Peter did have me do each scene in three different ways. Sometimes we'd do the outrageous take first, sometimes last, like dessert. It lets that instinct out. Otherwise it can back up

on you. At least you get it out so you don't feel like you didn't
get a chance to do it. Sometimes it works, other times no.

We did some improvisation with the boys as well. At times
we got really outrageous, as in the classroom with the Shakespeare bit. Some teachers perform for their students, so we
kept in the part where Keating talks about classical performances of Shakespeare done by Brando and John Wayne.

During that scene with Neil, when he tells me that his
father approved of him being in the play, I did try and make
him squirm a bit. I don't remember if this was Peter's idea or
mine. It might have been something he said, but probably it
was just an impulsive thing of mine. I wanted to push the
stakes. Put him on the hot seat, see what happens. Peter would
often say, "Try something like this and see what will happen."
So we did.

A Special Film

I knew that this film had a feel to it which was very
powerful. I knew it about halfway through. You just felt
something wonderful was going on and you didn't want to talk
about it too much because you don't want to mess with it. Just
let it be. Let it grow. Don't water it too much, just sit back and
experience it. It's a moving event.

There was a creative mood, a mood where you could try
anything. The boys were that way and it just spread. It was
difficult because we were shooting in Delaware in the winter,
but there was something about even that, it was quite powerful. There was a spirit, a bond between us that goes beyond the
making of a film.

There's a feeling that you want to work with these people
again. We still keep in contact with all the boys. They're
friends, they're family, you feel a closeness to them. Peter

checks on them, wondering how they're doing, are they working, are they okay?

Dead Poets Society tapped into an essential feeling we all have about finding that passion, that bliss that comes from doing what you love to do. People have stopped me on the street about it. I met a man in California who said it made him change his life, he left his business and now runs a gallery. I thought, I hope you're okay with that. He seemed to be.

But my favorite was one day in New York, there was a garbageman who saw me and he yelled out, "Hey—I *loved* that dead man thing!"

5
behind
the scenes:
collaboration
by
design

You'd be surprised at how much detail goes into even one little piece of film; it's much more than anyone could possibly imagine.
—Robert Grieve

The curtains open. The lights go down. Audiences settle into their seats and munch on their popcorn. The opening credits roll by. Two hours later the movie is over, and the end credits scroll across the screen. By the time they are done, the theater is virtually empty. Empty popcorn boxes litter the floor. The clean-up crew hurries to get ready for the next showing. Everyone else is headed for the parking lot.

While little noted nor long remembered, film credits none-theless provide a story all their own. The opening title sequence lists the studio first; the final three credits go to the writer, producer, and director. By contract and custom those that appear in between go to various collaborators, including the production designer, costume designer, and director of photography. Among those whose names appear at the end of the film are the people who do makeup, sound design, and special effects.

These six areas have each earned their own Academy Award category. Many books have been devoted to them. And while it may be difficult to lump them together, it can at least be said that they are all collaborators by design. These are the women and men "behind the scenes" whose crucial contributions often go unnoticed by the audience.

To shed some light on those contributions, a highly successful representative from each area was asked to explain what he or she does and to share some memorable and challenging assignments.

PRODUCTION DESIGN

"DREAM A LITTLE DREAM"

Production Designer Ferdinando Scarfiotti is best known for his extensive work with director Bernardo Bertolucci. The results of their collaboration can be seen in such visually stunning films as *The Sheltering Sky, The Conformist,* and *The Last Tango in Paris.* They won Oscars for their efforts on *The Last Emperor.* More recently Scarfiotti received warm critical praise and an Oscar nomination for creating the eccentric visual world seen in Barry Levinson's *Toys.*

The production designer is really the production dreamer, quite literally, the one who dreams. When I was working with director Nicholas Roeg he would always tell me, "Dream on! Dream on!" My dream team includes the art director, the set decorator, sketch artists, and construction people. They all work under me and are part of my department.

Generally I start preparation for a film about three to eight months before filming. With *Toys* I stayed on the movie almost two years. It was a very elaborate production to prepare, but I got a break when Barry Levinson decided to do *Bugsy* first. So I had all that extra time, but I think that was essential because that was not a movie I could have rushed through. There was a lot of research. Practically every scene had to be illustrated with a color sketch so the director knew exactly what kind of world I was creating.

It was just the opposite situation with *The Last Emperor*. I came into the picture quite late in the process. I barely had enough time to design the first two or three sets before shooting began. Then I was designing *during* shooting, which is never easy. I think I had about three months of prep, total; for a movie like that—a big period piece—three months is nothing.

Every film is different and requires something new. In *Love Affair* we had to design a Russian cargo ship that was supposed to be in the South Seas. Imagine building this huge boat on a stage! I'd never been on one before, so there was lots of research. Maybe tomorrow I'll have to build something else I've never seen before. Every film is a whole new world. You have to explore that world and give it your own sense of style. Because it may be a Russian cargo ship, but it is *your* Russian cargo ship, you know?

On Being a Production Designer

There's no formal requirement to be a production designer, but most of us are people who have some background in the arts. I studied architecture for four years in Rome, which was very useful for me. I've been interested in the arts since I was a kid. I was always going to the museums and making drawings in bed as a young child. My choice of architecture at the university has helped me with the technical background, which is really my weakest part. I rely heavily on my art directors for that, but still you need to know about structure and building. You have to know how to read a blueprint, to read technical drawings, otherwise you'll be in trouble. You also have to have a good sense of color. I feel at ease with color—this is one of my strengths.

From Script to Set

When I first read a script I generally try not to think about anything, I just let it flow through my head. That has always been a crucial part of the process because most of my ideas come from the first reading. Very seldom do I get other ideas from a second reading. So I have to be really relaxed in order to let the images emerge.

If it's a contemporary story, then you need more from the director in order to define the characters and know what their lives are like. If you're designing a house for a character, then you need to know more about that person.

Of course, we do go through the script many times, with the director, art director, and all my other collaborators. There are so many meetings that by the time that you finish your work and design the whole thing, you know the script very well. There's always little details, little changes. But the first impact is generally the one that counts for me.

Preparation

I begin by designing in my head. Then I'll do some very loose sketches. If the sketch needs to be a bit more elaborate, I use illustrators who do it very fast because I would take too much time. I have a group of set designers who make blueprints and technical drawings. The art director and I will supervise these. Out of the drawings come the models. I build them more for the director than for myself. Many directors are ill at ease when they have to read a blueprint or technical drawing. They don't know what they're looking at. You'll catch them looking at it upside down. So a model is really the best way to show the space and how the camera can move around inside it.

With *Toys* we tried a new computer program that can animate a whole set. You feed the computer a technical drawing with a floor plan. Then the computer builds the room on the screen, inside, outside, upstairs, downstairs, everything. Then you can move figures inside and outside, make every camera move you want.

To me it sounded like a dream. I got this computer wizard to feed all the sets into the computer for Barry to look at. But he didn't seem much interested in it so we dropped that idea. One day it will work, but at that moment it seemed like a cold way to envision the scene. So we ended up having a traditional storyboard artist illustrate the scenes.

You must do whatever research the movie requires. So I research, but then I try to close the books and do my own thing. The style usually comes from me, but it's also open to discussion. If it's a period movie you already have a sense of the style because of the period itself. You tend to see the script *through* the period if you know the period.

The Last Emperor

I knew very little about China. Because of the political situation, very little was available. Since there are very few art books in China, most of the research was done in Italy and London.

There is one excellent book on the Forbidden City that was helpful. And I researched Chinese architecture and Chinese artists. The subject is very vast but we were dealing only with the last few years of Imperial China and the coming of the revolution, so that made it easier. We also used the book written by the real-life English tutor who was played by Peter O'Toole in the movie. It didn't have any photographs but it did convey how people lived at that time.

When we went to China for location scouting I met some of the men from the imperial family. There were two brothers of the emperor who had family books and photo albums, which proved very valuable to us. They had pictures of the houses, which don't exist anymore. There was this Palace of the North where they were raised. It's now a clinic and you can barely see what it once was. Even buildings of the 1920s are very hard to find. They've been buried under concrete or rooms have been added to them.

Then there were the color problems. Imperial yellow is a special yellow that could only be worn by members of the imperial family. No one else could use that yellow. It's quite a true yellow, very gold. And there's a special red that had to be re-created for the set.

I brought a team of Italian painters and sculptors with me. We had to decorate all the ceilings with real thick decorations, as they used to do, especially in the Forbidden City. It was funny; the Chinese were in total awe of these people who were able to paint "authentic" Chinese decorations on the wall. There was no one there that could do it in the correct way. After the Cultural Revolution they quit teaching art. There was this backlash against art, artistic expression, and freedom. Many of the techniques used earlier in the century had been lost or forgotten. Finally we found some students from an art school. The challenge was enormous.

We were allowed to film in the Forbidden City in the courtyard but not indoors. So we built all the interiors. Most people thought that everything was shot inside the Forbidden City but it's not true. There was only one interior given to us at the last minute after a great deal of negotiation—the place where the little emperor was crowned. They let us in for half a day but with only five people. We couldn't bring lights inside because they were terribly afraid of fire.

Originally the script called for the interior with the door closed and then the door would open and the little emperor would come out and everybody would see these zillions of people outside. But if we had closed the door we wouldn't have been able to see anything. As usual in movies, when you have some problems they stimulate you to do something bizarre that you never would have thought of.

So I came up with this yellow curtain in the scene because that was the only way to light the place without closing the door. It was a canopy and you could lift it up. It worked wonderfully and had beautiful movement. I was real proud of it because it became a real focal point for the movie.

Toys

When I first read the *Toys* script I realized it had so many possibilities, it was totally open to interpretation. Barry Levinson left me completely free, so I thought of an old 1920s French play by Roger Vitrac, who was a member of the Dadaist movement. It was probably the only play written by a Dada artist. There was a very surreal style that seemed to fit somehow.

From there I decided to use the European avant-garde art of the twenties and thirties, which was quite famous but hasn't been used that much in movies. I thought of the surrealists and the futurists and the Russian constructivists, as well as the modernist movement of the early twentieth century.

Actually, the artist that I used the most is an Italian futurist called Fortunato Depero—one of the most important artists of the futurist movement. Research like this provides inspiration, but then I try to go off on my own and depart from the research.

There was an extraordinary series of events involving the outdoor locations. The script takes place in a heavily wooded area. But when you set a film in a forest, no matter how beautiful it is, there's always something very real about it.

I wanted something different so I envisioned this absolutely naked landscape, with really nothing but hills of grass. My idea was to find something like the Sahara, but instead of sand, have grass. So I drew it that way, but I wasn't sure such a location actually existed anywhere.

When it came time to find the actual location, we happened to find the exact look in Washington State, in a region near Spokane. There it was: no billboards, no telephone poles, nothing. Farmhouses maybe every ten miles. The rest is green hills, green hills, green hills. It's a farming community; they grow wheat, millet, and barley. So there were different shades of green and we controlled it a little, telling them what to plant so we would have a kind of uniform look. The planting had to be done twice because the picture was postponed for a year.

It had never happened to me where I designed something

out of my head and then found the reality exactly as I dreamed it. It was a miracle.

COSTUME DESIGN

THE LINES OF ILLUSION

Costume designer Marilyn Vance's résumé reads like a definitive bibliography of blockbuster Hollywood studio filmmaking. Among her credits: *Pretty Woman, Die Hard, Predator, The Breakfast Club,* and *Romancing the Stone.* She was nominated for an Academy Award for her efforts on *The Untouchables.*

When I first read the script, I'm looking for the setting and the story and what that story encompasses. I want to see how many people I have to deal with in my head. How many important characters are there? How do they relate to one another? Will they be driven apart?

Then you start asking character questions. Where would they live? How would they live? What's their income level? How would they represent themselves? Would they wear jewelry? Would they have a piece of junk on their wrist? Earrings? Makeup? You try to develop a sense of the kind of character they are. Mean nasty killer, he's looking one way. If he's blue collar, he's looking another way. The personality of each project can be found in the script.

For the costume designer, everything in life is psychological presentation. We all express ourselves through what we wear. I do character boards, which are like storyboards. I lay out the feeling and the look I'm going for. A lot of people know me for those character boards because they are a communication device. I can present them to the director and the actors, and they have something specific to respond to. Or maybe we'll take photographs of the actor or actress to see which colors are best suited for them and their personality. Very often the actors are appreciative. Other times it's too much for them. They'll say, "Oh, I suppose the next thing you'll do is act it out for me." It's always different.

Research

Research is always important. I'll start with traditional sources: books of costumes, art books, anything pertaining to the subject. I'll look at paintings. It depends on the project. You do whatever it takes.

For *Pretty Woman* I went to Hollywood Boulevard to look for hookers but I couldn't find any. They had cleaned up the street! And I needed the visual look to get it right. Then one night [director] Garry Marshall was driving around and saw this hooker wearing an old fifties' or early sixties' band jacket. It was perfect. So we used that for Julia Roberts—an oversized man's jacket hiding her little skirt and the boots up to here. Those boots, I had to have those boots! I had seen a pair in London so we sent for them. They were imported.

I researched strippers for *The Last Boy Scout*. Tony Scott, the director, had me in every strip joint in town. But I learned a lot. I'll put everything I've learned onto a character board with colors.

Usually I come on the project six or eight weeks before shooting, depending on the film. Sometimes you sit and wait and you're on the payroll for months waiting for casting. Other times you'll have three weeks to pull something off. Twelve weeks is a luxury.

Tricks of the Trade

I might dress hundreds, even thousands, for a film like *The Rocketeer* or *The Untouchables*. We had a thousand people in Santa Rosa for the flying sequence in *The Rocketeer*. We had to dress all the people in the stadium and all the flight people. Many times we have workrooms that will run for twenty-four hours a day. I'll have twenty or thirty seamstresses, plus people that are constantly keeping the clothing clean.

Sometimes the costumes are farmed out to so many places I can't even tell you. It could be shirts in one place, vests go to another place, suits go to somebody else. And maybe I'll make the shoes.

I take wool suits and dye them, just to break them down into a comfortable kind of a way because when you take things fresh off the rack, it's just terrible. You can't buy brand-new things and throw them in front of the camera. It's just looks so crisp and scary. All you're noticing is the brand-new clothes that people are wearing and it's a distraction.

Pretty Woman

When I did *Pretty Woman* I knew the Julia Roberts character would not think about fashion, but she had to be smart. This was about a girl who was a hooker, she was very gaudy and glitzy and had all this ridiculous amount of stuff on. How could she fit into this really understated, very wealthy, quiet man's life? I had her subdue the dress, pare it down. And it became very elegant. It showed that this was a woman smart enough to learn how to fit in. She realized how understated he was, she picked up on it immediately. In situations like this, less is more.

A lot of people remember her red dress. It started as a big ball gown because Garry Marshall wanted her to be a princess. But it was just too much. So I took it down and tried to do something else with it. I got the inspiration for the red dress from a period painting. It gave it that feeling of class.

We had to make Richard Gere's suits—all of them, because we couldn't find that simple, classy elegance. Everything we found was that Armani oversized suit look, but we needed a streamlined, classical character. I went with a French rather than an Italian look because we wanted him to have that kind of cool elegance, not too much fabric. The vests were deeper, to give him better shape in the shoulders. They looked wider, it gave him a really good line.

He went through torture for us. We had to fit him every day for weeks just to get the suits right. When you don't have a suit with texture, every little line shows. We did get the fabric from Italy though, because it had to lay just right.

Action Pictures

The problem with action films is that sometimes the character has to wear the same outfit for the entire film. We had to do this in the Die Hards, the Predators, *Judgment Night*. In *Romancing the Stone* she had twenty-four outfits in different degrees of degradation. The same outfit made twenty-four different ways! We had to rip them into various shreds. You ask the big questions. What would happen to this outfit as she swings on ropes and vines in the jungle? How would her coat fall apart? How can we make her sexy and appealing when we started with this dowdy girl who's on the bus? Her suit starts to rip and then her jacket goes, the coat, the shoes.

The most important thing everyone was concerned about was that Kathleen look sexy. "She has beautiful legs, we have

to show her legs." I had that wrapped skirt made of raw silk so
as it shreds, it shreds in the most elegant, beautiful, muddy way.

Take-offs and Put-ons

The Breakfast Club was another situation where you had to
do more with less. No costume changes. These people are in a
room all day! That's it. To keep up the visual interest, I had the
characters remove pieces and layers of clothing. Emilio gets
down to his tank shirt and Ally Sheedy has other clothing in
her bag. We had to make all her clothing from scratch because
we couldn't find any blacks that were interesting. She was a
dark character who had to emerge as pretty so we gave her a
pretty white camisole underneath that black. We also had to
make that pouch purse she carries so that she had something
to keep all her treasures in.

In The Untouchables they carried weapons so I had to
accentuate suits and clothing with much more fabric than we
would normally use. There were several sets of each costume,
all with different fits. One costume might be fitted for the
scene when the actor is carrying a gun. Another version of the
same costume would be for a quiet scene where the actor is
not actually carrying a gun, although you want to give the
illusion of the gun. A third version is for when the actor is
running. That suit would have a couple more inches of fabric
in the right places because the shape still has to be maintained.
It always has to look great, even when he's running or falling
down.

The Lines of Illusion: Make Them Look Good!

In costume design, you have to know how to make somebody look great. Many actors have real figure problems. Some

actresses are very boxy and have a high waist, but you want them to have the illusion of having this wonderful figure. So instead of showing the figure, you slim her body, use a little extra fabric. There's a hint of something wonderful happening. You're not quite sure what it is, but it's there. You get that illusion. Line is illusion in many ways. It gives you that feeling of something that you want to get across on the screen.

For *The Rocketeer* we had a very well-endowed actress and the director insisted that she wear white. I said, "White on camera—she's going to look terrible!" He said, "Not with the flesh and not with that baby face. It will all counterbalance. Each flaw will work against the other so it will be beautiful." Did it work? You tell me. White was a problem, and so were those enormous breasts. We had to make up special bras just to keep her tucked in there.

With men you have a different set of problems. A lot of men have narrow shoulders but they're wider in the chest. Some actors, like Bruce Willis, are short in the leg and longer in the body. What I do with him is make a higher rise on his pants to reduce the amount of his trunk, give him a feeling of longer legs. For both of the Die Hards and *Hudson Hawk* we made every ounce of clothing he wore because we needed to get his silhouette right.

Designing for men is so challenging. With women you know that you can always make that transition, from plain to pretty or whatever. But with men it's so subtle and the taste thing with men is so off. When you're dealing with a guy on camera and you really want to make a transition, a lot of it is subtle. But it's so much more rewarding because when it all comes together, it's very exciting.

Collaboration

At the beginning, you get all your information from the director. You need a clear idea of what he sees. A director like Stephen Hopkins (*Predator 2*) is very visual—everything has to harmonize. It's like a symphony going on here. Whereas Garry Marshall focuses on the story—that's his thing. Garry might say something simple like "she's in a ball gown, she turns into a princess" and I take it from there. Of course, the minute the actor shows up, things are bound to change anyway.

Then there is collaboration with the production designer. Surroundings are very important. In *Pretty Woman* the interior of the hotel and the uniforms had to harmonize. Everything had to be just so. That just-so theme was carried through in the uniforms of the elevator operator, the man at the front desk, the manager, everybody. And all of that was juxtaposed with how Julia Roberts looked walking through the lobby.

With the cinematographer, I have to know lenses and gels. Is he going to shoot in a special way? Are we going to use greens or blues? Only reds? Perhaps lots of warm whites or off-whites. Then we have to figure out how the lighting will alter the colors. It gets complicated.

For *Judgment Night* the yellow sodium light softened everything and our bad guys started looking really soft. Not a good idea. So we had to change the lighting. But we found that red and blue played beautifully in the film, it was amazing.

Sometimes with color, you begin by thinking warm and cool colors. But you must use a small palette of colors. You can't show off. There are times when you want to. But you can't. You're not doing this costume because you love it. You have to do what you feel is right for the movie. If it happens to take off as a fashion, that wasn't your intent. You just try to create this outfit for your character.

I see a lot of films now where the costume designers are trying to make a statement for themselves. Their concentration should be on the script and the character, not on the fashion. That's what I want from my team, from everyone. I can't afford to work with someone who has an attitude. We have to be a bunch of team players. It's about camaraderie.

PHOTOGRAPHIC DESIGN

THE DIRECTOR OF PHOTOGRAPHY

Haskell Wexler's work as director of photography on such diverse and memorable films as *Blaze, Colors, Matewan, One Flew Over the Cuckoo's Nest,* and *The Thomas Crown Affair* has made him one of the most respected and sought-after cinematographers in Hollywood. He received best cinematography Oscars for his work on *Who's Afraid of Virginia Woolf?* and *Bound for Glory.* He was also the writer/director/cameraman for *Medium Cool,* a groundbreaking film set against the backdrop of the riot-torn 1968 Chicago Democratic convention.

Many people think the director tells the actors what to do and the cameraman, the director of photography, takes the picture. This is true, but there is more to it. The transformation from script to screen happens through the funnel of the director of photography. Filmmaking is gathering together what's out there and filtering it through one device—the camera. Until that first frame is shot it's only contracts, ideas, concepts, scripts, and hopes.

My job is to help the director translate in an artful way the drama as expressed in the script and by the actors. This involves helping with the framing, staging, lighting, and utilizing all the mechanical devices necessary to make the images tell the story.

The cinematographer heads up a team. He works with the camera operator, who physically operates the camera. He executes the framing worked out with the director in rehearsal. The first assistant has many important responsibilities, some of which include focus pulling, changing lenses, setting the stop, dealing with diffusion and all filters, threading, and making sure that the camera is working properly.

The loader, or second assistant, loads magazines, keeps camera reports, and makes sure you don't mix up film stocks. He or she is the first to touch the film before images are on the emulsion.

The team the cinematographer heads up also includes the gaffer, who leads the electrical crew, and the grips, who handle the dolly or crane. The term grip often makes people outside our profession underestimate the creative collaboration that department has in the making of a good-looking film.

The look of a picture is only partially the province of the cinematographer. I won an award for *Bound for Glory*, but it was the plan that Art Director Michael Haller worked out with me that resulted in a beautiful subdued color look.

Preparation

There is no "right way" to prepare to shoot a film. I read the script first and decide if the ideas and emotions interest me and evoke images in my mind's eye. I talk with the director to get his general sense of the script and characters. This is an

important time because a good collaboration between director and cinematographer will make a better film, not to mention happier people.

In the beginning there is test shooting for wardrobe and
makeup. There may be screen tests so the director can see if
the actor is appropriate for the part. I also shoot technical
things in a controlled situation, to test for matches. You have
to maintain the same quality of light and density throughout a
scene. If you don't, the audience will notice something is a
little off. You have a color chart and check the degrees of
underexposure, overexposure, different film stocks, the
matching of lenses. It gets complicated. The main thing is that
when the film comes out, there aren't any mismatches.

Once the subject and location of the film are familiar, then
the images come quickly to mind. *Colors* was about street
gangs. It was shot in an area of L.A. that I seldom walk around
in. So I spent time in that area with Dennis Hopper, the
director. We just walked around and talked to people. I was
seeing what caught my eye and whether those things were in
concert with what Dennis saw. I don't try to just think of shots,
I'm trying to think seriously about what the whole movie
means.

The director and I are constantly discussing camera angles, color, lighting, blocking, movement of the camera. He
knows what he wants. How it gets done is usually up to me. I
might say, "We should see just a little bit of light on the
candlelabra over there because that's what John will have to
steal." You're looking for some way to dramatize or express
what's important.

Since visual ideas are not easily translated from written
script, we need frames of reference to communicate. Perhaps I
might see films with the director, or we will look at pictures or
paintings. I often use a video camera during rehearsals to

present my suggestions on how a scene could be shot. Of course, a cinematographer has to offer ideas and accept rejection. The director is the captain of the ship. How much or how little he wants collaboration is his decision.

Moving Camera, Moving Pictures

We have devices now which can move even the biggest 65mm camera in ways never before possible.

The main factor in camera mobility is the freeing of the eye from the eyepiece. A TV camera mounted to show through the taking lens of the movie camera allows for such great inventions as the Steadicam, Skyman Cam Remote, HotHead, Pogo, et cetera. Crane arms previously had to support the weight of a camera and at least two people. Now cameras can fly through the air on the end of a magnesium pole.

There are also helicopter mounts using video and gyroscopic stabilizers that allow for spectacular gyrosphere shots such as the end credit of the Paul Newman picture *Blaze*.

Lolita Davidovich comes out of the building where Paul Newman's character has died and the camera starts back. You see her on the steps, she gets into a car. Then the camera moves up the building, eventually you see the oil wells behind, the Mississippi River. All one smooth take.

In order to bring the script to the screen, the cinematographer has to be aware of the up-to-date technological advances and how and when to use them. You also have to know good people in all departments with whom you can work creatively in friendship. Most important, one always has to remember that good photography cannot make a bad picture good. Choose projects with some humanity.

MAKEUP DESIGN

THE SUBTLE ART

Makeup artist Peter Robb-King has worked on many of Hollywood's most famous faces. His credits include *The Fugitive*, *Sommersby*, and *Patriot Games*. It was Robb-King who provided makeup for the humans who found themselves in Toontown in *Who Framed Roger Rabbit?*. He was nominated for an Academy Award for his contributions to *Legend* and won the BAFTA, the British Academy Award, for his work on *The Last of the Mohicans*.

When I first read the script, I'm checking for what the concept is that was in the writer's mind, as well as the concept of the director. With any script, there's a huge range of possibilities. Until casting is complete, it's not always guaranteed that a character will stay the same race, religion, ethnic background, or even the same age.

So many times these days you don't get the actors until fairly late in preproduction. Without the actors you really are in the dark. It's very difficult to try out any kind of special makeup on a different person. A double or a stand-in won't work. You need the actor who's playing the part to make the final effect and show it to the director or the producer.

A lot of production companies would like you to start a day before shooting, but realistically it should take anywhere from a week on a contemporary piece, to a month on something more complicated. On something really complex, where you're going to be manufacturing prosthetics and other special equipment, it could take months.

Even on a "normal" project you need to start experimenting with the actor as soon as possible. At least a week before. In addition to hair and facial hair, there might be injuries, or old wounds or scars the script might call for. You want to set these up before you start.

Working with the Stars

When you're working with stars, you are mainly aware of a presence. Stars are really people whose audience appraisal of their work gives them the right to be a star. Normally they have gone through a lot to get to that position. There are very few overnight successes. They've learned a lot along the way and have less of the problems of somebody who's up-and-coming. The worst is someone who's *trying* to be a star when they're not. They can be tough.

In my experience, stars are the easiest people to work with. They've worked through the ranks. Yes, they realize their image is important, but they don't spend all their time worrying about it. They're very comfortable in their situation.

Much of my work with stars is enhancing what they have, bringing out the best in them. Which is basically all makeup can do. Sometimes you're trying to make them look correct for that particular story. But a lot of actors want to change their appearance, they don't like to appear the same every time. Occasionally you'll get the opposite, actors or actresses who are locked into a particular look. Usually this happens with the older performers who had a look years ago that they liked. They tend to get locked into that image. It's like somebody gets married and twenty years later they're still wearing the same makeup they got married in.

They'll insist on a particular range of makeup or a particular style of eye makeup or foundation. Nearly always, you're trying to improve things and bring them into the nineties, or into whatever you're trying to accomplish in the film. But you have to tread very carefully.

On the Set

We're often the first people there in the morning. Usually about six A.M. The hairdressers come in at the same time and sometimes the costume people as well, if the actors need to be in costume before they get made up.

You get used to the early hours. Most makeup artists have a certain kind of personality. I think that the job involves a fair degree of psychology. You've got all these personalities to deal with, you've got to get them in makeup and on the set looking good and feeling good. If you create a bad atmosphere every morning it would be unlikely that you'd stay in the job for too long, even though your makeup skills may be perfect.

In terms of time, for a man the minimum is ten minutes, the maximum, maybe thirty minutes. For a woman it can go from a half hour to an hour and a half. It depends on the script requirements and the look that you're creating. You can create a modern look but you may be putting false eyelashes on an actress, which takes longer than putting no lashes on. Or you may be doing a particular lip shade which may take longer than a standard lipstick. You may be doing more remedial work on one actor than another.

Some actors could sit in the chair all day, others want to be out in seconds. It's not that they don't like you, they just want to be out of the chair and on to something else. You can't control it. People assume that you always want to keep them there longer than you need to. It's not true. You would never be able to work in the industry if you kept people longer than you needed them.

But sometimes you can see it from their side. Some of the *Legend* characters took more than two hours to make up every morning. In *Roger Rabbit* Christopher Lloyd's character took two and a half hours. He had a lot of prosthetics. People may have thought that Lloyd looked like that in real life; luckily he doesn't!

We extended his face and made it look longer. There was a chin extension, nose and ear extensions, an Adam's apple. His head was shaved and some hair added when his hat wasn't on. All of this goes on while he is sitting in the makeup chair. He had that look every day and he certainly didn't have that look coming in off the street. It was a long, involved process, but he was great, he enjoyed playing that role.

You can add prosthetics to the cheeks, either from the inside or the outside. A small addition to the skin can make a huge difference to the look on the screen. The subtleties of makeup are never ending. And it's really all about the small differences. It's a subtle art. You can do something small and it can change someone's appearance quite radically.

Great makeup is a real asset to a production. It's not something the audience should be aware of. The best compliment for us is that our actors look good because they look perfect for the part.

The No-Makeup Makeup

Sometimes the director will want a no-makeup look, which can often take longer than a full makeup because you have to achieve a result on the screen that makes the audience *think* that they're looking at a person with no makeup. But you've also got to satisfy the actors that they'll look good on the screen.

It's complicated because the no-makeup look still demands makeup to correct whatever is happening with the actor that you don't want the audience to notice. He may come in in the morning and be flushed, have a rash or a zit. Realism may be great, but if somebody has a zit one day, they don't necessarily have it six weeks later when they're shooting the scene that will appear next in the movie. So if you use natural things, you're going to have to re-create them weeks later. You're always worried about continuity. People don't show up looking the same every morning, and you have to present them to the camera looking the same as they did the day before.

In Case of Violence

There are many scripts where people have things happen to them that are, let's say, unpleasant. There are accidents with injuries, illnesses. People get hit or wounded. A lot of things can happen to the human body, so you're changing appearances all the time.

This is where research comes in. There's a lot of medical material available, and illnesses and injuries have to be dealt with in a correct manner. We rarely re-create it totally to life, because the audience wouldn't want to see it. The real effects of gunshot wounds would be too devastating. I believe filmmakers would go further if the audience would accept it. But would they? The reality is much worse than they might imagine. Generally, when we create a wound, we need to pull back.

For *The Last of the Mohicans* I needed to do research to learn what would happen to the body with a particular caliber bullet. Period firearms cause different types of wounds. The velocity of the bullet wasn't as fast, the wounds weren't as clean.

Special Challenges

Period films present many unique challenges. *The Last of the Mohicans* was an epic film made under difficult conditions. These days a makeup artist rarely has the opportunity to work on a project of this size and scope.

We're talking about 1,500 actors on the screen in an eighteenth-century environment; the battle scenes, the sheer volume of work in re creating a time and place that is long forgotten. There were fully tattooed bodies. The characters didn't wear as many clothes as we do today. So the whole body shape was important, muscles, everything. All of this in addition to the usual makeup problems that had to be solved if the script and story were to work.

Legend was difficult as well, but for different reasons. It was an amazing fairy tale full of goblins and strange characters. The extensive makeup effects included foam rubber appliances and multipiece prosthetics for almost everyone. It took five solid months dealing with those actors.

Aging a character is really one of the most difficult things we do. It's hard to know what someone is supposed to look like in the future. If we did we'd all be geniuses, and that isn't the case. Too many films go to extremes in this regard. In the makeup world we know that it's a bit over the top. But the studios like obvious things, they prefer to see what they're paying for. The reality is often less. It's subtle, but it's there.

That's the thing about makeup in general. As I said, it's a subtle art. Actors think—why am I going through all this if it's just a little bit different? But that "little bit" is what we do, and it can make all the difference.

SOUND DESIGN

"I CAN HEAR IT NOW"

Supervising sound editor Robert Grieve has contributed to the success of a number of classic films. His work can be heard in *Grand Canyon, Children of a Lesser God,* and *Body Heat.* If it seemed to you that you really were in Sherwood Forest while watching *Robin Hood: Prince of Thieves,* it was Grieve who helped put you there.

When I was very small, my parents thought I had a hearing problem. They took me to the doctor who had this machine where you put a headset on and they tune you in to these frequencies and say, "Can you hear it now?" I said, "I can hear it now." And I remember the doctor saying "You can't hear that" because it was higher than the usual frequency that the human ear ordinarily hears. It was actually my ability to tune out my parents by selective hearing. This comes in very handy as a sound editor.

I know that the more you train your eye to see beautiful things, the more things like that catch your eye. I find that the more I listen to things, the more I strengthen all my senses. Training any one of the senses trains them all. An increased focus on sound heightens your sense of touch, taste, vision—everything. If you want to heighten your senses, concentrate on one of them and the rest will follow.

From Script to Sound

As soon as I get the script, I start thinking about the sound of the film. There's a spotting session, where we literally "spot" the places where sound will come in during the film.

Some sounds have their source in the script—a car radio playing, or thunder as the character approaches Dracula's castle. Then there are sounds we add to enhance the mood suggested by the script. There will be music on the radio, but I will also add whistling wind and the sound of the car's tires. Sure, there is thunder as we approach Dracula's castle. But exactly what kind of thunderstorm is it going to be? Is it just beginning? How fierce is it? A lot of the mood will be determined by the sounds that the audience hears.

In choosing sounds, I try to think of something that will add psychological flavor to the story without drawing too much attention to itself. It has to work on a subliminal level, and enhance the mood that the director and the script determine.

We start with the natural sound that was captured during filming, and we do what we can to control that as well. In the restaurant scenes from those old movies from the 1930s, there's often flowers in the middle of the table. The actor leans over when he talks because the microphone is hidden in the flowers.

We never want any extraneous sounds while shooting. If we do a restaurant scene, all the extras will be mouthing silent words so we can add whatever sound we want later. If the actors are in a car, usually the car is being towed so the natural sound doesn't have any car noise. This is done so there is no interference with the main dialogue. We add the sound of the motor later when we do the soundtrack.

We usually start on a job two or three weeks before the

director's cut is finished. The first thing to be done is a quick, rudimentary preparation of the dialogue. Let's say a scene was filmed on a street, and the actor was miked. You can hear car sounds in the background. Every time the editor cuts from one angle to another or one actor to another, you hear a "kkkk" sound. That's because the mike is in a slightly different position for each shot. So we have to smooth that out.

The other thing I like to do right away is to fill the scene out with background noises so that you get more of a sense of place. If you're in the woods, parking lot, et cetera, there will be specific sounds used.

Sometimes I might want to try something a bit offbeat so we'll try that in the temp dub and run it for the director to get his ideas. Then we'll start perfecting the temp dub. Often this means going out and shooting some new sounds for the final cut.

The soundtrack looks exactly like film, it has sprocket holes and it travels back and forth with the film. When we start recording, we do a separate track for each sound you hear in the film. There can be as many as 150 tracks per reel. When it's mixed together we decide how loud each sound element should be, and whether it should pan left or right, center, or surrounds.

Creative Sound

When I talk about getting creative I mean adding those little touches that help tell the story. In *The Vanishing* Kiefer Sutherland's character is approached by the man who kidnapped his girlfriend five years ago. He's never been able to find her, not one clue. This guy appears and he jingles her lost keys and says, "I'm the man you're looking for." Her key ring had this special little Bullwinkle toy on it, which Sutherland immediately recognizes.

The director was looking for something that could re-create a sound from when she was kidnapped. We didn't want to get corny or be obvious so we settled on a sea gull. You know how they sort of laugh and squawk when they are trying to steal food from one another? We put that in there along with the sound of the keys. And it worked perfectly to bring the audience back to the moment of her abduction.

Grand Canyon

In *Grand Canyon* we used a lot of helicopter sounds to give the feeling of being watched in the neighborhood. Of course, there were the baby cries and the sound of Mary McDonnell's character going through the bushes. That dream sequence gradually became a nightmare. In order to enhance that feeling we started putting beetles and bug noises and all sorts of buzzing sounds that kept getting louder.

You never know what will work. In one scene where she's running along she sees that bum in the alley. She's frightened. And then off in the distance you hear this ice cream truck playing its silly little song. The innocence and "normalcy" of the truck's sound contrasted nicely with the character's fear and tension.

There was also an earthquake sequence. We had a lot of fun with that. We wanted to make it as real possible so we thought a lot about what happens when one hits. Just a moment before it hits you hear dogs baying off in the distance. Then you hear all the car alarms going off at the same time, and every dog in the neighborhood starts to bark.

Body Heat

One of the things I remember about *Body Heat* was that the wind was blowing a lot. The sound of wind is usually cold and yet the script called for humid heat. Even though it was filmed in Florida, it was about fifty degrees during the shoot. The thing everybody remembers is how the film makes it seem so hot, everybody is sweating. In reality it was freezing when they shot. And the wind was blowing all the time. So I'm thinking, how can we make the audience feel a warm summer breeze just by the sound? I started doing layers of crickets, then all the wind was recorded through palm fronds. It's sort of a clacky noise, a little thicker than wind through grass. These sounds are associated with palm trees and tropical warmth.

Kathleen Turner's character had those wind chimes outside the house. I remembered the ones that I liked the best were my grandmother's. She had old tubular chimes with lots of interesting minor notes. Some of the ones in the film were those old clay chimes, but all of them sounded pretty horrible on the mike. We had to go out and rerecord them all. The studio interior sounded too "roomy." So we went out to the middle of the desert and found this old log cabin. It had this . . . different kind of quiet. We recorded four hours of chimes and matched each sound with the right psychological moment in the film.

Robin Hood: Prince of Thieves

Any period piece poses special problems and *Robin Hood* was no exception. At one point I had a sound crew of forty-four people. That's including editors, assistants, all the people we needed to prepare all the tracks. That's the biggest crew I've ever had in my life.

When you're recording period dialogue out in the field, you've got a problem because I can't think of anyplace in the world that doesn't have a car or a plane going by. In Sherwood Forest, it wouldn't do to have a plane fly over. But they did. We were only able to use about 50 percent of the location dialogue, all the rest had to be looped [replaced] later.

I wanted Sherwood Forest to sound exactly like it may have sounded back then. At that time they had wolves in the forests. Those wolves disappeared hundreds of years ago, but they were there during that time. And bears are virtually extinct in England, but back then they were part of Sherwood Forest. We had to do a lot of research to find out what sounds were present during Robin Hood's time period. We generated a fairly extensive list of sounds and used them for backgrounds.

We had foxes, and English birds. We used an English robin, which sounds quite different than it does in the States. We added the robins because they have a really pretty song that seems to say "forest" right away. Robins in *Robin Hood*. It seemed appropriate. We sent away to England for a lot of what we used on the soundtrack.

One of the birds that is actually there today is the cuckoo bird. And they sound just like the clocks. So I said, "Great, let's put that everywhere." It's subtle, mind you, I mixed them down pretty low. But there's a certain humor in *Robin Hood* and the cuckoo bird reinforces that. There's one scene with Maid Marian and these goofball villains. They're trying to rob her and she ends up capturing them and forcing them to lead her to Robin. Throughout that scene, if you listen closely, you can hear the "cuckoo" in the woods.

Children of a Lesser God

For *Children of a Lesser God*, director Randa Haines asked
how we could intensify the feeling of the character being deaf.
To achieve this I accented each sound just a little bit more than
your ear would actually hear it. When William Hurt's character first drives up to the school, the truck passes by and we
hear some leaves scratching along the ground. Then when he
meets Sarah, there's the sound of her mop.

In another scene there was rain on the window, and you
can actually hear the individual drops on the windowpane. To
get that sound, we recorded the individual drops and then
edited them one at a time. There was a general kind of a rain
sound and then there were these very specific larger drips
coming from the top of the windowsill. I wanted to hear each
one. Sometimes to enhance the mood I work directly with the
score. There's one scene where William Hurt's character is
getting on a ferry to go to the school, and there are sea gulls
flying around the boat. We took their "caw," and changed the
tone of it with a harmonizer so that it was tuned to the musical
score that was playing in the background.

In the swimming pool scene I wanted to get a feeling of
that sound you hear if you block your ears very hard and try
to cut out all sound. You begin to hear a tone, a little like a
seashell but purer than that. Then we shaped that tone,
changed it gradually, because we didn't want it to be monot-
onous. Later in the film, Marlee Matlin's character yells out
that first word. It was a big moment. We recorded her sound,
but we wanted to make it uglier so we raised the level of the
sound, just loud enough to make the audience jump in their
seats.

At the very end of the film, the dance was going on in the
background. Matlin was down at the dock and Hurt was at the

top of the hill. We spent a long time balancing that sequence between music and silence. You could still hear the dance going on in the background, but we had to get out of it in such a way that you didn't miss it. Then suddenly you're alone and it's very quiet.

A lot of it has to do with pace and timing. I added the sound of the waves lapping against the shore and crickets singing in the night to help the mixer fade out the music without the audience ever hearing it go; it was just subtly replaced with the sounds of the night. You'd be surprised how much detail goes into even one little piece of film; it's much more than anyone could possibly imagine.

ILLUSION DESIGN

THE WORLD OF SPECIAL EFFECTS

Ken Ralston is one of the most accomplished of the new breed of special effects wizards. Currently he is associated with George Lucas's Industrial Light and Magic. Though ILM is located in northern California, it is Hollywood's most renowned source of special visual effects. Ralston's four Academy Awards reflect his contributions to *Death Becomes Her*, *Who Framed Roger Rabbit?*, *Cocoon*, and *Return of the Jedi*.

I probably have one of the few jobs in the business that is almost as involved as that of the director or producer. We work in preproduction, production, and postproduction, so we get to see every phase of the process. Our work is usually complicated, detailed, and can take a long time.

A large part of our job is creating effects that have never been done successfully before. Technology is advancing so quickly in this area that we were able to do effects for *Death Becomes Her* that would have been impossible to do just a year before.

The World of Visual Effects

I grew up watching special effects, from *King Kong* to all those old dinosaur and monster movies. Some were pretty poor, some were better. *King Kong* was state of the art for the 1930s and was a knockout. *The Ten Commandments* had some powerful effects work. Everybody remembers the parting of the Red Sea. In science fiction films there's great work in *The Day the Earth Stood Still, Forbidden Planet, Metropolis, War of the Worlds*, et cetera.

One of the reasons I'm even in this business is because of the work of Ray Harryhausen, who did effects for *The Seventh Voyage of Sinbad, Mysterious Island*, and *The Three Worlds of Gulliver*. Maybe they're not great movies, but they had some of the most ingenious effects works being done at that time.

There are also some great films where you may not know that you're watching special effects. *Citizen Kane* is loaded with effect shots, probably over a hundred. Almost every shot of *Xanadu* is an effect shot. They're either models or matte paintings. Sometimes they would use the bottom section of a big set and then do a matte painting for the entire upper ceiling area. So half is real and the other half is illusion.

Another famous special effects sequence is the burning of Atlanta in *Gone With the Wind*. I think what the studio did was burn the great wall down from their *King Kong* set, on the back lot, and use that as part of the fire. Then they added miniature buildings, matte paintings, et cetera, to complete the shot. The first floors of some of the buildings were real, but the upper part, which was the imcomplete set, was blacked out to camera, and later, miniatures or paintings were inserted.

The famous sunset shot of Tara is all special effects. Scarlett is in silhouette and the background is a matte painting. There are miniature trees in the foreground. It's another example of how, if we do our job well, you often don't even know those are special effects.

Creating Visual Effects

I begin by reading through the script and marking the scenes that look like potential visual effects. Then I meet with the director and the production team and go through the whole script to get a feel for how complex or how impossible it will be.

At the simplest level, special effects include smoke, fires, and explosions. More complex effects involve blue screens, miniatures, paintings, optical enhancement, computer graphics animation, et cetera. Often these scenes require the filming of two or more scenes which, when superimposed on one another and blended together so they appear as one shot, can create magic.

Often you work with models that are built to look like the real set. The miniatures have to match the live sets perfectly, so when composited together, they look like it's all the same setting. In *Back to the Future III* we crashed a train. That was a big, quarter-scale, complicated miniature.

At ILM we also do a lot of manufacturing of creatures, body parts, and unusual mechanical devices for operating aliens. Other times they are done with live actors and makeup, simple puppets, and now, with the new technology, brought to life with the help of computers.

Who Framed Roger Rabbit? combined cartoon characters
with live-action characters. For two years I worked very
closely with Richard Williams in England, who supervised
most of the animation. I had to design a new system that could
combine live action and animation, take what had been done
before, and, using new technology, develop better techniques
to add shadows, color shifts, and blends.

There were so many details. I had to check the actor's eye
lines to make sure they seemed to look directly at the cartoon
character. The lighting on the cartoon characters had to look
the same as the lighting on the live set.

For *Cocoon* we did the effect of the sky opening and the
spaceship coming down that was seen at the beginning and
end of the film. You see clouds and a white beam come down
through them and illuminate porpoises in the water.

The porpoises and spaceship were miniatures. The clouds
were shot in a water tank using a latex mixture for the clouds.
We also created the aliens for that film. The aliens are rather
anorexic actresses in costumes. Then, in the optical printer,
the device that combines all these elements, we created that
wispy look and the smoky feeling. In this case, the aliens were
never on the same set as the actors. So the actors on the set
were always reacting to characters that were never there.

The same thing applies to *Hook*. The blue-screen technique has been around for years. All of Tinkerbell's flying
scenes were filmed in front of a blue screen. Julia Roberts was
never on the set with the other actors. Afterward, the blue-
screen "Tink" element was rephotographed to add all of her
flying action, and the wings were miniatures shot to match her
every move.

Our job is to deliver whatever the director wants. In *Back
to the Future* Robert Zemeckis took us to a location and said,
"Here's a street and I want a Delorean flying through the sky."

Writer Pen Densham *(center)* with Kevin Costner and Morgan Freeman on the set of *Robin Hood: Prince of Thieves*. "I started out with one line which was 'Robin Hood, à la *Raiders*' [*of the Lost Ark*], and that sat in my computer bank for five years." *Courtesy Trilogy Entertainment Group*

Writer-director Ron Shelton with Paul
Newman on the set of *Blaze*. "I won't
start a script until I have my characters'
voices." *Courtesy Ron Shelton*

Writer-director Lawrence Kasdan: "I work out of my own interests, enthusiasm, obsessions, and neuroses." *Courtesy Lawrence Kasdan*

Writer-director Oliver Stone: "I try not to impose my own view from the outside. I really like to take it from the inside…I work as a professional—but *I feel it.*" *Courtesy Ixtlan Productions*

Producer Richard Zanuck *(right)* with director Bruce Beresford on the set of *Driving Miss Daisy.* "You can't just make an ordinary picture—you have to make an *extraordinary* picture." *Courtesy The Zanuck Company*

Producer Gale Anne Hurd: "A film takes on its own life and you have to be serving that." *Courtesy Gale Anne Hurd*

Producer Kathleen Kennedy: "Very few people get to have a job where you create something that generates immediate feedback. That's quite unique, and that's what's addictive about this business." *Courtesy The Kennedy/Marshall Company*

Producer David Puttnam: "The one element that doesn't have a voice is the original screenplay.... You have to remain true to the original vision." *Photo by David Appleby; courtesy Enigma Productions Limited*

The creative team responsible for *Dead Poets Society* includes director Peter Weir *(above, with Robin Williams)*, producer Steven Haft *(below left, with Wier)*, and writer Tom Schulman *(facing page, bottom)*. *Facing page, top:* Robin Williams as Keating exhorts his students, "No matter what anybody tells you, words and ideas can change the world." *Photos courtesy of Peter Wier, Steven Haft, Tom Schulman, and Touchstone Pictures*

Director Ridley Scott *(right)* with cast
members Michael Madsen, Susan
Sarandon, and Geena Davis *(in car)*
on the set of *Thelma and Louise.*
"Unfortunately, filming is all against
the clock. So it's a constant battle
between commerce and creativity."
Courtesy Ridley Scott

Director Martha Coolidge: "You're always looking for a metaphor that is extremely visual and dramatic so that it becomes a picture and not just words on a page." *Photo by Jane O'Neal; courtesy Martha Coolidge*

Director Norman Jewison: "Every film has its own life, its own destiny that must be guided." *Courtesy Yorktown Productions*

Inventor Garrett Brown with his Steadicam. The small, handheld unit gives the director the flexibility to follow the action into difficult and confining places.

Edward James Olmos: "I believe that intent equals content, and therefore it doesn't matter how intensely buried it is, the intention will inevitably come out." *Courtesy Olmos Productions*

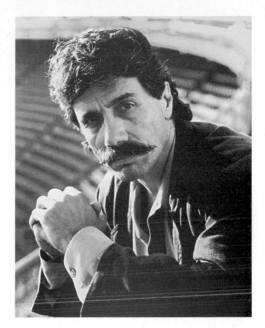

Mary McDonnell: "A very wise director once told me before opening night in the theatre, 'Go out there and make some mistakes.'" *Courtesy Mary McDonnell*

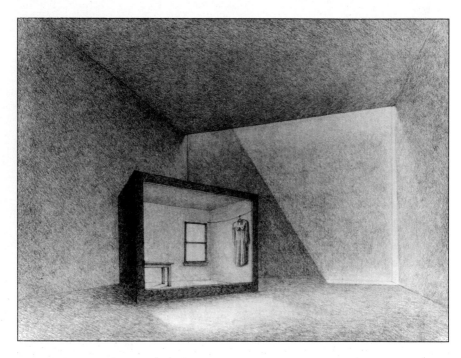

Ferdinando Scarfiotti's work as production designer on Barry Levinson's *Toys* earned him an Academy Award nomination. His original sketches for some of the most memorable sets are *(above)* Alsatia's Office, *(facing page, top)* The Old Warehouse, and *(facing page, bottom)* The War Room. *Courtesy Ferdinando Scarfiotti*

Final composite of Meryl Streep sitting at piano with head twisted 180 degrees. Computer graphics reflection of head in mirror.

1. Background plate

2. Clean plate used to fill in background behind blue hooded head.

3. Bluescreen head match-moved to live action plate.

4. Bluescreen ponytail replaces ponytail in head element.

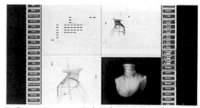

5. Computer-generated replacement neck.

6. Precomposite; head removed and replaced with clean plate.

Ken Ralston's special effects team at Industrial Light and Magic faced a formidable challenge in bringing *Death Becomes Her* to the screen. *On the facing page,* Meryl Streep stretches as an actress, thanks to computer technology. *Above,* Ralston with the mansion model used in the film.

Actor Bob Hoskins *(below)* is adrift in a blue background as he "talks" to his animated co-stars in *Who Framed Roger Rabbit?* Ralston and his team make sure he hits his marks. *Photos by Kerry Nordquist; courtesy ILM*

Composer Henry Mancini: "Once you know your material, it's like you're going to build a house. Style comes into it, attitudes, tempo." *Courtesy Henry Mancini*

Steven Spielberg wanted that bicycle to fly across the sky in
E.T. First we shoot the street. Then we build a model of the
bicycle or the Delorean. The model is set up in front of a blue
screen and shot. Then we create a black silhouette of the
object called a black center. You may remember that you saw
the bicycle in silhouette in E.T. Then the color positive of
the Delorean is printed in that black silhouette area.

So you're combining three different images—the set, the
silhouette, and the color object. In the final stage we use the
optical printer to combine all these separate pieces of film into
one image. However, using computer graphics has changed
this procedure substantially.

Live Action Versus Special Effects

If you're doing live action on a set, you just roll the camera
until the actors get it right. You might shoot miles of footage.
But for special effects this is prohibitive because many effects
are time consuming and can be costly.

Another problem is that effects necessitate a reversal of the
usual filmmaking process. You need to know how everything
is going to be cut in the editing room before you can do most
effects. And it's very hard for directors and editors to make
those decisions in preproduction. But they have to commit
themselves because I can't change things dramatically in the
last month or so because of technical limitations. We are
locked into a deadline and there's no playing around with
shots at that point.

To help the director we'll use animatics, which is a process
of shooting the sequences on video using models. On Return
of the Jedi we had sequences using funky space models shot on
sticks against a black background to give George Lucas something to edit with. And we made up some rough little models

of what the speeder bike and storm troopers would look like. We shoot miles of video. Then George cut that together to give us an idea of exactly what the final sequence would look like.

Shooting it in rough form tells me where everything will be in the shot—the size of things, the lighting, everything I need to know to make the shot work. It gives us the initial information of a scene so that we can plan the basic approach—scheduling, action, cameras needed, people, time, and budget.

In *Roger Rabbit* we shot the five-minute sequence of Toontown on our stage here at ILM in Marin County. We shot blue screen with Bob Hoskins interacting with all the cartoon characters. The process took weeks and weeks. Then, as soon as we had a rough composite with the rough animation, we gave it to the director, who checked the timing and the position of the actor and his relationship to the cartoon characters and backgrounds in the scene. Then we sent it to the editors. The process repeated itself over and over again, always refining. Little by little everyone started to get a feel for what was happening dramatically. In the end I think it worked very well.

State of the Art: Death Becomes Her

With *Death Becomes Her* we were fortunate to have had enough research and development time to test out some new theories. Everyone seems to remember the scene where Meryl Streep's head is twisted on backward. You could always do an effect like this in a schlocky way for certain films, but this had to be way beyond that.

In the beginning I went out and bought a Barbie doll and turned its head around backward. This was a low-tech start, but it helped because it's a hard image to keep in your mind. In a way, creating some ten-headed creature from Mars would

have been easier. So I sat there and looked at that and started
to come up with a rough possible direction to go.

Then I went to the folks in the computer division and
talked through my ideas. We did some tests with one of the
women here at ILM on a little set that we built. At that time we
ran through all the possible ways of doing the shot. We didn't
know what would work best. We had her on the set doing
dozens of different actions against a blue and a black screen.
Then we started to narrow it down.

We studied the director's storyboard of the sequence.
Then we went down to Los Angeles where the mansion interior was being constructed. We spent a day there and shot the
whole twisted-head sequence on video with a stand in. Bob
Zemeckis, the director, edited the sequence as closely as he
could to the final edit. That gave us an idea of what the shots
were going to be like, and gave us our blueprint for planning
all the techniques, people, time, and equipment necessary to
pull it off.

There's always the budget to consider. Much of this type of
work is so abstract that it's difficult to budget without actually
starting to do it. You can talk about it for a year. You can
pretend you know. But then that first day on the set, everything changes, it all goes out the window.

This was one of the rare times where many of the effects
scenes were shot on video, while the film was still in preproduction. It helped because the scenes were so complicated and a bit frightening for all of us. We had to get a head
start, no pun intended, to get a feeling for what we had to
accomplish.

To create the look of the head on backward, the neck was
created in a computer. That object doesn't exist—except in
the computer. What's real is Meryl's body. But because of the
way we had to distort the neck, we had to replace the chest

and the neck with a computer piece which was blended in with her real head, shot blue screen.

It was pushing the effects envelope because shots were so long you could analyze our work very closely. Usually, with effects films, you have quick cuts or crazy explosions or bizarre alien things. Things that are happening are so wild that it's distracting and can make it hard to focus your attention on any one "trick." But here, the audience had plenty of time to scrutinize the effect. It had to be perfect.

First we shot her body and she did the whole scene as if she had her head on backward—which was an incredible acting job! Then we shot the area behind her head without her on the set. Then a month later she wore a blue leotard and we shot her head, blue screen.

I then sat down with the rough cut of the sequence and plotted frame by frame by frame, every position her head would be in. It was very labor-intensive. She sat in a chair and roughly duplicated each head position for every frame. And we also had to add the exact lighting to duplicate the lighting on the real set.

Then there was the ponytail factor. When we shot her close-up in front of the blue screen, her real ponytail was cut off or hidden behind the blue outfit she was wearing. As we started to work out the head positions, we realized you'd have to see the ponytail. So we had her hairdresser send us one of the ponytail wigs. We had to take the ponytail and match it frame by frame as close as we could to what her head was doing in every frame. In the end it was one of the things that no one will ever know because it works so well.

I don't want to get technical, but you shoot film at twenty-four frames a second. If the scene is over three minutes long, you're looking at five thousand or so frames and you're doing

behind the scenes:
collaboration by design
239

everything frame by frame. It gets complicated. The work is so time-consuming and there's an intense amount of concentration on the smallest little detail. Eventually everyone went kind of bonkers. I know I was.

The project took about six months from start to finish, and it's a good thing we started early because the final version of the scene was not done until the bitter end of postproduction. We needed every second of time.

The effects team for the whole movie was 250 people. That includes our model shop, which built all the miniatures, and our optical department. There's the computer graphics team, the editors at ILM, as well as the people who work with the film and production crew. Many others. We put everything we had into it.

Cause and Effects

This job definitely requires a lot of discipline and concentration. It helps to have a strong background in art, filmmaking, the whole general process because you touch on every aspect of it when you're working on a film. It helps to have a good knowledge of computer graphics, but to develop the computer literacy you need you have to actually be working in the field. The systems we use are not the kind that you can go buy at the software store. Maybe someday.

In a nutshell, the first 95 percent of what we do at ILM is manageable. But that last impossible 5 percent, that's the part that separates us from everyone else. That's the hard part. But it's that last little bit that allows us to pull off things that maybe haven't ever been done before. It takes the whole film to a different level. And maybe the audience never really thinks about it, but I think they appreciate it. That's good enough for me.

C L O S E - U P

SANDY VENEZIANO, ART DIRECTOR
DEAD POETS SOCIETY

I got a call from a friend of mine at Disney who said that Peter Weir was going to be directing this film *Dead Poets Society*. Would I like an interview with him? I knew his films and really wanted a chance to work with him. His wife, Wendy Stites, would be the production designer, so as the art director I would be working with her to execute the look of the film.

Usually I read the script before meeting with the director, but when I met with Peter I had no idea what the movie was about. I went in and sat down and he started telling me the story, which was wonderful. Then he started talking about the sequence in the cave and how it played.

As a designer I started thinking about how we could get this light feeling that he wanted. So I suggested to Peter that the cave should have a fissure at the top and you could have the light pouring in as they read the poetry.

And I think that is what got me the job because without seeing the script I couldn't talk intelligently about anything else. He called me back and said "please do the movie." I was delighted.

From Script to Seeing

I got the script and digested it and then started going through it line by line. The first thing I look for is what is required by the story: what has to be built and what might be available at the location. Then I focus on what the overall look of the film is going to be.

I thought of the overall look as romantic—that rich,

warm, academic feel of the school and what that tradition entailed. When I got to Delaware, I met Wendy, the production designer, and John Seales, the cinematographer, and they had very specific ideas about how they wanted things to look.

Color was very important. Color was dictated to us partly by the school. It was very rich and warm with dark woods so we wanted to carry that throughout. It's sort of a moody feel. And it was such a good period to work with—it was old enough that it had a flavor. John Anderson was our set decorator and he worked with Wendy and myself, choosing all the furniture pieces. We were very careful to choose everything from that period.

A Touch of Class

In designing the classroom, I researched what boys' schools looked like in the 1950s. Some of them had the little anterooms, with a wash area for the teacher, so I incorporated that into the design. And it also gave Robin [Williams] a place to go into and come out from.

We were able to use the school for all the exterior shots, such as the soccer field. The chapel, foyer, and cafeteria were also used. But we couldn't use the classrooms or dorm rooms because they weren't large enough for us. You have to have plenty of room to be able to get the camera anywhere you want.

So we had to build those sets with wild walls, walls that could be removed to accommodate the placement of the camera. Usually we have eight to twelve weeks of prep before we hammer the first nail. You need about six weeks to build the sets. The classroom and dorms were built at the Disney lot in Burbank and then taken apart, piece by piece, and trucked to Delaware. I remember it was really tight. We worked twelve to fifteen hours a day to get them there on time.

But when they arrived there was no room for them at the actual school. So we found an old school nearby and put the dorm set inside the gymnasium there. Their old cafeteria was converted into a space large enough to accommodate the classroom set. It was kind of funny, you know, the dorm was in the gym and the classroom was in the cafeteria. But it worked. A third space at the old school was used for the cave interior.

The classroom was supposed to have windows which look out onto the courtyard. So what I did was take a panoramic photograph called a translite of the courtyard outside the real school and put it behind the windows we had constructed for the classroom set. We had people walk back and forth between the windows and the photograph so it looked like the real school.

With the windows, the change of seasons presented another problem. For some of the seasons, we just took another picture of the campus. But by the time we got to the fall scenes, it was winter. We must have spent close to a week pasting the "autumn" leaves on the trees before we could shoot the pictures.

The sets had to match the boys' school exactly so the audience would believe that the classroom and dorms were at the same location as the exteriors. I matched every mold, every nuance.

Neil's house was easier. It was an actual house near the school. We re-dressed the whole place. What was tricky was the relationship of the upstairs and the downstairs. Peter felt the wood was important, and it was already there in the office. We changed the furniture and completely redid the bedroom. I remember I wanted to change the wallpaper but Peter said it was fine.

Re-creating Nature

Building or redecorating a room is not as difficult as building a natural setting. One of our biggest problems was the cave. We had to find an exterior for the cave and build the interior set so the transition from one to the other worked smoothly.

For the exterior, we found a historical landmark where the Indians used to go, and we got permission to use it. It looked like a cave but in reality it was an entrance. In the film you see the boys approach the entrance to the cave in the real place and then when they move inside, it's our set.

There was a sequence where Peter wanted Robin to be reading poetry in front of a frozen waterfall. We found this little stream, all right, but the problem was it wasn't frozen. We dammed it at both ends and had the special effects people construct icicles to turn it into a frozen waterfall. After it was all finished Peter decided that the scene would play better in the cave so it was never used. It happens all the time.

Costume Design

A lot of the ideas for the costumes came from research and a lot of them came from Wendy. Wendy and Peter had very specific ideas about how they wanted the costumes to look— especially those hoods and coats. Wendy is excellent with costuming and supplied all the touches that helped bring the characters to life. We spent a lot of time shopping for the exact fabric and blankets to use on the beds, because the rooms were so bare.

We also had to create the Welton insignia—the lion motif that was on their jackets. That was a real important symbol for the whole movie. It also appeared on the books, in the corridors, everywhere. To create it, I went through fifteen lions in seven different positions. Lions laying down, lions growling, you name it. Finally we came up with the right symbol.

Collaboration: A Team Effort

Peter is a genuinely warm human being besides being a brilliant director. He knows exactly what he wants and he directs you to his vision. And that's what we were all there for, to give him his vision. It was one of those rare movies where everyone got along famously with everyone else.

Working with Steven Haft, the producer, was like working with a friend. I really didn't have any money problems with him at all. He was very supportive.

Some actors are very specific about what they want—the house they live in, their environment. Robin was not. But each time they would shoot on a new set, Robin would take the time to personally thank me for helping him with his character. Which was great. It's the kind of positive feedback you don't get very often, even though the environment is really important to the actor.

The cinematographer can make or break you as a designer. If the lighting is too bright it's going to look horrible, it's not going to look real. If he does something strange with the camera angles, the sets can look terrible.

John Seales and I talked a lot about color. He would say, "I think I'm going to use this lighting because it makes Robin's face look better so let's make sure that the color of the walls is more like this tone than that one. What do you think?" It was very collaborative. We worked together to get the best look, discussing texture and color. Sometimes we'd put an actor in front of the wall before it was painted, to check various shades of yellow or green.

My team is mainly the costume designer, cinematographer, and production designer. The special effects people work under me. Then there is the set decorator, the construction coordinator who builds the sets, and the painters and plasterers who work under them. All of them contribute.

I worked closely with the prop master on so many little details, even down to what kind of books to use for the poetry readings. What color are they? The prop master would show me four or five examples and I would show one or two to Peter because ultimately everything is his responsibility. I tried to limit the number of examples to save him time.

A lot of people remember the photographs in the foyer of all the old Welton students from years gone by. We couldn't use any real photographs from the school for legal reasons, so we had to fabricate them. We dressed up extras in period costumes and took pictures and then made them look like they were shot forty years ago. With everything from set construction to the last photograph, my theory is that I hope you never notice my work. The environment can't come out and grab you. We all work hard to make sure that the audience always feels that they are exactly where the scene takes place, even though most of the time it's an illusion.

Filmmaking is about illusion, but mostly it's about what is going on in the scene and the actors, not the walls behind them. If you watched *Dead Poets* and it seemed perfectly natural, like we simply found a school and shot it exactly as it was, that's perfect. To me, that's a job well done.

C L O S E - U P

JOHN SEALES, CINEMATOGRAPHER
DEAD POETS SOCIETY

One of the first things I remember about *Dead Poets Society* was the last week of preproduction. Peter set aside the time from eight in the morning until noon every day and the two of us would go through the script, endlessly talking, taking notes. We'd talk about how scenes would flow, how certain scenes might combine if there were two that were similar.

Peter would scribble stick figures for storyboards, mulling them over. By then we knew every square inch of every location so we'd decide where the camera would actually go. But Peter's not cut-and-dried on this. He always works on a what-if system. What if the camera were over there instead of here?

He would be quite happy to change it if it enhanced his feelings for the scene. And of course I'd be ready to change with him, because as the cinematographer, that's my job.

Maybe all of this sounds like any conversation a director might have with his director of photography, but with Peter there is always something special. It's hard to describe. He carries these strong images in his mind, yet he's very open to collaboration.

You have your own ideas about where to put the camera and Peter is extremely interested in your ideas. He wants to hear them. I'll come up with an idea and he'll mull it and mull it, I swear he's got the entire movie going in his head. He'll run that little piece of idea backward and forward through his mind's moviola and he'll come out with an answer. Maybe he'll use it, or maybe he'll say, "John, it's a powerful idea but I'm going to need that power later. We'll hold back for now and use it in a later scene."

That's why I think his pictures are so perfectly balanced in the performance, in the emotion, in the editing. Because he's always thinking about the whole movie. Before we had shot one frame he said, "I'm counting on the power of the editing room to make this film." And I think it did.

On the Set

When we started filming, we began with some of the easier scenes so the boys would get to know each other before getting into the more dramatic scenes. We shot the soccer game on the first day. Then we did some work with the classroom scenes, and then worked our way quietly to more dramatic scenes.

With the indoor scenes, you tend to get a bit of them here and there, you don't want to use them all up at the beginning. If you chew them all up too soon, you don't have them to fall back on when the bad weather comes.

We'd discuss the day's scenes in the morning on the way to work. Peter would always ride to work with the first assistant director, the camera operator, the continuity person, and myself. We're his command vehicle.

We would be fresh and he would lay out the day's shoot. He would say something like, "Scene 53 is an 'A' scene and scene 72 is a 'B' scene." A "B" scene meant it might not be in the film after editing. He would know that the "B" scene could go if he had to shorten the film so he'd rather spend more time on the "A" scenes.

He'll still shoot the "B" scenes, and shoot them very well, but he won't waste time on them. Peter's very unusual in that almost every shot he does helps build the story. Unlike most directors, he doesn't do master shots all the way through. He'll only do them up to the point that he intends to use them in editing, then he'll move on to his close-ups.

You can almost see where he'll cut—on the head turn, whatever. He'll know that ahead of time, and so my composition is better because he knows where he wants to cut and he'll commit to it right there on the set. It saves a lot of time and of course on the set, time is money.

Keep It Moving

About a week into filming, Peter said to me, "John, you're not a slow cameraman but can you go any faster?" He explained the problem, and it was formidable. "I've got eight stories to tell, seven students, plus a teacher and a girlfriend. I need to have all of those stories to work with in the editing room." So we really started moving. After shooting was over the production office happily told us that we averaged twenty-one set-ups a day over the entire film.

That's quite an average. The usual is about three to five. Five to nine is moving right along. Sixteen is regarded as pushing it a bit. In TV they might do that many, but not in features. So when it was all over I asked Peter, "Which story-lines did you drop out?" And he just smiled and said, "I got them all in. All I had to do was trim them."

The Music Scene

Another unique thing about Peter is his use of music. He selects music for each scene, which gives us a rhythm and pace for that particular scene. It plays while the crew is lighting, rehearsing, getting all the equipment in the right position.

Sometimes he'll let it play until the last second before the

behind the scenes:
collaboration by design
249

actor speaks. Then he'll fade it out very quickly and leave the actor with this music in his head. Afterward the actors say what an amazing thing it is because the music kind of controls the speed of their movements and their reaction time.

It helps me as well because it will determine the speed at which I move the camera. I knew how fast to pan the camera, or tilt it or track it. Peter doesn't have to explain it with words, the beat of the music does it for him.

If you listen to the music he uses as you're doing a particular shot, you can pretty well work out where the cuts will be. So the music really gives you a feeling for how the film will be edited.

Seeing the Image

Peter's films are characterized by his use of images. With *Dead Poets* there were some memorable ones, like the birds. Not just the flocks swirling but that scene of the owl on the night run to the cave. We trained an owl to fly from A to B, then when one of the boys stopped suddenly it was like the owl fluttered through this patch of time into the past. And there was that long run through the trees where the mist was hanging low—all these hooded figures. It was very powerful.

A lot of people remember the scene in the classroom where Todd [Ethan Hawke] comes up with his poem and Robin is spinning him round and round. We used a Steadicam to get it. The cameraman kept circling them, walking in an eight-foot diameter around Robin and Ethan.

We were both worried that this spinning background might be detrimental to the emotional connection between them. So we shot the same scene with a static camera. But when we saw the dailies it was obvious that the spinning shot worked perfectly and, of course, that's the one he used in the final version.

During the suicide scene, we used some subtle slow motion intercut with normal speed to give it a sort of floating feeling. This suspends time, manipulates time, it takes the film to a different level.

When the boy takes the crown of thorns off his head and puts it down, we're running the camera at 128 frames a second, which creates slow motion. But we also intercut with the normal speed of twenty-four frames per second. What it does is suspend him in that final mellifluous moment of his life.

Seeing the Light

The lighting on *Dead Poets* was as natural as we could make it, very realistic. The only time we would do something a bit different was when the boys went to the cave or were running through the mist at night. The school had to be lit much like in real life, so we started with what was there and enhanced it to a level that would enable us to film. Tom Schulman's words were enough. I didn't have to do much to enhance them.

I often feel that when the words are good and the actors are fairly humming on those words you could almost light up a movie with a flashlight. The cinematographer is there to enhance as much as possible but certainly not to override or overcontrol or start doing ridiculous commercial-type tricks that can detract from the real emotion. The classroom had seven little bulbs hanging down, I didn't mind that because that's reality. Same with the houses, they were just real houses the boys went to, where they had parties, so they had to be lit as real houses.

I found it very difficult to lay smoke into the classroom in order to get a sense of shifting sunlight. There was one scene

where Robin and the math teacher were having a cup of tea
and the math teacher was smoking a pipe. So I just dropped a
little bit of smoke in to give it a sort of ethereal look. The rest
of it I just photographed as reality.

When the boy actually commits suicide, it's winter with
snow outside, so that was done in cool moonlight with cool
lighting. The available lighting came from the night outside.

In the father's bedroom when he awakens to the sound of
something, the windows are cool, but it's not cool lighting
inside. His bed lamp is warm lighting. Same with Neil's bedroom when he makes the fateful decision, his bed lamp was
left as a warm lamp. It worked as a counterpoint against the
emotion the boy was going through. Otherwise, you're using
cold lighting to agree with the bleak feeling in his mind, which
is really too much.

A Special Film

When we watch dailies, Peter will play the music he used
on the scene. He says it helps him emotionally. I remember
this one day I'm watching the rushes and the music is playing
and I thought—that looks just right—and I turned to say
something to the gaffer and he was crying. I couldn't believe
it. I said, "You're a hard-bitten, twenty-five-years-in-the-
business, Los Angeles gaffer. You're not allowed to cry in
dailies!" It was a wonderful moment.

For all the effort we all put into the film, I think it all comes
back to the script and the story. I remember Peter saying that
Tom Schulman's script was just about perfect all the way
through. Deep down I'll always believe that Tom's Academy
Award was well deserved.

6
the
editor:
"a way
of
seeing"

Imagine a gigantic reel of film spilling its contents as it threads its way down the freeway. The first frame is in Hollywood and the rest stretches all the way to the ocean, then works its way south through the suburbs, along the beaches. It continues through San Diego and crosses the border into Mexico, finally arriving at downtown Tijuana. In a car, that's a three-hour drive spanning 170 miles, approximately the same as the distance between New York City and Philadelphia.

That reel of film, some 900,000 feet in all, represents the amount of raw footage given the editors of *Scent of a Woman*. Their job was to take these miles and miles of film and shape them into a cohesive two-hour story. How do they do it?

Editor Carol Littleton (*Grand Canyon, Body Heat*) sees a similarity between her job and that of a musician.

Dialogue, visuals, story all have rhythm. It's the editor's job to pick up on those rhythms that are internal in the scene and to make them play. Like the musician, you're going over the same material again and again, finding the nuances, making the slight changes, working on it until you feel you've extracted the best technical interpretation and emotional tone.

The Big Picture

Editors are also like artists, painting the big picture from a palette of scenes, each with a slightly different hue of expression, meaning, camera angle, shading, camera movement, emphasis, and perspective. Eventually all are blended into a final impression. "The editor is like an artist, working with light, color, and composition," says Joe Hutshing (*Indecent Proposal, JFK*). "You might want a love scene to be warmer, so you pump more gold or red into the print. It's subtle, but it affects the reaction to a scene.

In *Born on the Fourth of July* there's a scene in the opening credit sequence where young Ronny hits a home run and it's just pumped with color. That was a process that we went through to enrich the color. It gives it a great feeling. Or it might be a memory and you want it to look like an old photograph, so you might remove much of the color, give it a sepia tone.

"It is like painting, but when you're editing, you have a limited palette," Hutshing explains. "You can only work with the shots you've got. But there's an infinite variety within that restricted palette. The goal is to create an intensely satisfying emotional experience. The difficulty is staying fresh to the material."

Musician? Painter? Yes, and then there is the writing analogy. Hutshing says the film editor must also act as a storyteller.

> You have to have a good sense of story. You have to be excited by stories and know what will happen if you structure them in certain ways.
> Does the audience see the bloody dagger before or after the door is opened? How will that affect the story? Maybe it should never be seen at all. How long do you hold on the shot? It's about rhythm, timing, pacing. And it all affects the story.

Carol Littleton agrees. "My job is to enhance the writing and to make sure that everything is clear in the final version. I decide what to include and how much focus to give it." Like most editors, she feels a special kinship with the writer. "I think that writing and editing are very closely related. Both jobs are more monastic than social." Like the writer, the editor labors alone in a room, a solitary world. Says Hutshing, "You're in the room twelve or fourteen hours every day, but if you're working on something that you really like, you don't really think about that."

From Script to Screen

Like most collaborators, Carol Littleton starts with the script. It will be her responsibility to help bring the project from script to screen, and there are always certain things to look for.

I use the script as my main criterion for whether or not I
want to do the picture. I like to see a really good strong
story with well-defined characters. I look for structure. I
don't always get it. At the very least you have to see a
possibility for restructuring in editing. There are so many
variables over the course of a film being shot and edited
that you really want a good script for your bible.

Veteran editor Bill Reynolds's credits include such classic films
as *The Turning Point*, *The Sting*, and *The Sound of Music*. He
looks for "entertainment value" and those troublesome little
warning signs.

When I read the script, I'm thinking, "Do I want to do this
picture?" I try to visualize it and think, "Is this going to be a
good picture and be good entertainment?" When reading it,
I'm very much aware whether the characters are alive,
strong, or funny. If you read a script and think "This is meant
to be funny but it isn't," then you know you're in trouble!

There are also scripts that represent such a challenge, the
editors wonder if they can pull it off. Joe Hutshing admits to
his own short attention span: "I'm bored easily." So what
happened when he got all two hundred pages of *JFK*?

Oliver gave me a shooting script and it took me four days
to read it. It was interesting but still so dense, almost
unreadable. I got bored. You had to concentrate so much
to get it. I knew it was going to be an incredibly tough
editing job. I wondered if it could even be made watchable, it was so incredibly complicated.

On the other hand, there are those rare occasions when a great
script can simplify the editor's job. Thom Noble encountered

one when he was asked to work on "a different kind of road movie."

Normally, when you get a script and start talking with the director, you realize there's a whole bunch of stuff that you can lose—there's a lot of fat in most scripts. But Callie Khouri's *Thelma and Louise* was such a perfect script. You actually could read it and say, "There's really not a word wasted in this entire script." And, of course, the women were just fantastic characters.

Production: The Dailies

Once the editor has read the script and made the decision to come aboard, the first day on the job usually coincides with the first day of production. Carol Littleton has edited almost all of Lawrence Kasdan's films. Her experiences with him are somewhat unique.

Usually I start work on the first day of principal photography, but Larry allows me to be present during the rehearsals. At rehearsals, I'm looking to be a quiet auditor. It allows me to have a sense of the film, to experience it somewhat before it is actually shot.

I also get a better perception of the problems that the actors encounter, as well as the delight they take in pulling it together and making their characters work. I take notes so that when the moment comes that I'm no longer fresh with the material, I can reexperience the emotional arc of the film. I'm able to use that when I'm cutting to help bring out the best in each scene and performance.

It's interesting to note that Littleton's presence at rehearsals rarely extends to the set during shooting. "Usually I have too many other things to do. The set is about sitting around and waiting," she says with a laugh. "All I can think of is all that time that's going to waste."

Thom Noble is on the set "as little as possible" and with good reason. "You see them setting up a shot and it takes a whole morning to do this one incredibly intricate tracking shot. The danger is that you might feel compelled to use it when you cut the sequence."

The raw footage comes in each day, and the editor shows these "dailies" to the director. For Littleton, it's an opportunity to get inside the process. "I'm hoping to be able to see in dailies the essential focus of the director's attention, what he was going through on each take. Sometimes it might be a practical consideration—such as perfecting a camera move. Or sometimes you see that each take is so different you're going to just choose what you like."

Bill Reynolds explains the steps the editor goes through as the actual cutting begins.

As soon as you have a complete scene, whether it's the beginning, middle, or end of the movie, you can start putting it together as a scene.

When you first look at the picture, you're looking for the story. The number one object is to keep the story moving, reveal the details of the story, and get the best performances. You make the actors look as good as you possibly can but most of all the objective is clarity.

Littleton reveals how she collaborates with director Kasdan during this initial period. "Many times Larry doesn't say what he likes, more often he'll say what he doesn't like. I can see visually what works and what doesn't work because it's pretty obvious after you've looked at so much film."

Thom Noble begins plotting how he is going to be able to integrate the best aspects of each take. "Every take will have a moment in it you want to keep. You might see that one take is lit more brilliantly, it looks great. So you think to yourself—I have to use this, somehow I've got to put this in."

At the same time, Noble explains that the editor must resist the temptation to "overcut" in an attempt to get in every cherished moment.

Sometimes a scene is perfectly performed in the master shot and you can let it sit there. At the same time there's a moment of a close-up of somebody that you've got to try and get in. Ideally you'd like to integrate it into the whole without there appearing to be a cut. In other words, you try and make it all appear as seamless as possible.

Assemblage: "The First Cut Is the Deepest"

Once the production has wrapped, the pressure shifts to the editor to produce an initial cut of the film. For Carol Littleton, there are a lot of personal choices.

The first cut is pretty much the editor's cut, assembling according to what the script says. You put everything in on the first cut, you see everything that was shot and everything that was considered. I try to choose the best from each scene. This is my interpretation: dialogue, mood, character, everything.

Of course I'm cutting during filming, but I'm cutting

in the order in which it was shot, so it's a little bit disorient-
ing. Throughout, I'm trying to cut the scenes as lean and
to-the-point as possible. I'm not just assembling shots and
stringing them together. I'm always trying my best to deal
with performances and analyze the story.

In the first assembly Joe Hutshing tries to follow the script as
closely as possible. "I try to be true to what was written and try
to make it work, exactly as the script has it. Once that has been
done then you can start making interpretations of it, refining it."

Carol Littleton reveals that there comes a time when the
editor must be willing to let go of the script. At some point you
realize "the script was a wonderful guide and that's what was
used for the shooting, but now we have to forget that and just
deal with the film we have."

Even at the assembly stage, maybe *especially* at this stage,
creative decisions are made by the editor that will largely
determine if the movie will "play." Carol Littleton tries to
follow the director's lead, but many decisions must be made
on her own.

With the first cut, I'm following the lines of the director's
work visually. But which shot to use? The two-shot? Over
the shoulder? Long shot? And for how long? The duration
of the shot. If there's camera movement, obviously they
want to be able to use that section. The director and the
director of photography have decided the visual design,
the lens sizes, the angles, the movement, the composition.
The rest is up to me.

The parameters vary according to the director's instructions.
Many directors prefer to use the same editor in project after

project; a shorthand develops between them, an instinctive •
communication. Littleton has worked with Lawrence Kasdan
so often that she anticipates his preferences. Since Kasdan
usually writes his own scripts, she tends to return to them for
guidance as she seeks out the emotional moments.

When you're reading the script, you know who the main
character is in the scene and you know what the emphasis
is. For instance, in *Grand Canyon* Danny Glover finds his
nephew under the staircase. Who's more important—
Otis, the kid who has seen some horrible thing in his life
that has shocked him? Or is it his uncle?
    In this particular case, we had singles of both, wider
shots too, but as it turned out, I used mostly the two-shot
that was moving in, it ended up in very tight shots of him
because the emphasis of the scene was on the kid's pain
and this incredible realization in his life. That's where the
emotional moment is.

Joe Hutshing explains that there are also those times when
the script can't be followed. "What works in a script doesn't
always work filmically. Maybe the location has fallen through,
maybe the lighting is off, or an actor is sick, and you have to
make do with what you have."

It's a matter of redefining the purpose of the scene and
making it work. I look at the film as a viewer. With *JFK*,
since the subject matter was dry, although it's an exciting
story, I was trying to keep from getting bored.
    It's important to keep the audience riveted on the
story, so I watch it and try to keep it from getting slow.
There was a lot of wonderful footage and a lot of stock
footage, and a lot of our work involved how we could

creatively get to this point or that point and keep the story moving.

Littleton begins by cutting out the repetition. "The biggest sin is to be redundant. The next biggest is to have things that are truly extraneous." Inevitably it gets back to what to leave in and what to cut out. She tries to cut "things that really do not contribute to the through-line of the picture."

At the same time she warns that "you can cut it down too far and leave out the emotions. You need to create the moments that allow the audience to come inside the story, to participate and be a part of the dramatic moment."

Thom Noble, who rose to prominence for his work on *Witness*, stresses that the best editing is usually invisible. "The effect that I always try for is that it looks as if it comes straight out of the camera that way, so you're not aware of all the cuts."

Of course, with some sequences it's important that you *are* aware of all the cuts. If it's an action sequence and it's all hectic, busy, and exciting, then obviously the cuts matter.

But if you're doing intricate dialogue sequences, peo ple in a car or sitting at a table or having a dinner party, you've got to try to get every wonderful moment that the actor has given you and integrate it into the film. *Thelma and Louise* was like that. There were magical moments that Susan [Sarandon] would give and you just have to try and get them in. That's your job.

And what a job it is! The editor must assemble the film in ten to fourteen days after the production wraps. So much film, so little time. Do directors appreciate this monumental feat? Not as a rule. Their minds are occupied with differences between script and screen, between what they thought they shot and what they actually have shot.

Leonard Nimoy made this painful discovery as he made the initial transition from actor to director.

> I discovered when I directed my first picture that perhaps the low point in the making of a film is sitting through the first assembly of footage. It's disastrous. It's shapeless. It's formless. It's toneless. It's boring. It's long. It's wrong.
>
> It's not funny. It's not dramatic. It's just one long session of pain. When you've done it a couple of times, you're prepared for it, but when you come in as a novice expecting to see your movie, forget it!

Carol Littleton agrees that after seeing the first cut, "There's the reality of what one might imagine shooting and the reality of what's actually on the film." She smiles. "Very often they're not the same. So it becomes truly collaborative at that point. Some directors just want to talk. Some are the monkey on your back, you can't get them out of the room."

The Director's Cut

During the next eight or ten weeks, the director and editor will work closely together to shape the film into its next incarnation, the director's cut. How close this version is to what is released will depend on the degree of the director's clout with the studio as well as other contractual obligations.

Thom Noble explains how the process begins. "My first cut is really more than an assembly because every scene is cut as I would hope it would finally be. In the morning I show the director what I've done and we go straight through it. Then we'll have lunch and talk about it."

Then we'll go back in the afternoon and start running it reel by reel. We're looking at every sequence. You've got ideas about what scenes should go, so when you come across those scenes you both agree to cut them. And then it's "I think we'll come into this scene a little bit later and come into this one a little bit earlier."

We know that some scenes are holding up the action of the picture, maybe they're not interesting or not good enough to stay in. So you'll lose them. Just in the first sweep through, you eliminate ten to fifteen minutes.

At this point Noble usually needs about a week to make the director's recommended deletions and additions.

Then you run the picture again and you look at it and you realize that omitting certain things has really improved it. Then we look at each scene individually and see how we can pare it down.

By the end of the second week you've got another five or six minutes out of the film, and if you're happy with it and you feel that the film is going in the right direction, you'll try and put a soundtrack on it and get it out and preview it.

The preview process affords the audience its first opportunity to watch the movie. If you've ever attended a "sneak preview" that was early in the process, you probably noticed that some scenes didn't quite fit together, maybe there were sound problems or the music seemed a bit off.

Yet even in these earliest screenings the director will begin to gauge the audience's response. Are they restless at some point? Are there things that were supposed to be funny but failed to get a laugh? Noble continues:

> You assess the audience's reaction and you start paring it down some more. Then you take it out and preview it again and see if your results [the audience approval scores] come up at all. In theory the studio has to stay away while the director's cut is being completed.
>
> Finally you show it to the studio, but first you add some music and temporary sound effects. That takes another couple of weeks. By now we've taken our eight weeks.

The crucial "studio run" will help determine the amount of publicity and advertising support the film will receive. And of course there will be the inevitable studio suggestions for change. Noble says this is where the director plays a pivotal role.

> Depending on the strength of the director, he either listens to them or not. Or he may listen and not act on any of the suggestions. Or he may say, "Let's do these things . . ."
>
> Then we'll show it to the studio again and they'll say, "We'd like to preview it in this shape." If it scores really well then we pat each other on the back and send it to the composer.
>
> On the other hand, if it's a disaster in preview, we may do all sorts of things in an attempt to please the public. Take that scene out or add that scene or restructure it in some way, make it more clear to the audience what the story line is.

JFK: The Ultimate Challenge

It's difficult to imagine a project with more elements than *JFK*. There was footage from the networks, the famous Zapruder film, material from the Southwest Film Archives and from numerous other public and private sources. Mixed film stock of eight- and sixteen-millimeter video, a conglomerate of visual images, each one capturing a unique piece of the most violent, gut-wrenching event in modern American political history.

Director Oliver Stone, renowned for his painstaking penchant for duplicating reality, had delivered the raw elements for a masterpiece. Somehow editor Joe Hutshing had to make it come together to tell a long, difficult, and controversial story.

I knew it was going to be incredibly tough. I wondered if it could even be made watchable because it was like looking at a schematic for a television set and then imagining actually watching the television. It was so incredibly complicated.

There was so much information, really much more than there is in the final version. You overshoot intentionally to see what works and what doesn't work and then you pare it down and try to choose your best moments.

Was there ever a moment of his own when he felt overwhelmed by the task? Hutshing smiles a knowing smile that says there were probably more than a few.

Bill Brown, who was in charge of postproduction, thought of this great analogy of what it was like working on this film. He said, "Joe, did you ever see those pirate movies

where they're out at sea with these sixty-foot waves, and
there's the ship but the sails are all down and no one is on
deck and the wheel is just spinning?"

I just thought that was the perfect analogy for this. It
was so much beyond what anybody had done before.
There was so much footage and so many ways to go with
all of this stuff. It was a little bit scary. There were times
I felt like I was drowning, that I was in way over my
head.

In this case the life preserver turned out to be the energy of the
film itself. Eventually Hutshing, working with three other
editors, began to piece together a story that cried out to be
told.

We had a lot of wonderful footage to work with. A lot of it
was how we could creatively get to this point or that point
and keep the story going. Each scene has to work on its
own, and then it has to work through the common thread
of the structure of the film.

Eventually you let the film find its own pace and you
kind of work through it. Filmmaking is a very social activity for everyone except the editor. Editing is about taking a
huge chunk and reducing it to something, making it coher-
ent and pacing it correctly, making it smooth.

Hutshing pauses for a moment, trying to remember. "I think
our first cut was about five hours long. The final version is
three hours and eight minutes." In between there were a lot of
crucial decisions to be made. "In between" became a classic
example of the art and craft of editing film.

Visual Language: The Tools of the Trade

At every stage of the editing process, it is the editor's responsibility to help make the story clear to the audience. This is accomplished through the use of a visual language. Since the best editing often goes unnoticed by the audience, the editor's manipulation of images is vital but somewhat invisible. Joe Hutshing traces the modest beginnings of this art.

Originally in film, somebody would shoot somebody sneezing or a fire truck going by and people would pay to see that. Then editing started because they put two shots together. Then years later somebody invented the insert shot, so you'd have a wide shot of somebody looking at a watch and then you cut to the insert of the watch. At first people didn't understand that. Eventually they accepted that as part of the language of film.

Asked about the language of editing, Thom Noble is willing to summarize it in a single word. "Timing. Everything is timing. It's that intuitive sense of what the correct rhythm and pacing of any moment is."

Carol Littleton agrees. Her response is enthusiastic, and takes on a kind of rhythm of its own.

Timing is a big part of it, it has to do with musicality. The timing of a piece of music. The timing of a language, how it flows, how it goes from one moment to the next. The speech patterns of an actor have their own rhythm and musicality.

It's timing in the musical sense, not in the sense of a punch line. It has to be a question of focus and intensity. The editor needs to have a rigorous discipline, to know why you're doing the picture; it's about sensitivity and selectivity.

There's the flow of images within the scene. Sometimes editing has to be seamless. Other times things need to be revealed in a sort of jumpy way. You might go from a moving camera to a static camera and back to a moving camera. Maybe somebody is looking around a room. You need to see things from *their* point of view. All of these things have their own musicality, rhythm, timing.

Littleton constantly seeks "the right combination of things" that will tell the story effectively. The quest is a never-ending one, but the tools of the trade remain the same.

You need to understand all the tools that you have at your disposal—image size, quickness of the cut, using camera moves, juggling the sequence of events around, staying with the linear sequence without interrupting the action, cross cutting. . . .

These tools are learned in school or on the job; their effectiveness is honed by each project, their proper use discovered over a lifetime. In the end, they are all that the editor has to create the visual language that produces screen magic.

The Invisible Language

Since the visual language of editing is mostly invisible, is it possible to ascertain the editor's contribution when seeing the final product? This question surfaces each year at Oscar time as editors attempt to select their peers' best work. The rest of us must look to our favorite films, those we have seen again and again, and think back to their most memorable scenes. It helps if you have the editor available to walk you through them!

Thom Noble was called in five weeks after *Witness* went into production. Director Peter Weir was unhappy with the way it was being edited, and Noble had the opportunity to recut the opening sequence of the Amish farms as a kind of audition. As he began to look at the shots, he realized the film's extraordinary potential.

> There is a sort of rhythm that the shots have and it kind of dictates how you have to do it. With the opening titles, that rhythm was dictated by the actual shots I selected. I used the ones with the long lenses, which made everything that much slower because you had to hold the shots a bit longer. This gave these first scenes a sort of dream quality.

Excited by what he had been able to accomplish, Noble screened the segment for Weir.

> Peter and I were sitting on a rattan couch and we put up the first reel and I remember thinking, This is actually a great reel. I've never cut a reel better than this opening.
>
> The dreamlike quality started with the Amish coming over the hill and everybody going into town and then the railway station and the little boy's journey with the balloon going by.
>
> And I'm thinking I've really got this down and if he doesn't like it, I'm just going to slash my wrists right here! I was feeling very nervous and kept on looking at Peter, hoping he would look my way and sort of give me a

thumbs-up sign or smile, but he was just looking intently at the screen.

We got to the end of the reel and there was this long pause and I know that I was trying to stop shaking because the rattan was making all this noise and he said, "It's great, it's so European." That was the major breakthrough.

Another one came as he and Weir worked on the film's much-discussed "lost scene." The experience demonstrates the nature of collaboration between editor and director.

The first editor included in the first thirty-five minutes a scene of Book's sister Elaine and Rachel, where Rachel cleans Elaine's house. It's about six or seven minutes long. I recut that scene but almost immediately we decided we didn't need it. We had to get to the Amish farm fast.

When you look at the picture as a whole, I'm not really that interested in the sister. The scene in the home was really the weakest scene in the entire movie, because it doesn't have anything to do with the real point of the film and Elaine is not a main character.

In the opening title sequence of *Grand Canyon*, Carol Littleton found a metaphor for the urban angst that the film explores so effectively.

Grand Canyon is an overall mosaic of life as we live it in L.A. At the beginning, you see the basketball game being played first on a backyard court and then the same game being played at the Forum. And you realize this whole sort of synergy of lives is being played, the same game, we're all playing this game.

I saw it as a beautiful metaphor, going from the bodies

in slow motion to a Forum full of fantastic athletes. And that same idea is reprised at the very end when Danny Glover and Kevin Kline play their friendly game at night in their backyard court.

The story really begins when Kevin Kline's car breaks down in a dangerous neighborhood near the Forum. Littleton says, "You could call that whole sequence an action sequence, from the time that he turns off the boulevard on to these dark streets until the time that Danny Glover comes to rescue him and they're in the tow truck."

That was a sequence that was storyboarded, and it had a certain logic. Certain things were going to happen before Danny got there and certain things were going to happen after Danny got there. Action sequences have an internal logic. You're thinking of pacing and rhythm, making it as exciting as possible.
    In this scene, it had to do with how isolated you could make Kevin seem. I chose shots that show the threat, that show his anxiety, the most dramatic lighting. Where the gang of kids came up, there was a dolly move, the camera dropped down from where the kids were over to the top of the car to look in the window.
    It conveys a certain claustrophobia, a sense of being hemmed in. So you're going from a medium shot up to a tight shot during their dialogue.

Littleton's next decision was perhaps the most important one in the entire sequence.

The big decision involved how to reveal the gun. Are we going to reveal the gun casually, just a flash of the gun, or were we going to let the kid literally pull it back and show it, maybe reveal it over a line? But in the footage he actually didn't say a line there, so I had to move one of his other lines over it. That way he reveals the gun when he's saying his most threatening line.

The gun is especially crucial as the scene plays out. Eventually the kid asks Danny Glover if he respects him for who he is or simply because he has the gun. Glover's memorable reply: "Son, if you didn't have the gun, we wouldn't be having this conversation."

Though there are a number of memorable action sequences in *Thelma and Louise*, it is the dialogue in the car between Geena Davis and Susan Sarandon that carries the film. Thom Noble explains that editors have long struggled with ways to make these talking scenes more interesting.

In these situations I think the reaction shots are as important as the dialogue. If you just cut to whoever is talking, then back when the other person says something, well, that's a hopeless way of cutting a dialogue scene. The reaction is often much more interesting than what the person is saying.

It's a lot more than just looking at the material and saying, "This is a great reaction shot." I have to find the ideal moment to come off the speaker's dialogue to get the other person's reaction in. Sometimes you might overlay the dialogue. Action sequences you can do most easily, but to actually get somebody's dialogue perfect, that's tough.

With *Thelma*, Noble had an unexpected luxury. Director Ridley Scott had come up with a way to run all three cameras at once, so the soundtrack was always in synch, no matter which shot Noble ended up using.

Every scene in the car would have a camera on Geena, a camera on Susan, and a camera on the two of them. So you actually had one common soundtrack all the way through. The overlaps that are usually a nightmare were no problem because they could "interrupt" each other seamlessly.

I'd work it through in my mind, all the various places and the moments. You learn to go with the flow. The performances are so good in that film, they kind of just run away with it. Let the camera run, be on Susan at that point and be on Geena at the next point, and just let it play. There was always the opportunity to play a reaction shot rather than hurry it along.

Themes and Things

Sometimes the genre or subject matter of the film will help determine the appropriate editing style. Carol Littleton reveals that Lawrence Kasdan's *Body Heat,* his directorial debut, was really a homage to film noir.

It's a certain genre with certain strict rules. Not only the visual style but the storytelling has to fit within the genre.

In that film, you had to have the entrapment of the man and the unraveling of their plot to kill her husband. They had to be interlaced so there was a sense of the eroticism and the mystery. You had to know what to reveal, how much, and when to reveal it.

My role was as a sort of built-in censor to make the film erotic rather than pornographic. Larry shot a lot of footage that was rather explicit, and it was up to us in the editing room to determine how far to go and how much could be tolerated by the audience.

I think Larry wanted to make the film as erotic as possible, and there's always that question, how much do you show and how much to withhold. I think that suggestion is far more erotic than being totally explicit. The time that these characters are apart is just as erotic as when they're together.

"For me, Oliver's movies have a theme you can say in one word," says Joe Hutshing. "*Wall Street* was about greed. *Born on the Fourth of July* about sacrifice. With *Talk Radio* it was hate. Conflict was *JFK*, conflict between people and the government, between truth and fiction. With *The Doors*," he says with a laugh, "it's got to be *excess*." He points out how editing is influenced by genre and theme.

With *The Doors* we used a lot of dissolves because it was this hallucinogenic, drug-induced life-style.

For *Wall Street* Oliver used a lot of camera movement to give a predatory feeling, like sharks. You can cut anywhere with a moving camera. There has to be a reason for the cut, but we found that a moving camera was so much fun to cut back and forth with.

On the other hand, with *JFK* we used hard cuts and transitions that stood out, things that were in your face. Somebody would be watching television, watching Oswald being processed at the police station—and then you'd see the close-up of the TV—and then all of a sudden there would be a mirror where somebody would walk in and it would go full screen with stereo. It was like you were there.

Finally, there are those scenes that the editor must "save" if the film is going to work at all. These often result from problems encountered during filming or decisions made in postproduction. With *JFK*, Hutshing was asked to combine two scenes where Mr. X (Donald Sutherland) reveals crucial information to investigator Jim Garrison (Kevin Costner).

> In the script there were two separate scenes. First, in the middle of the movie, he goes to see this guy X. Then at the end of the film, after the trial, he goes to see him again. And X says things like "You were right about that."
>
> The problem was there were too many endings! When Oliver decided on another ending, we had to take the second X scene and combine it with the first one.

The combining of two similar scenes in similar locations should have been relatively easy, but there was one major obstacle.

> The problem was in the second X scene they were dressed entirely differently. In the first scene he's in a blue suit, the second scene a brown suit. I couldn't use any of the dialogue. So I took all the information that was in the second scene and shifted it into the first one.
>
> That's why you see a lot of stuff played off of Costner, over the shoulder, because we were putting totally different words in Sutherland's mouth. Then we added stock footage, like the plane flying over to add some variety to the long scene. I tried to go back to Sutherland when I could, but it's heavily weighted on Costner listening. It had to be!

Hutshing is quick to point out that the scope of *JFK* required a unique collaboration *between* editors, since there were four of them assigned to the project. "It's a little unnerving for older editors to have to work with a lot of editors on a project, but I'm used to it," he says.

Indeed, the use of multiple editors has become something of an Oliver Stone trademark. Hutshing doesn't mind. "I enjoy the collaboration and I also like to see what other editors can do. I make a pass on a scene and give it to somebody else. I can get bored with scenes so if you're switching around with another editor, for me, it's actually a lot of fun."

Increasingly, the image of the editor working "alone in the dark" is being replaced with the reality of multiple editors. Hutshing attributes this to postproduction time pressures. "I think the studios want to see a return on their money faster, so a way of shortening the time is to put multiple editors on each project."

If actors do their best work when inspired by one another, why not editors? It provides another example of how the art of filmmaking is increasingly collaborative in nature.

Beyond the Cutting Room Floor: Collaboration with the Actor

Is there anyone who has a more comprehensive view of the actor's film performance than the editor? Every take is viewed, then seen again and again as the editor makes creative decisions. With this in mind, it's interesting to ask editors about their view of the acting process and how it relates to their own work on the film. Hutshing stresses continuity, a familiar editor refrain.

Everyone has a way of approaching it, but someone like Martin Sheen is the same in every take and every take is excellent. He gives the same readings every time; you can transfer the words from one take into another because he gives them at the same pace. He's an editor's dream.

Tom Cruise tends to know his character well and keeps it a certain way each time.

Other actors experiment more. Robert Redford does things differently each time. And maybe the actions don't always match, but I enjoy the fact that Redford gives you the option of all these different takes. He'll give you a lot of choices about which way you can go.

Even the looping sessions, where actors have their dialogue rerecorded to match the picture, can demonstrate certain unique performance abilities. Hutshing explains that most actors can loop only a few words or a sentence at a time. "Donald Sutherland is a very studied actor and he would come in and do his looping in whole paragraphs, pages at a time. He'd watch himself once or twice on the screen, then do it perfectly."

Continuity is also a major consideration for Carol Littleton. "I want the actor to be decisive about the character at all times, to give a truthful performance."

But often it's ragged. Maybe they picked up the glass with the right hand and then in the next take they pick it up with the left hand. It's better if the actor can remember continuity and *still* give a truthful performance. If they don't remember their continuity, the editor's choices will be greatly diminished.

For Littleton, "Being technically accurate can be as important as being emotionally accurate. I get crazy over this." Actors often think of the editor as the enemy, someone who is likely to leave their best performance or their *entire* performance on the cutting room floor.

The actor has to realize that we are not sitting here passing judgment on what we like and dislike. We are their best friends, trying to do the best for them. But we can't present their best work if it's compromised by technical incompetence. We are a very respectful lot, we editors. But if we're not able to cut it, we'll have to compromise, and it will be at their expense.

Bill Reynolds points out that editors are often asked to compensate for an actor's performance problems. "You can save a bad performance by placing a part of his dialogue on his back or on the cut-aways to other actors. You might place the dialogue offstage or have somebody else react to what is being said offstage."

Since editors see every mistake and are often frustrated with the actor's work, it's always interesting when they are impressed by a performance. Carol Littleton admits to a personal favorite:

Mary McDonnell is incredibly alive and real in the moment. You really feel it when you see her dailies; you really know the takes when her skin is tingling and the takes where she was either confused or trying something that didn't work.

It's a palpable difference between the takes that are truly successful and the ones that don't really make it. Because she's experimenting, she's allowing herself to find something that works for her within the character.

And as long as the director is patient and she feels comfortable and free and secure, she'll thread herself right through all the mine fields. Not many actors can do that. It's part talent, part hard work. And when she hits it, it's pure with incredible emotion. And it's so exciting to see that. She can be very still, very concentrated, and completely in the moment. *That's* a movie actress.

Collaboration with the Director

Editors and directors tend to form long-term relationships and work together on many projects. Each knows what to expect from the other. Each has certain needs that must be fulfilled if the collaboration is to be successful. For Bill Reynolds it's about flexibility.

What the editor really wants from the director is coverage—enough material to work with because the director is producing the material from which a movie is going to be made. If you have coverage, you have flexibility.

There are always unforeseen problems; maybe some scenes are overwritten and say more than they need to say. If you've got good coverage you can still create a perfectly smooth flowing scene that serves its purposes. Of course it will be much shorter than it started out to be.

Carol Littleton seeks an understanding of the material she is given to work with—and that can come from only one place.

From the director, I look for continuity—particularly continuity of performance. The actor has a very big job. He's the custodian of his own character, and he has to know how to feel now, how he was supposed to feel before this scene, and how he will feel coming out of this scene.

The director's skills are honed in recognizing a good performance and knowing how to move from take one through take two, three, four, et cetera. He needs to elaborate on a specific idea and to refine it through each take.

I'm looking for the subtleties of the take to see what the director was actually attempting. You'd be amazed how many directors do not know how to judge performances while they're being shot. They shoot a lot of stuff and say, "We got it in there someplace!"

But where? That's when things become difficult. "I'm stuck with this endless footage," she says. "And I'm doing the director's work or the actor's work. Why did they do twenty of this? What were they trying to accomplish? And I haven't got a clue."

Joe Hutshing's experiences with Oliver Stone speak to the need to generate excitement in the audience.

Oliver is open to suggestions and encourages collaboration constantly. The worst thing he would say to me was "Joe, that's so conventional!" That's one thing he really hates. I learned that early on, not to give him anything conventional. In a scene where he had more conventional coverage, he would have me junk it up. He'd say, "It's too clean, make it dirtier, make it seedier."

Hutshing's experiences on *Born on the Fourth of July* proved very instructive in this regard.

In *Born* when Tom Cruise first gets to Mexico, he goes to this outdoor cantina and they're all drinking shots of mescal and smoking cigarettes and playing poker and there's hookers around.

That scene was shot with various angles and had clearly shown the poker game and everything the guys were saying. Tom was coming in, a little bit shy, trying to get to know the guys. He didn't speak the language. He was confused. I kept cutting the scene and bringing it to Oliver and he kept saying "This is so boring, I can't even watch it."

Finally I was desperate. I said, "What am I supposed to do?" He says, "Just cut it *in half!*" I said, "Yeah, but it won't make any sense." He just told me to try it. So I just kept making the scene more and more shredded, jarring, discordant, chaotic, and that's exactly what he was trying to get out of it.

The cuts were to make sure the scene *didn't* flow because if it flows, it doesn't duplicate the emotion you were after with respect to the character.

At the end of the day editors and directors are trying to accomplish the same thing. Their collaborative success comes from a deep understanding of one another—almost an empathy. Hutshing pauses for a moment. "You know, Oliver Stone could have been a great editor. He's extremely visual and has a very good story sense." Coming from an editor, this is the highest tribute any director can receive.

The Audience: The Final Collaborator

Editors often say that they are the "first audience" to see a film. The audience remains uppermost in mind as they go about their task of trying to tell the story in the clearest, most cohesive and visual manner. Perhaps the single greatest concern among today's editors is that they are required to accomplish this at an increasingly rapid rate. Bill Reynolds sees an alarming trend in this regard.

In recent years the pressure has gotten greater and greater and the postproduction time has gotten shorter and shorter. Many times when I'm about to do a picture, I'll ask what the schedule is, and they'll say we shoot for so many days and there will be x number of weeks for postproduction. Then some decision will be made that the picture isn't quite ready to start and they'll delay it by a couple of weeks, but they don't push back the postproduction time, they *subtract* it.

Joe Hutshing sees the current studio practices as definitely detrimental to the final product. "It means that the movie is going to suffer because it's now become a sport to studios, to see who can shrink their postproduction schedule the most. It's almost like they're wearing it as a badge of macho one-upsmanship."

Days of Thunder and *The Godfather Part III* are mentioned often as examples of films that obviously lacked adequate postproduction time. For Hutshing, "It's like serving a meal half cooked. We've got all the ingredients, let's just stick it in the microwave. Yeah, but it makes bread chewy and the meat unevenly cooked. And it's not visually satisfying. If you want something to really move you, you better do it right."

But is there really ever enough time? Hutshing would have liked to have had more on *JFK*. "There were a lot of things I was really unhappy with when the movie came out but I just didn't have time to redo them. Little things." In this case there were some interesting studio politics at work as well.

The problem was we kept showing it to the studio and they would say things like "You can't show that much of

Kennedy's brains on the table," so we would change that. After a couple of screenings, it was clear that we were starting to take out more and more of the "offensive" stuff.

Oliver is sensitive to people's wants, but he starts getting worried that he is sanitizing his own movie. So he told us it was up to us, do we want to work seven days a week and get it out earlier and have a rougher movie or take longer on it and have a more sanitized version. There was no question for us, we said, "Let's get this out now, let's do it." And maybe it was a little rougher for that but it was a stronger statement that way.

Embodied in this story is the spirit that accompanies Hollywood's most successful editors as they come to work each day, bringing their unique vision to the cutting room.

"Some directors say all editors care about is if the cut works," says Hutshing. "And that's not true at all. We have to worry about everything. You worry because you love film, and because it's important to visualize how something will be. It's a way of seeing."

Like all of film's collaborative artists, editors probably will fail more often than they will succeed. Nevertheless, armed with nothing but a sense of story and a few tools of the trade, they speak the visual language of film. When they do succeed, their work touches us and moves us in ways we can't even begin to describe. Editors may be invisible, but what they do leaves an indelible impression on the lives of the rest of us— the audience "out there in the dark."

C L O S E - U´ P

WILLIAM ANDERSON, *DEAD POETS SOCIETY*

I agreed to do *Dead Poets Society* without seeing the script, which is not unusual, given my relationship with Peter. He had another editor on the film and decided quite early on that he wanted to change.

They had already been shooting for a couple of months when I arrived in Delaware. I started by cutting fresh dailies, rather than going over what had already been done. Peter doesn't always make selections during dailies. Sometimes he'll say "Oh, I like that" or "That was great," but then he might say the same thing on the next take. Having worked together on so many projects, I don't really need for him to say anything. Just from sitting with him I can sense what he likes and what he's going for and then I take it from there.

The Performances

I remember being impressed early on with the boys. They were young but they were incredible actors, all very talented. I think a lot of them will go on to greater things. Never for a moment did you get a sense that they were acting. The performances that Peter got from them were amazing.

Of course Robin Williams is a unique performer. Peter told me about the three different performances for each scene, and he trusted me to just go with whatever I felt was right. On the one hand there's Robin being Robin, ad libbing, which can be over the top. Then there's Robin close to the script, and then there is Robin somewhere in the middle. I just followed my instincts and found a balance between all three. There was a scene that I didn't use initially when Robin was in the class, doing his John Wayne impersonation. Peter decided that we should try it at a screening. The scene played well so we kept it. Other than that Peter mainly went with what I selected in my first cut.

It's Never Easy

Peter basically leaves the first cut to me. He doesn't want to influence me or tell me how to put it together or even be in the cutting room. He'll come in after I've cut it and we'll start looking through and deleting scenes we don't need. Perhaps the scenes may be repetitive or they just don't work. Other than that I'm on my own. Working with Peter is always special. We discuss changes and then he leaves me to it. He has a great respect for people's creativity and for people that work hard and get the job done.

I can't say Dead Poets was any more difficult a film to edit than others I've worked on. They're all difficult. I've cut more than twenty-five feature films now, and they don't seem to get any easier. I don't know if that's because I'm fussier about the end product or what. Dead Poets was definitely a challenge. We had a tight schedule but fortunately there were no structural problems with the film, which indicates to me that Peter was very focused and the script was on line.

The rushes of Dead Poets were unique though. On other films, often the only people who show up for dailies are those that really have to—the director, producer, camera, continuity. But in Delaware just about every night was a packed house, a real party atmosphere.

"The Famous Final Scene"

The one scene that really sticks out in my mind was the final one where the boys all climb up on their desks. One of the second editors initially put that together, and when Peter saw the rough cut he was very disappointed.

I took the scene, locked myself in the cutting room, and spent a day or two going through all the material. I selected everything in the rushes that I thought might be useful in building the emotion of the scene. At that point it was several times longer than the final version. Then I started cutting.

Some editors talk about editing as a technical exercise, but that is certainly not true for me. From the time I first started cutting on a moviola, I would notice myself smiling as the actor smiled in the scene as it ran through the machine. My editing is almost always guided by my emotions.

And that's how it was on that final scene. I spent a couple more days with the endless possibilities of looks and reactions in the footage I had selected. When I arrived at a cut I thought was working, I put some temp music with it, sat back, viewed it, and thought, "Yeah . . . okay." It actually brought tears to my eyes.

When it was almost time for the first screening I said to Peter, "Don't look at it now, wait until the screening." And that's what happened. The first time Peter saw the scene was at the screening. He really liked it. I think everybody did.

7
the
composer:
invisible
bridges

My job is to take over where the director left off, to tell those things that you can't tell in pictures or in words, and to do it elegantly.
—Hans Zimmer

"Have you ever seen *Chariots of Fire* without the music?" Composer Hans Zimmer's smile speaks volumes. In his spacious music studio, he is surrounded by odd instruments of every conceivable description, not to mention a mind-boggling array of synthesizers and computers capable of producing virtually any sound. Zimmer was originally from Germany, although his accent also bears the traces of his years in London.

> You're the first person the director can't really talk to about what's going to happen. He doesn't know about it. He can speak about the scripts, the actors, he can look through the lens of the camera. But when it comes to the music, suddenly he loses control.

Watching Zimmer work, it's easy to understand what he means. To enter the world of the film composer is to enter a techno-environment that seems a world apart from that of any of the other collaborators. To alleviate this problem, Zimmer begins by getting to know his directors as well as possible.

> I try to hang out with the director, find out what makes him tick. With Ridley Scott in *Thelma and Louise,* we spent forever just going out to dinner, talking about friends, talking about other books we read, and somehow talking around the gritty subject of the movie.

Generally the last artist to work on the film, the composer begins when everyone else is finished. The director hands the composer a "final" version of the film. Final, that is, except for the music.

Going last has its hazards. The collision of art and commerce that is the Hollywood studio production process accelerates as the project nears completion. If ever there was very little time, it's now. With multiple millions of dollars at stake, the pressure to deliver a final print is intense.

"About 99 percent of the time we're brought in too late and we're always doing eight weeks' work in three weeks' time." Veteran composer David Raksin smiles. "You have to have a certain versatility and a kind of idiotic innocence to be a movie composer."

The Sound of Music

Raksin, forever remembered as the man who created the haunting theme for Otto Preminger's classic murder mystery *Laura,* has worked with many of Hollywood's best directors. A body of work spanning many decades has taught him a fundamental truth about film composing. "We're manipulators. It's about affecting the audience subliminally. The manipulation involves the music that helps tell the story."

Don Ray can describe his job in three words. "Serve the story." He explains, "I compose music that serves the dramatic purpose and also serves as music in its own right." David Newman says, "Your job is always to get inside what the film-maker is trying to say. You're looking for what the film is doing."

Bill Conti has a knack for knowing "what the film is doing." Though his credits are many, it was *Rocky* that cata-pulted him to the top of his profession and into the loftiest tax brackets as well. When the movie scored a knockout at the box office, that "low-budget job" turned out to be a film composer's once-in-a-lifetime opportunity.

The result is a sprawling home, complete with medieval paintings and tapestries from the far corners of Europe. "This is the house that *Rocky* built," he says with a laugh, though it is hard to imagine Sylvester Stallone's alter ego amid such splen-dor. When it comes to the music, Conti chooses his words carefully to convey the essence of the paradox that "comes with the territory."

> It comes from inside. It's unique, original, and interpre-tive. Above all, it's entertainment. We're looking to enter-tain. You have to use artistic means to do something that is really not artistic, in the classical sense. Mozart didn't write just to entertain. He wrote as art, *and* it entertains. We're not confused about why we're doing this—we're entertainers.

To Read or Not to Read?

Every other collaborator begins by reading the script. Yet by the time the film reaches the composer, it can, quite literally, be a different story. Some composers read the script beforehand to familiarize themselves with the story. Others prefer to preview the film before meeting with the director.

Buddy Baker was responsible for the music that lent magic to many classic Walt Disney films. Today he heads the film scoring department at the University of Southern California.

> It takes longer to read the script than to see it, so I can get into the story more by reading the script. To write music, you've got to look at the characters.
>
> You also get the directing notes—pictures of what's coming up with this person. What's happening and going to happen and how's it going to be shot. I underline certain lines of dialogue. Or I may make little notes to myself about certain situations.

For David Raksin, the key is the contrast *between* what's in the script and what's on the screen.

> There's a great difference between the script and the movie. I usually read the script, but not always. Directors are often under the impression that they've said certain things or done certain things that are simply not there.
>
> You're a lot more useful to them if you come in without having accepted any of that. I want to be inspired by what they have on the screen, not what they *think* they have on the screen.

Sometimes the director prefers to have certain musical segments completed before the film is shot. Director Barry Levinson explains how this worked with his ambitious *Toys*.

> We needed music for this Christmas pageant, and we
> needed about four or five songs written in advance so we
> could actually use them while shooting the movie. Those
> songs became thematic throughout the piece in terms of
> score.

Henry Mancini's name has been synonymous with memorable
film scores since he created the music for *The Pink Panther*
movies. "The main reason to read the script is to find the
source material that needs to be written before filming begins," he explains. "But when I read the script ahead of time, I
forget it because there is many a slip between the page and the
screen."

UCLA's Don Ray advises his composing students to *avoid*
reading the script before they begin.

> As a courtesy, the production office will offer to send you a
> script, which you will gratefully accept but will not read. If
> you read the script, you will have preconceptions. You
> need to see the film as it was shot, not as it was intended
> to be.

Bill Conti says the process can begin while the film is still in
production. "Sometimes the director sends me dailies on vid-
eotape, just to familiarize me with what's going on. I deal with
the vision of the director, even though the writer has begun the
process."

Buddy Baker also sees a connection between writer and
composer, the first and last collaborators on the movie. "We're
all, in a funny way, pleasing the writer. The writer starts it and
nothing would happen without the script."

Hans Zimmer says, "Your responsibility is to the movie
and it has to be the director's movie, not the writer's." At the

same time he laments, "One of the tragedies of making movies
is that there is such little regard for the written word. What a
film should do is to tell you a story. Music can really help that
process, but unless you're careful, it can also undermine it."

The Temp Track

Before the composer begins working, the director or music editor will create a temp track. This consists of music that
seems to fit the film and provides hints at possible directions
for the final film score. For Barry Levinson it became a vital
part of the collaborative process in *Rain Man,* the Academy
Award–winning story of an autistic patient (Dustin Hoffman)
and his con-artist brother (Tom Cruise) who hit the road
together.

When I do a temp track, I work with several different
music editors. I'll have discussions about what I'm thinking. Then the music editor will give me many suggestions.
I may wind up with six hundred songs and I may be
looking for two. A lot of things kick off ideas.

In *Rain Man* I had to figure out how to do a score
without strings because I thought that strings would be
too sentimental. And I wanted to eliminate guitars because you always associate guitars with road movies.

I was sent some pieces from Johnny Clegg—called
"Scatterlings of Africa." I loved them and said they would
be great to play in the movie when the car is driving to
Palm Springs and the windmills are there. I told Hans
Zimmer, "That's the sound of the film—the music is very
rhythmic." It fit because in one of my discussions with

someone involved in autism, they mentioned that autistic people respond to rhythms.

So before I shot the movie I knew I would use "Scatter-lings" and "Dry Bones" for the end. I played the movie with the temp track for Hans. He would bring in some-thing, we'd try it, then go take a look at the movie and keep molding it and changing it until it became a sort of cohesive piece.

Often music from the temp track seems so right the director will keep it. In *Platoon*, Oliver Stone had chosen Samuel Barber's "Adagio for Strings" for the temp track, and its impact, when combined with the footage of the burning village, was perfect. "Someone had suggested the adagio to me, and although Georges Delerue did score the film, much of the temp track was used and combined with Delerue's music."

Peter Weir's use of Mozart in *Green Card* is typical of what can happen when a director falls in love with the temp track. Many composers agree that if they've already been hired (and if they're very smart), they will try to avoid a temp track with Mozart—played by a ninety-piece orchestra.

Buddy Baker's advice makes sense. "I ask the music editor to track it with my music as much as possible, take my music from other movies. Don't give him the Philadelphia Orchestra playing Mozart because he's going to fall in love with that."

Alex North's experience with *2001: A Space Odyssey* pro-vides another example. North did an original score, but direc-tor Stanley Kubrick threw it out and kept the now-famous temp track that included Johann Strauss's "Blue Danube" and Richard Strauss's tone poems.

Nevertheless, there are many times when temp track music is very inappropriate. When David Newman listened to the temp track for *Hoffa,* he felt it didn't work because it was "either too gangstery or not rich enough."

Finally, some composers prefer that there not be a temp track at all because there are simply too many associations possible with *any* music that's used. When David Raksin was asked to compose the music for *Laura,* they were going to put "Sophisticated Lady" on the temp track. "I could see, with them using 'Sophisticated Lady,' that they were going to use the old cliché with the saxophone or muted trumpet. Not too much of the theme, in my opinion." Instead Raksin responded by composing the main theme song in a weekend so the director would never hear the scene with "the wrong music."

The Spotting Session

In theory at least, the composer's actual work begins with a "spotting session" where she or he will sit down with the director (and sometimes the producer) and watch the film to determine where the music will go. Like most composers, Bill Conti prefers to preview the film. "I'll watch the film before the spotting session. The more you look at the movie, the more thoughts start to take shape about what you want to do."

Buddy Baker explains that as the spotting session begins, the role of the music director is crucial:

> The music editor is the composer's right hand. In the spotting session, the director is saying what he thinks about a certain situation, how it should be played, or he might even be asking "What do you think about this?"
>
> As a composer, I'm there with no music paper, just a notepad making notes. But my music editor is not only

listening to what we're saying, he's watching a footage
counter and making a little note of where that cue starts.
And he makes a brief sketch of all the music that's going to
be in the picture. Then, after we get all these notes, he will
even make little notes about what the producer or director
said.

Composer Shirley Walker (*Memoirs of an Invisible Man*) reveals that these notes can become important later on, in case
there is a dispute regarding what was agreed upon.

The notes are a protection for all of us so they're sent to
the director and the producer. Then as we're discussing
these things and someone says, "I thought that was going
to be a murderous rage-filled moment," we can look at the
spotting notes and see that the consensus had been that it
would be a tender moment. Of course, we might mutually
decide to rethink this.

Buddy Baker describes the give-and-take that continues as he
moves closer to the actual recording session:

When we get all through the picture and go back over
these notes, then we fine-tune it. Maybe the cue doesn't
start at the note he sketched down, maybe it starts ahead
of that a little bit.
Then I decide what I'm going to do and relay all that
information to the music editor so he knows how to set up
the film so we can record.

Bridges and Houses

Once the spotting session is over, the composer begins
searching more intently for the musical options within the
film. Don Ray is always looking for possibilities.

You might look for short musical bridges that merely link
scenes so only an occasional love scene or chase is under-
scored. You might alternate the dramatic intensity by underscoring whole scenes while leaving others without any
music at all.
    You might decide to use music very sparingly, which
can be particularly effective in verbal films, such as court-
room dramas, or very naturalistic films where silence
speaks volumes.

Since each film is different, the need to recognize the
essence of the story and follow through on it is at the heart of
the process. Shirley Walker begins by identifying what she
calls a "core concept."

If I don't have a core concept of the story and the characters, then I'm just spewing out a bunch of notes. The core
concept is always something about the story and the story
telling.
    Once I get that core concept in place, then I start
letting it turn into music. It's like having a skeleton first
and then the music is the flesh and the muscle. I'll sit and
create numerous different emotional contexts. I like to
play those into a tape and just listen to it again over a
period of a few days, get that material cycling around by

⁄ itself. Then I take it into the director and say, "Here's what
I'm going to base the score on."

Buddy Baker prefers to start by finding the tempo, then building on it.

> You watch the movie, look at a scene and just go, "La de
> da . . . this tempo feels kind of good." It's kind of intu-
> itive. Then you tell the music editor that you want to go
> at this tempo and then he figures out, for a two-minute
> scene, how many bars of music you need to write at that
> tempo.
> Once you get through all the technical part, the notes
> come easy because it's all laid out. You will have already
> established your themes or how you're going to do it. It's a
> blueprint. You make a blueprint for each piece of music
> and then apply the music to the blueprint, just like you
> would build a house.

"I may spend several days trying to get material that I think is
right," says Henry Mancini. "Once you have that set, once you
know your material, it's like you're going to build a house.
Style comes into it, attitudes, tempo."

The analogy surfaces yet again as David Raksin describes
the inherent structures of film composition.

> There is always an architecture. There is a certain struc-
> ture, and you have to find out what the scene is about and
> what position it occupies in the whole film. When I get the
> scene breakdown, I circle with red everything that is really
> important, things I can't overlook.

Like writers, directors, and other film collaborators, Raksin
will seek out the emotional moments in the story and attempt
to find a way to portray them honestly. Often this does not
come without an internal creative struggle.

> You have to figure out the emotions and the flow of the
> scene. You hope you can write chronologically so you have
> a sense of it as it develops. I'll be working on a long scene
> and I'll say to myself, "It doesn't sound like this is going to
> work." But I'll just keep writing.
>
> For *Laura* that weekend I must have written forty or
> fifty themes and not written a bunch of others which I
> thought of but which weren't good enough to write down.
> Finally on Sunday night, as a result of all of this, I came up
> with the real thing. When I played it for Otto Preminger,
> he realized it was something special.

The Theme's the Thing

Many composers think in terms of composing specific
themes for the main characters that can be played in many
different styles. Sometimes the theme might be scary, played
with bassoons, or romantic, played with violins. As the film
goes on the themes might be put into minor keys or given
different harmonies.

With *Hoffa,* David Newman recalls, "I used three themes
for Hoffa himself, one low—kind of tough, but still lyrical.
Then there was his motoring kind of theme and his compas-
sionate theme. I take the theme, repeat it, set it in a different
way, develop it, take a few notes in the theme and expand
upon it, sequence it, turn it around."

Hans Zimmer tries to keep the process as flexible as possible.

I often have themes for what the characters are going through. But I never stick with my themes. My themes are always changing.

Rain Man is actually the craziest theme of them all. Because you never really hear a theme. You'd only hear it if you took every piece of music in the movie and bundled them all together, then you would get a complete tune.

Here is where the music becomes more than a mere emotional blueprint for the movie; now it actually serves to illuminate and underscore the story.

The whole idea is that Raymond [the autistic brother] goes on and on, and you never get the whole picture. So the tune begins with the first note on the first reel and it's never complete until the last note of the end titles— so it's this huge arc but it's always interrupted by mayhem.

Some of the most memorable movie themes originated with other characters or even other projects in mind. Henry Mancini actually developed The Pink Panther theme before the panther was ever conceived.

"The Pink Panther" was actually written as a theme for David Niven, the jewel thief. He was a roguish character, very light on his feet, and I just happened to come up with the opening of "da dant, da dah" before the sax comes in. Then Blake Edwards, the director, wanted an animated main title, and the theme was perfect with the sax and flutes. It keeps winding through the picture, constantly changing.

In the best of all worlds, theme changes can work in tandem with the main storyline to help viewers piece the story together. David Raksin managed to accomplish this in *Laura*.

> *Laura* is a monothematic score—a score with one real theme. The other themes are fragments which I didn't develop. There are about five or six of these fragments in *Laura*. Remember the Laura character is not seen until reel six. It's all a flashback.
>
> So what you're trying to do is create in the music something which evokes the way you see her spirit and try to arouse that feeling in others. I realized that it had to have a quality of evoking a beautiful, wonderful girl. There was this romantic idea of love, a peculiar kind of love because the girl is dead. I had to make the point that the detective was falling in love with her. It's a detective story milieu, but musically, I treated it as a love story.

Hans Zimmer explains that, like other creative people, composers start to get ideas, then live with them. Under incredible time pressures, they are stretched to their creative limits. The process is more about feeling than thinking. Each project tends to occupy the mind night and day.

> I digest it, sleep it, dream it. Try to see what it smells like. What the scent of it is. Searching for themes is like hunting animals. You hunt, you hone it down. I have to get all of my rationalizing out of the way first. It's got nothing to do with thinking.

Music and Pictures: Together at Last!

With the main themes established, it's time to review each scene and decide how the music will be used. Often this involves working closely with the director to make sure that the music not only complements what's on the screen but provides a requisite tension or underlying emotional context that contributes to the story as a whole.

How much can the music convey? How much *should* it convey? There are a number of schools of thought about this. Shirley Walker might be classified as a minimalist. "I don't like music in your face. I come from the school of film composing where underscoring is truly underscoring. In *Memoirs of an Invisible Man* the music is more of an invisible presence than a manipulative force."

To get a feel for how this works, David Newman suggests a new way to look at a favorite film.

Notice where the music comes in and where it goes out. Then, more importantly, where it comes in again. One cue has to relate to the next, and the next, and so on. Keep in mind ways in which they juxtapose. How much time elapses until another music cue comes in? This is how music performs one of its major functions, to give the film unity.

David Raksin echoes the words of most composers. "Music can't save a picture, but it can help hold a picture together. It can tell the audience on a subliminal level what is happening." Most difficult are the times when the music must somehow convey something that may not be completely executed on the screen. These are the moments when music speaks, though words and pictures fail.

Bill Conti faced a real challenge scoring the famous montage scene near the end of *Rocky,* the one where the underdog fighter prepares for the big championship match.

> Director John D. Avildsen had about five miles of film with Rocky [Sylvester Stallone] doing one-arm push-ups, running, jumping. We worked our way up in thirty-second increments till we had about three minutes of montage.
>
> Our objective here in the tenth reel is to make the people think, right before the fight, that this guy has a chance, although in our exposition and development of the film story this guy doesn't have a prayer. So somehow we have to say "This guy might have a shot at it." Obviously it worked.

Another more subtle challenge came as Hans Zimmer worked with the producers and director of *Driving Miss Daisy.* The simple, leisurely paced period film went on to Oscar glory. Most critics felt the score was a big part of the reason why. Zimmer explains how it happened.

> The score that director Bruce Beresford wanted for it is very different from the score I actually wrote. I have a feeling that Bruce wanted a far more classical score. We're dealing with old people, there has to be some dignity involved. Bruce is a huge opera buff. If I had pulled out a couple of tunes from some opera, he would have been deliriously happy.
>
> But co-producer Lili Zanuck got me thinking when she said, "The problem with old people is the way we see

them as tired and sitting on the sideline somewhere. We young people make them into this. But they have a lot of energy, they have a lot of zest." And Miss Daisy [Jessica Tandy] is definitely feisty.

As with so many composing dilemmas, Zimmer finally found that one creative breakthrough, the moment of clarity that brings together all the elements and sets the tone for the entire film score and for the film itself.

I was looking for a rhythm and I looked at the way Miss Daisy walked—those feisty little steps as she walked to the Piggly Wiggly. The way her face was, the way her feet moved, the way it was lit. That was it! When I saw her walking, I heard the tune.

I thought of the clarinet as the solo instrument for Miss Daisy. I wanted to have this one, crystal-clear line that goes all the way through. Just the way her stubbornness goes all the way through.

Because for better or worse, if she's right or wrong, pigheaded or not, she always has an opinion, she always has a very straight line. The way she walks, the way she reacts, the way she has an answer for everything. And it is only her voice.

I specifically stayed away from that soothing pretty music with lots of strings. There are no strings in the whole thing. The whole score is electronic, and I think it helped carry what was really a very slow but wonderful movie.

Creative breakthroughs can come at any time but don't always lead directly to the perfect film score. With *Rain Man,* Zimmer encountered a very different predicament.

I'm sitting there and I start to write this tune and I start to get a little buzz and I say, "Wow, this is happening." So the producer, Mark Johnson, walks by and hears it and says, "This is a great tune," and he tells Barry about it.

The only problem was by this point I'm listening to it and I'm having my doubts. "This isn't right, but Mark thinks it's wonderful and says we have to have it everywhere in the movie." So Barry Levinson, the director, comes and says, "Okay, let's hear it." Finally by the fourth bar, he doesn't have to say anything. Maybe it was a great tune, but it had nothing to do with his movie.

The creative relationship between the director and composer is at the heart of the composing process, and like all other collaborations, it doesn't always go smoothly. Zimmer recalls a fundamental misunderstanding that led to near disaster on *Backdraft.*

I nearly got fired off the movie because I kept writing the wrong thing. I wrote the fires like an action film, having forgotten our conversation about bringing them to life. Ron Howard, the director, realized these fires could have a personality, that they could have a spirit of their own.

When he heard the music for the first fire, he was totally freaked out because it was all wrong. I changed thirteen bars and suddenly it was all perfect, because once you press the right emotional button, everything else falls into place. It's like building houses, it's all wrong until the roof is on, or actually until the windows are there and it has its character.

Sometimes it doesn't take a long time to get an idea because there's all that subconscious work that goes on beforehand. As it turned out the main theme of *Backdraft* was composed in about three minutes. There are tunes in the fires, which is not how you ordinarily write an action sequence. But in the end, I think that's what helped make it work.

Zimmer's German background has occasionally led to misunderstandings on his American projects. There's nothing more American than baseball. "I know nothing about baseball, so for *A League of Their Own* there was a point in the music where I let the wrong team win. Director Penny Marshall said, "You don't understand. When they hit the ball, that's good!"

At the same time Zimmer recalls occasions when he feels his background has worked for him.

You have to remember I know nothing about America other than what I see in the movies. If you think about what Barry Levinson did in *Rain Man* by getting an Australian cameraman and a German composer to be the eyes and ears of America—it worked because we look at America and think, "Wow, how wonderful, look at this place!"

You've seen it all, we haven't; we're still awed by it. So by giving it a slightly different twist, America might see the wonder of its own place again. With *Thelma and Louise* it's the same thing because Ridley Scott, an Englishman and a great visualist, is having a good look at America.

Cut to the Chase!

One of the staples of big-budget American action films has always been the chase sequence. The complex visual nature of these sequences calls for the kind of music that can stir the audience. The composer strives to create this music amid a number of constraints. Buddy Baker explains why it took him awhile to learn how to do it.

> If you have a chase scene, you're aware that the sound effects guys are going to load that up there so you write around that. It took me years to learn that I couldn't have a tempo going when a lot of horses are running because you can't hear the rhythm of the music. So I write sustained music, perhaps with the French horn, and let the horses provide the rhythm.

Zimmer keeps the audience uppermost in mind as he considers each note that will go into the final version. "In car chases, you often go with every cut to make it very exciting, to make it visceral. You get the anxiety level up in the audience."

At the same time he cites a fundamental truth about chase sequences that helps him create something original out of an all-too-familiar movie situation.

> The car chase is taking place because of something the character did as opposed to something that is being done to the character. So you might use the character's rhythms and emotions as opposed to the story's rhythm and emotions or the traditional car chase rhythms.

Point, Counterpoint

According to Don Ray, every composer has two basic options in each scene. "You can add emphasis to whatever is already there—such as playing exciting music under a chase sequence or romantic music under a romantic scene. And that's fine. But you might also play counterpoint, which is used for irony and contrast."

Unnoticed by the audience, except at the subliminal level, counterpoint provides one way for music to add texture and layers of meaning to the film.

Perhaps we hear the tacky little corrida band in the distance as the matador dies in the arms of his childhood sweetheart. Maybe it's a music box that delights the little girl as, unseen, the monster approaches. The distant blaring radio constantly intrudes into a tenement drama.

In *Pacific Heights* Hans Zimmer used counterpoint to juxtapose two movie staples: sex and violence. "Every time there's some nasty violence I play seductive music. If everybody is going *bang, bang* and the music starts going *bang, bang,* it doesn't do anything. You're just overloading."

Bill Conti's scoring of love scenes has always contained a special quality. "There are so many ways to work the emotions. The film says 'they're going to get up and kiss' but the music can say 'we don't want them to do that, the kiss is not right and they know it.' What's amazing is that the music alone can do that."

Writing the Score

Once the major creative decisions are made, it's time for the composer to get down to the business of writing the score. The length of the score for each film varies. There may be as little as fifteen or twenty minutes of music in a two-hour film, or as much as a hundred minutes. The average is about fifty to sixty minutes.

Interestingly, films that are best remembered for their music are not always those that contain the most of it. Henry Mancini reveals that the scores for *Breakfast at Tiffany's* (which included "Moon River") and *The Days of Wine and Roses* each contained about forty musical minutes. The two projects netted him three Academy Awards.

The memorable score of *Driving Miss Daisy* contains less than thirty minutes of music and took Hans Zimmer about two weeks to write. The amount of music required generally determines how long the composer will be on the picture, but there are exceptions. More ambitious projects take more time. Zimmer worked on *Toys* for about a year, though he also completed *A League of Their Own* and *The Power of One* during that period.

Henry Mancini tends to compose very quickly. "I average about three to five minutes a day. That's as fast as you can go and still be good. Most pictures take two or three weeks, it depends on how panicked they are."

Oboes and Options

As final deadlines draw near, the composer's choice of instruments becomes a significant part of the creative decision-making process. Each instrument is chosen with the story and the characters in mind. USC's Buddy Baker points out, "Different characters might have different instruments. Each instrument evokes different emotions, so an oboe or an English horn can be plaintive, lonesome, sad. In *Peter and the Wolf,* the wolf was always the French horns, the duck was the bassoon."

"You have to know instruments' sounds, what they can do and not do," says UCLA's Don Ray. "For instance, what key can they play in? Can they trill? Do a glissando [a rapid slide through a series of consecutive musical tones]? What mood do they add? Dark? Light? Music *means* something. Some instruments blend better than others.

Most successful composers are not afraid to experiment with nontraditional and unorthodox instruments, as long as they fit the mood of the picture. In 1962 Henry Mancini used an autoharp in *Experiment in Terror.* "It was being used in hootenanny groups at that time. You hit a note and it sounds like it's an echo chamber. It worked great because of the echo." The African locations in *Hatari!* led him to use African thumb pianos, giant pea pod gourds, and shell gourds.

Bill Conti is also noted for his use of unusual instruments. "I have a history of finding that unique little instrument, a funny little sound, a whistle. We all want to compose a distinctive story. Instrument choices are one way to be unique."

Shirley Walker explains that often the composer works closely with an orchestrator who will assist in finding just the right sounds.

On projects where I was the orchestrator the composer might say, "I want the brass to have the melody until the kiss and then during the embrace the violins should soar and take over and carry the emotion." And I'll execute that.

Other times I might go back and say, "I like your idea of using the strings here but what about the possibility of French horns in this line?" It warms up the sound. And when it works, the composer is giving you permission to make a contribution on that level.

Throughout the process the composer always deals with one fundamental dilemma. This is precisely why movie work is so

different from that of a recording artist. "You only get to hear
our stuff once," Conti explains, "so we've got to catch your
ear. If it works once, that's all we care about."

Take It from the Top

It's late afternoon on the Disney lot in Burbank. Bill Conti
stands on a sound stage in front of a huge orchestra. It could
be opening night at the symphony except that everyone is
dressed casually, and of course there is no audience except for
a dozen sound technicians and crew members. It is the final
day of recording for the three-hour film *Bound by Honor,* a
project Conti has been working on for nearly a year. Again and
again the scene is projected on a large screen so the musicians
can match their performances with each visual cue.

During the seven-hour session the same piece of music will
be played over and over again as separate soundtracks are
recorded for the guitars, brass, percussion, and finally for the
full orchestra.

Conti gives the musicians a break and explains that to-
night's final session will be devoted to the music that will play
over the end credits. "Of course no one will ever hear it!" He
laughs. It is ironic that so much time and money is devoted to
music that will play to a mostly empty theater.

There is time for one more question. How does he know
how many musicians are required?

I hear what the film should have, there are blocks that
come into your mind. A symphony orchestra—eighty-six,
ninety-six, a hundred. A chamber orchestra, Mozart,
thirty-five. A wind ensemble, rock 'n' roll. I'll have some-

thing in mind and I'll say it's going to be around fifty or sixty players. Why?

Because the things that I'm hearing in my mind can't be done unless there are fifty or sixty players. If they say, "It should be like a forties movie." Boom, eighty-six comes right to mind, eighty-six players will do this because they didn't do this with less than that in the 1940s. That's what it takes to be effective.

Buddy Baker has probably been through this process as often as anyone in Hollywood. Most of the time he labored on the Disney lot.

Each musician puts on headphones and listens to what's called a click track. The "click" is actually a glorified name for a metronome, which gives the musicians a *tick, tick, tick* to follow with every beat. I decide on the tempo and everybody in the orchestra is hearing that tempo through the little earphone. In some cases, the composer uses free timing, where he or she conducts to a clock which either shows seconds or the footage of the scene. Without the click track, you can't keep a tempo going for two or three minutes and come out exactly where you need to.

To the untrained observer the recording process goes so smoothly that it's hard to believe there is little or no rehearsal time. Yet none of these musicians has ever seen a note of the music until they all come in for the session. Don Ray says that "Los Angeles studio musicians are the best in the world. They sight-read. They don't have an attitude. They come and do their job and then go home."

Shirley Walker concurs.

Here in Los Angeles we have musicians who are third-generation film music performers. And remember, film music is a very different type of performance than symphonic.

People get the two mixed up because they're both orchestra. But it takes a hell of a player to play film music, and most orchestra musicians are very timid. Some producers might want the London Symphony, but L.A. musicians are the best.

Collaboration and the Composer

As each piece of music is recorded, it will be played for the director. Some directors also make it a point to attend recording sessions so they can get a feel for what's going on. Nevertheless, it is a rare producer or director who has any technical musical knowledge. Bill Conti says as a result, the collaboration process that ensues is not always pretty.

The director is the master sergeant that makes decisions at all levels. But could he possibly be qualified at all levels? No, he can't be. I have to play a piece of music for him and he has to respond. The guy that equivocates is the guy that really hurts everybody.

If he says "I don't know. Could you try it more like this?" Now that's more difficult. I want him to know his own feelings enough to say "I like this. I hate this." I might go to the piano, "You mean like this?" But you don't want them to start talking notes or instruments.

Buddy Baker agrees. "I try to read the director's emotions, the way he's thinking, but it's very difficult to work with someone

who doesn't know what he wants. The thing is he doesn't want
you to know that he doesn't know. He's trying to tell you
things and you're trying to figure out what he really means."

> You don't want to give a producer or director too many
> choices because they really get confused. You can no
> longer play a piano track and tell the producer, "This is
> going to be strings here and woodwinds here." They won't
> understand that. Usually at Disney I would use a small
> orchestra to play and make it sound professional.

Henry Mancini uses a similar technique, but tends to record
rather than perform live. "I make a demonstration tape for the
director so he can get an approximation. Orchestral themes
can be hard to play on piano, especially if you're an in-
between piano player like I am. I don't have the technique."
Composers who have worked extensively with a particular producer or director tend to develop a relationship that
helps them understand one another. Baker's years at Disney
paid handsome dividends when it came to the collaborative
process.

> I always loved working with Walt Disney because, even
> though he didn't know anything about music, he had an
> uncanny sense of what was right for a scene and he would
> express it in very plain terms, which meant a lot to me.
> He would say, "This should be a big symphonic sound,
> maybe a chorus in here?" or "This would be kind of light
> and cute." That's all I needed to hear. Eventually we knew
> all the instruments that bothered Walt. He didn't like
> piccolos—high-pitched sounds. He had a philosophy that
> the real high-pitched sounds bothered women, and that
> bothered him.

Walt didn't like oboes either. You never wrote an oboe
solo behind any dialogue because it's going to cut through
and the audience will be listening to that oboe and missing
the dialogue. Almost any solo instrument used in its high
register will intrude.

There was a Disney sound. All the music had a little
sparkle to it, it's always kind of happy music and always
ends up with a lightness.

John Cassavetes (*Faces, A Woman Under the Influence*)
was neither happy nor light, but he was regarded as Hollywood's premier independent film director during the 1970s.
His reputation as an experimental and sometimes self-
indulgent director notwithstanding, Bill Conti found him an
ideal collaborator.

When I worked with Cassavetes, I would ask him what he
had in mind. He'd say, "I don't know, that's why I hired
you, you're the musician." I said, "Thank you, John," and
went away and did my music. When you played it for him
he would say yes or no. It was wonderful.

Ideally, the give and take of collaboration will produce the
best possible music for the project. David Raksin advises a
strong working relationship with directors, but warns against
being too flexible.

"You have to be able to argue your point to have their
confidence." And how does the composer respond when the
director's ideas are not good? Raksin simply says, "You're
kidding . . . you want to get some guy who's willing to ruin
your movie? Get somebody else!"

At the End of the Day . . .

At the end of the day, all composers realize that their contribution to the film will always be limited by what they are given to work with. Shirley Walker stresses, "Music can't save a bad film. We jokingly refer to those situations as 'dressing the corpse.' If it's dead it's dead, and all we can do is dress it up and give it a pretty surrounding. But a good film can just be put over the top by a great score!"

Given this, it is a paradox that the best scores aren't noticed by the audience because the emotions aroused are subliminal. "The idea of a film score is not to call attention to itself," says David Newman.

> The idea is to take this mass audience and beeline it toward the director's vision. The function of the music is to describe or illuminate the "unspokenness" of whatever the scene is. These recurring themes or textures will take you through the movie. You'll be engaged from beginning to end, without thinking in terms of each little scene.

Buddy Baker also emphasizes the background role of the composer and of the music itself. He shares a lesson he learned many years ago from a man renowned for his ability to anticipate audience response.

> Once I did a score and it seemed appropriate to use a triangle at the end. We recorded it and it was lovely. I'm sitting the next day with Walt Disney and he says, "Hey, Buddy, what's that damn telephone doing in there?"

Baker laughs. "He thought it sounded like a telephone ringing on stage. And he was right."

Emotion in Motion

The audience serves as each film's final collaborator. We all sit in our seats in the dark and watch the worlds go by. Since the movie is nearly complete by the time it reaches the composers, they are really the first audience members to preview a film. The difference is that it is also their job to provide the last coat of paint—the invisible musical bridges that pull the audience into the experience.

We all remember our favorite film moments. The best composers seek them out for us and provide the music that leads us to them. They also take us all the way back to those "footprints in the dark," the glowing remnants of the original vision that began when the writer typed FADE IN.

To accomplish this, composers must get in touch with their own emotions. Bill Conti reveals that the process is not without peril.

Unfortunately, to write sad music, you have to feel sad. I'm feeling the feelings that I'm supposed to feel because I'm writing the music that makes me feel them. A project that is depressing depresses me when I'm doing it. I'm numb. I'm in that place.

That I use intellect to write music is without question. But I have to drag the music up from someplace. No one knows where it comes from. It's a physical, emotional thing.

Suddenly a smile returns to his face. "Of course the day I wrote the *Rocky* theme, I felt like I wanted to go punch someone in the face!"

When all is said and done, we have to translate emotions into a particular style, using melody, instruments, and textures. We're counting on the fact that we all share our emotions because of our humanity. I'm hoping that when I write the music that makes me cry, you'll cry. Our stock in trade is to scare you, make you excited, laugh, feel alone, feel alive. We're musicians. That's what we do.

CLOSE-UP

MAURICE JARRE, *DEAD POETS SOCIETY*

Peter sent me the script for *Dead Poets* and asked if I liked it, and of course I did. We had already worked together on several projects including *Witness* and *The Year of Living Dangerously*. For me especially, it's always interesting to work with Peter because he's very musical, he has a tremendous sense of music culture, which makes communication very easy. He knows classical, avant-garde music, new age, electronic, opera, ethnic music, everything. And that's so rare for a director.

He knows exactly what kind of sound he wants and where the music's supposed to be. He knows if he wants an orchestral or electronic score. Best of all he knows what the music is supposed to do. Other directors might say let's try this with oboe or trumpet, or they might want to keep improvising, but Peter always knows what he wants.

You can't arrive at the recording studio and experiment with a different way of orchestration. Even at the spotting session, Peter is prepared to tell the composer what he wants. At the same time, he's very open to ideas, always willing to try something new. It's a very rare form of musical collaboration.

The Process

During the shooting I go to the location to see how the director is working. What is his aim, what does he want to say with his theme? I'm constantly in contact with Peter during shooting; he keeps me up to date on the progress of the film.

Between the time I read the script and when the final cut is ready, I'll do my research. Maybe there is an ethnic influence in the film, I might have to research an instrument or a style. I need time to digest that.

With *Dead Poets,* the first thing Peter said was "I don't think we need a lot of music, probably not more than thirty minutes." He already knew the film would be better if it wasn't overloaded with music. You don't want the music to get in the way. Often you have to explain this to a director, but Peter knows.

If you've seen his films, you may have noticed that they usually don't have too much music. He understands that the music is supposed to say something, not only to illustrate the film, but to be used as counterpoint. Music is not just "there" like wallpaper.

Musical Choices

I used the bagpipe for the beginning procession, and then a solo bagpipe, very dramatic, right after Neil's suicide. It was so dramatic, so touching, because it was the only sound and because we hadn't had any music for a long time. That makes it special.

For the character of Knox Overstreet we used a Celtic harp with metal strings. There are two kinds of Celtic harps; one has regular strings, but I used the one with metal strings because it has more reverberation. It's more poetic. At the beginning, when Knox rides the bicycle, it's like the wind. It's almost like the instrument is coming from the wind.

The Famous Final Theme

From the beginning Peter stressed that the music should be very subtle, except for the last five minutes of the film. But he said that when it came time for the final five minutes, "That's where you have to save my ass."

Let me explain. If the music doesn't work at the end, the whole picture fails. Here is where the music is a counterpoint. If you think of it, Keating is the real hero, and he's defeated at the end. He's been fired. He has to leave the school. But the music has to say what we *don't* see in the scene—that somehow it is a victory for him.

Maybe he was fired. Maybe he does leave the school. But something will stay in the minds of these young kids. They have learned something that they will cherish their whole lives. So it was quite a challenge. I used a musical form called "passacaglia," which is basically the same form of music I used for the barn-raising scene in *Witness*.

You start with a little bass line, and then you gradually build. You add another line, another level. It's like Ravel's "Bolero." I built it instrumentally, first by using the Celtic harp playing just solo, and then all the instruments of the orchestra come in; the strings, the woodwinds, the brass, all coming in, playing the counterpoint, and then percussion and then the drums, and at the end, when you have no more orchestra instruments available, I put in six bagpipes, which gives it a tremendous climax.

In the film, when Williams has to leave, suddenly these kids start realizing what this man has given them, so one stands on the desk, and then the second one, and the third one, it's a growing thing. So with the music I tried to do the same thing. It grows and grows to a crescendo, and finally, it says triumph, it says victory.

8
the
last
collaborator

The journey from script to screen can be seen as its own epic adventure, a quest as vast as *Dances with Wolves,* as political as *JFK,* as whimsical as *Driving Miss Daisy,* and as inspirational as *Dead Poets Society.*

In the first act the writers, directors, and producers, armed with only a script, must test the courage of their conviction that these hundred or so pages can be magically transformed into a wonderful movie.

In the second act they go forward to assemble an army of collaborators who will share their vision and contribute their talents to the cause. The army labors day and night, and when the battle is over, all that remains are a few images captured forever on frail strips of celluloid.

As with all third acts, pressure mounts as the adventure nears its conclusion. Millions of dollars are at stake. Will the film be delivered on time? Will the spark of the original vision make the final cut? Everyone hopes so. Everyone has done his or her best.

As the climax draws near, it is time for the final collaborator, whose last-minute appearance will determine if there is to be a happy ending. That "last collaborator" is the audience. The fate of each and every film rests squarely on their shoulders.

To gauge audience response, filmmakers and studios hold previews of soon-to-be released films and obtain quantitative feedback via response cards. Filmmakers are sharply divided on the utility of previews. Many feel the more important aspects of the filmmaker/audience relationship involve social responsibility. In their view it is about qualitative concerns, not quantitative responses.

Quantitative Response: The Preview Factor

In legitimate theater the tradition of holding preview performances in order to fine-tune new works and actors' performances in them has long been widely accepted. In motion pictures there is a tendency to view the process with a certain trepidation.

Hollywood lore is full of stories about how a studio, buoyed by data from preview performances, butchered a great film by changing the ending or injecting more sex or action into the final version.

Editor Bill Reynolds says, "Previews are helpful because you can find out what audiences like or dislike, what they understand or don't understand."

Often they will think something's funny that isn't supposed to be funny. Of course, if it's dramatic and they're sitting on the edge of their seat holding their breath, you get a sense that it's working. Even previews cards can be helpful, if there's a certain consensus. But that was the old style of previews. Today the emphasis is on analyzing how to sell the film.

Editor Carol Littleton agrees, while noting that the crucial
distinctions between the production and marketing previews
have been lost.

Production previews have always been useful in helping us
make the best possible film. We need to know what the
audience is getting and not getting.

Marketing previews are another matter. The emphasis
on numbers is an attempt to quantify a film, and I've seen
wonderful movies destroyed by this process. The studio
will insist that you cut the film for the lowest common
denominator.

Often the studio will use focus groups to try to get a sense
of how the audience will feel. For Littleton the problem is
that, "One loudmouth can take the discussion and pervert it,
so you're cutting the movie for that one jerk. And the reason
you are doing it that way is because he has a louder mouth or
because he's more articulate than someone else."

It's very frustrating to see the original vision of a film
successfully executed all the way through production, only
to be lost when marketing previews are used to determine
the final cut. The magical moments that make a film
unique are often lost.

One reason why so many movies are unsuccessful today is that they've gone through this process six or seven
times. What you end up with is a movie that will offend no
one, and move no one.

The studio bought the original vision, but now instead
of figuring out how to market that movie they want to turn
it into a different film—something that they think will be

easier to sell. Movie-making is about intuition and alchemy, it can never be a science.

Producer Kathleen Kennedy says that she finds the preview
process valuable to a certain point. "The trick is knowing
when to shut it off and go with your gut."

> The point is that, as a rule, the movie is what it is. Unless
> you are willing to go back and spend a lot of money
> reshooting scenes and taking the movie apart, you're not
> going to be able to do anything to change the picture that's
> really significant.

Kennedy says that stories pitting the studio against the director are often the result of filmmaker frustration about power
plays. While these situations still exist, she contends that they
are increasingly rare.

> Most studio executives are not really going to go in and
> take the movie away from the director. The result would
> be that those people would never come back and work
> with them again. It's a small town.

Kennedy feels "The atmosphere today is more collaborative. I don't see the studio as an adversary, I see them more as
partners. There are some very intelligent people working at
the studios, and they have contributions to make that can be
very helpful."

Qualitative Response: Social Responsibility

Predicting the responses of "the last collaborator" can be a very tricky process. In their attempts to bring classic films from script to screen, Hollywood's most successful and distinguished filmmakers walk a fine line between keeping the audience in mind and pursuing their own unique vision. While their methods of accomplishing this may be diverse, the common theme uniting their efforts is a tremendous respect and affection for the audience. There is also a willingness to accept responsibility for what is created for those "people out there in the dark."

You may remember it was writer Tom Schulman who said, "If you write about things you feel deeply, you're bound to touch people." Producer Richard Zanuck noted that "You can't just make an ordinary picture—you have to make an *extraordinary* picture. Find a subject that is exceptional and people are going to be attracted to it because it is unique."

Director Ron Howard talked about "the force within us to be better people. We have it within our power to actually phase out certain behaviors, such as violence, and create viable alternatives." The work of Howard and other socially committed directors explores these themes in a dramatic context that entertains and informs the audience.

The most highly regarded actors and actresses are aware of the power of the medium and are committed to harnessing that power to move our society forward. Mary McDonnell feels a "tremendous responsibility to find women's roles that I want to be out in the world. I don't want my work to feed into

the old clichés about women that we have been struggling for
decades to eradicate."

I certainly don't want to put those clichés up on the screen
for millions of young women to get attached to. That
doesn't mean every woman I play is a heroine. But the
dilemmas of the women I do play must be those that I can
support. They must be truthful and provide the audience
with an opportunity to see how women can make a difference in our world.

Actor Edward James Olmos's message contains a plea for an
awareness of the awesome power of the medium and the
responsibilities that go along with it.

Film is the most powerful medium ever created by human-
kind. It will affect the subconscious mind like no other
medium can. No live performance, television show, or
book can quite match up to the power of the audio-visual
event projected on a big screen. It's literally larger than
life.

The artist must take responsibility for the work that's
up there, period. "Who did that? I did." When I speak to
young people I tell them to educate themselves and then
get into this medium. It's open. You can learn it all.

But you always have to remember that intent is content, so examine your own intent. If your goal is to be
rich and famous, do something else. Greed and economics too often drive our industry. That's why Hollywood makes so few films that truly make a difference.
You've got to take the long view, think about how your
work will be assessed hundreds of years from now, because it will still be there.

These concerns run through the work of all of Hollywood's best collaborators, from famous actors to those "behind the scenes." From costume and production design to cinematography and special effects, each collaborator feels a certain responsibility to the audience. As Ken Ralston said, "Maybe the audience never really thinks about [what I do], but I think they appreciate it. That's good enough for me."

Every classic film is the net result of the work of all who helped bring it to life. Sometimes the most difficult decisions are made by those who sacrifice their own needs for the greater good. This was the case when editor Joe Hutshing and his team were asked by Oliver Stone to work around the clock to make sure that their collective vision of *JFK* could emerge successfully. "Maybe it was a little rougher for that, but it was a stronger statement that way."

In assessing his own contribution to the filmmaking process, composer Bill Conti said, "We're counting on the fact that we all share our emotions because of our humanity."

It is precisely this oneness with humanity that surfaces again and again with respect to the audience's role as the last collaborator. Perhaps Oliver Stone says it best as he considers the larger lessons he has learned during his own filmmaking career.

In this business it's easy to be consumed and surrounded by it all and to be cut off from experience. You must never forget that the umbilical cord is to real life, real people. In this way you become more human, more humanistic through the work.

Of course it's about collaboration with your cast and crew, but you also have to be collaborative with mankind. You have to be out there in the street sharing everyday experiences as an artist with other people. It is only by doing this that you are able to reflect the fears, concerns, desires, and joys of the human experience.

The epic adventure that is the journey from script to screen begins with the word and spreads outward to millions of theaters around the world. There, in the dim light, you can see the tears and laughter of humanity reflected on the faces of the last collaborators.

index

about
the
authors

DR. LINDA SEGER has become Hollywood's premiere script consultant since founding her own consulting business in 1981. She has worked with many of the industry's best-known writers, producers, and directors as well as several of the major studios. Seger is the author of the best-selling *Making a Good Script Great* as well as *Creating Unforgettable Characters* and *The Art of Adaptation: Turning Fact and Fiction into Film*.

DR. EDWARD JAY WHETMORE, associate professor of communications at California State University, Dominguez Hills, is the author of the college texts *Mediamerica, The Magic Medium*, and *American Electric*. Currently in its fifth edition, *Mediamerica* has been adopted at over three hundred colleges and universities across the country and has been read by an estimated half-million students. Whetmore has written feature scripts for Warner Brothers and LTL Entertainment.